ASPECTS OF EUROPEAN MONETARY INTEGRATION

Aspects of European Monetary Integration

The Politics of Convergence

Alison M. S. Watson
Lecturer in International Relations
University of St Andrews
Fife

First published in Great Britain 1997 by
MACMILLAN PRESS LTD
Houndmills, Basingstoke, Hampshire RG21 6XS and London
Companies and representatives throughout the world

A catalogue record for this book is available from the British Library.

ISBN 0–333–64522–7

First published in the United States of America 1997 by
ST. MARTIN'S PRESS, INC.,
Scholarly and Reference Division,
175 Fifth Avenue, New York, N.Y. 10010

ISBN 0–312–17479–9

Library of Congress Cataloging-in-Publication Data
Watson, Alison M. S., 1967–
Aspects of European monetary integration : the politics of
convergence / Alison M.S. Watson.
p. cm.
Includes bibliographical references and index.
ISBN 0–312–17479–9 (cloth)
1. Monetary policy—European Union countries.   2. Monetary unions–
–European Union countries.   3. European Union countries—Economic
integration.   4. Foreign exchange rates—European Union countries.
5. Interest rates—European Union countries.   I. Title.
HG925.W37 1997
332.4'566'094—dc21   97–5339
                                                              CIP

This book is printed on paper suitable for recycling and made from fully managed and sustained forest sources.

10   9   8   7   6   5   4   3   2   1
06   05   04   03   02   01   00   99   98   97

Printed and bound in Great Britain by
Antony Rowe Ltd, Chippenham, Wiltshire

For my Mum, Peggie, and in memory of my Dad, Tom
With much love

Contents

List of Tables

Preface

'Is not the life of Europe today the cry of a terrible contradiction, the great mystery of a harmonious yet at the same time divisive process of evolution?'

Sartorius von Waltershausen, 1907[1]

It is a paradox of European history that the sentiments of von Waltershausen, written almost ninety years ago, could have been written with the same relevance today. Each member of the European Union has, in recent years, undergone a process of review concerning its position in the future Europe. For some countries, such as Britain, this review has manifested itself in feelings of discontent over how much sovereignty the future Europe entails giving up. For others, the process has been one of taking stock and appreciating changes in their domestic, political and economic environments.

In addition to these types of review, there has been a wide degree of discussion at every level. From state, regional and local dialogue to debate within political parties and between political parties, the European Union has been scrutinised by economic and political analysts and considered by geographical and social commentators. Of all of the policies so far pursued by the European Union, the most far-reaching will be the Economic and Monetary Union (EMU) of Europe, proposed in detail in the Treaty of European Union (TEU), as signed in Maastricht on 7 February 1992.

Many books have been written on the subject of Europe throughout the history of the integration process. When we look back on the history of Europe, we shall see that more analysis will have been devoted to the question, 'Whither integration?' than any other. It is, then, with a degree of trepidation that the author approaches the issue of European monetary integration and the politics of convergence. What more could be added to an ever-burgeoning literature?

It is the purpose of this volume to address some of the major issues arising in the issue of European monetary integration, specifically those concerned with the convergence criteria, from an international political economy perspective. In particular, it is hoped that this book will provide students of politics, international relations and international political economy with a perspective on both the economic and political issues which are of relevance to the way in which policy-makers will achieve the economic and monetary union of Europe, particularly with regard to the issue of economic convergence.

The first three chapters of the book, representing Part 1, provide an outline history of the European monetary integration process as well as an introduction to the economics and international political economy relating to this issue. Many books have been written on European history, so it is not our intention in these initial chapters to provide an exhaustive account. Rather, these chapters will serve as the background references for the analysis of convergence which follows.

Part 2 makes up the remainder of the analysis and consists of two chapters on the convergence criteria dealing respectively with the issue of inflation and budgetary conditions, a chapter on the international political economy of exchange rates and interest rates and a chapter on the convergence of European exchange rates and interest rates. In some respects, however, such a division of the analysis is an artificial one. Anyone who has made any study of the contemporary economy will realise that these criteria cannot truly be separated, so fundamental are they to the workings of any contemporary economic system, a fact which should be borne in mind throughout the analysis. Chapter 8 concludes part II with a review of current developments and likely future events.

Many people have offered their support and encouragement in the writing of this book. In particular, I would like to offer very special thanks to Professor Ronald MacDonald for his continued advice and guidance; to Peter Macmillan for reading so much of this material and for providing so many useful suggestions; to Bruce Hoffman for his much-valued support and advice on writing style; to Magnus Ranstorp for his encouragement and help with the references section; to Gina Wilson for helping me to clear my administrative decks; to Mark Brewer for grammatical reminders; and to my editor, Annabelle Buckley, for her very large amount of patience. The usual disclaimer applies.

I reserve the final words of gratitude for my family (particularly for allowing me to moan down the phone!); for Isobelle for providing some lovely distraction; for Angela Black, for her ever-valued friendship; and for Peter, for everything.

Alison M. S. Watson
St Andrews, October 1996

NOTE

1. Sidney Pollard, *European Economic Integration 1815–1970* (London: Thames and Hudson), 1974, p. 170.

Part 1
European Monetary Integration: Reasons and Consequences

1 European Monetary Integration: Scope and Method

The past on pedestals, girnan frae ilka feature,
    We granite frouns
They glower on the present's feckless loons,
Its gangrels tint i the haar that fankles the future.
                    Alexander Scott, *Haar in Princes Street*, 1949

INTRODUCTION

When the signatories to the Treaty of Maastricht 'resolved to achieve the strengthening and the convergence of their economies and to establish an economic and monetary union including, in accordance with the provisions of this Treaty, a single and stable currency',[1] they were embarking on one of the most significant episodes in European financial history. This was a significance not lost on the then President of the European Commission, Jacques Delors, when he noted that economic and monetary union 'is the political crowning of economic convergence. It is a perfect illustration of the joint exercise of sovereignty . . .'[2]

In this chapter we will first of all examine some of the broad economic costs and benefits of this policy of monetary integration in Europe. However, if an appropriate examination of the monetary integration process is to take place, it is the interface between economics and politics in European monetary affairs which must more fully be explored. For the European Union (EU), perhaps more than any other actor, we must be concerned with

'how the state and its associated political processes affect the production and distribution of wealth and, in particular, how political decisions and interests influence the location of economic activities and the distribution of the costs and benefits of these activities. Conversely, these questions also inquire about the effect of markets and economic forces on the distribution of power and welfare among

3

states and other political actors, and particularly about how these economic forces alter the international distribution of . . . power.'[3]

For this reason, after our analysis of the economic reasoning behind economic and monetary union (EMU) in Europe, this introduction goes on to explore some of the basic issues of the international political economy of EMU. For example, throughout our analysis we must consider who the important actors in the process are and what factors influence their decision-making over the future role of monetary union in Europe. In turn we must also examine the role of Europe within the international monetary system.

The significance of contemporary efforts towards economic and monetary union in Europe can be seen in even greater perspective when viewed alongside some of the early attempts at monetary integration. The latter are briefly examined in this introduction and they, in turn, set the scene for the historical analysis which follows, beginning with the mood for change in economic and political relations which existed in the post-World War II period and continuing with an examination of the European Coal and Steel Community (ECSC) and the origins of the European Economic Community (EEC). Our final section in this chapter sets the scene for the historical origins of the current policy of European monetary integration which we will begin to examine in chapter 2.

THE NATURE OF EMU

Monetary union can exist in either a strong or a weak version. In its weak version, the members of a monetary union agree to irrevocably fix their bilateral exchange rates (either rigidly or within bands) whilst at the same time allowing their national monetary authorities to undertake the necessary monetary policy in order to defend this exchange rate. In its strong version, monetary union implies that the individual national currencies are replaced by a single currency which will be in use throughout the union, and national monetary authorities are replaced by a single central monetary authority. The national monetary authorities thus effectively relinquish their control of national monetary affairs.[4]

We can see from the following definition given in the Delors Report of 1989 (which set the blueprint for the economic and monetary union described at Maastricht) that the monetary union which the European Union intends to pursue is the strong version:[5]

'Economic and monetary union in Europe would imply complete freedom of movement for persons, goods, services and capital, as well as irrevocably fixed exchange rates between national currencies and, finally, a single currency. This, in turn, would imply a common monetary policy and require a high degree of compatibility of economic policies and consistency in a number of policy areas, particularly in the fiscal field. These policies should be geared to price stability, balanced growth, converging standards of living, high employment and external equilibrium. Economic and monetary union would represent the final result of the process of progressive economic integration in Europe.'

The degree of control which this statement seems to entrust to the single monetary authority would appear to represent a significant threat to the ability of an individual nation state to adopt a national monetary policy position (although how much authority any individual country actually has over national monetary policy in an increasingly globalised financial system is a matter for debate, and a point to which we will return throughout our analysis). In addition, a country's currency has, since the earliest days of coinage, been a symbol of national independence in financial decision-making. It has long been the blood of the body politic.[6] For example, it is a powerful symbol of French identity that a resident of Paris can use French francs in Toulouse but not in Barcelona. Similarly, it is regarded as a strong symbol of the national identity that Scotland still produces her own bank notes. Why, then, are states willing to give up national monetary policy-making and a national currency in favour of a centralised European monetary authority and a single European currency?[7]

The first, and one of the most significant, discussions of the economics of monetary integration was by Mundell, who pioneered the so-called 'theory of optimum currency areas'.[8] This theory focuses attention upon the costs and benefits of forming a monetary union. The former arise largely as a result of the loss of monetary policy as an instrument of adjustment. The main concern here lies in whether the costs of losing this instrument for the individual member country outweigh the economic benefits of monetary union. If the economic benefits exceed the economic costs, then the countries taking part in the monetary union are said to be within an 'optimum currency area'.

When a monetary union is formed (according to the strong version described earlier), the central bank of that union has control over the monetary policy instrument for the union as a whole; national monetary authorities cannot conduct their own individual monetary policy operations. So, for example, if world demand for Italian goods declines (leading to unemployment for Italian workers and an Italian balance of payments deficit as exports of Italian products fall), the Italian monetary authorities can no longer devalue the lira in order to increase Italian competitiveness. They have lost that instrument of adjustment.

Whether or not this situation is beneficial for the countries in a monetary union depends upon three distinct considerations. The first of these is concerned with labour mobility. Consider as a simplifying example a two-country model (Italy and Sweden). An asymmetric demand shock will result in a decline in demand for Italian goods which will exactly offset an increase in demand for Swedish goods (so that the Italian balance of payments deficit is matched by a Swedish balance of payments surplus). If labour is mobile within the two countries, unemployed Italian workers could migrate to Sweden where there is excess demand for labour (to meet the increase in demand for Swedish goods). Such labour mobility reduces unemployment in Italy, reduces the inflationary pressures which have been caused by the increase in demand in Sweden and reduces the current account disequilibria in both countries. If, however, countries within a monetary union have less mobile labour forces, which find it less easy to move between countries, then losing the instrument of exchange rate adjustment will be more costly for the members of that union. Thus, for example, Italy's unemployment problems will remain, as will the inflationary pressures in Sweden.

The second consideration to be made when deciding whether a monetary union is beneficial or not amongst the member countries, concerns wage flexibility. If wages are flexible, then, in terms of our previous example, unemployment in Italy should bid down wages, while the increased demand for labour in Sweden should bid up wages – in other words, for firms in Italy wage costs will be lower, whereas for firms in Sweden wage costs will be higher. Italian competitiveness is improved (since output prices have fallen) which stimulates world demand for Italian goods, and Swedish competitiveness is reduced (since output prices have increased), suppressing demand for Swedish goods. Both countries should therefore find their economies returning towards the previous equilibrium. If, however, wages do not move easily (that is, if they are sticky – particularly in a downwards direction) then countries who take part in a monetary union will find that it is more difficult to adjust to changes in demand than it is for other countries who have maintained their national monetary authorities and can thus adjust their currencies in order to bring the forces of supply and demand into balance once more.[9]

Finally, there is the consideration of whether or not fiscal policy can be used as an alternative to monetary policy when instituting macroeconomic adjustments. How much national authorities can use fiscal policy as an adjustment mechanism is dependent upon the degree to which countries are willing to trade off inflation against employment.[10] For example, if shocks to demand are random then the Italian government can increase its budget deficit (thus causing inflationary pressures) in order to finance an increase in government spending. This would increase demand in Italy, thereby reducing unemployment. However, if shocks are not random or are long-lasting, or if governments cannot borrow sufficient funds from financial markets, governments may then find it difficult to reduce government budget deficits.[11] One solution to this problem is to allow for a fiscal transfer, as in our example between Sweden and Italy. After the demand shock, the Swedish authorities would increase the tax rate, reducing demand. These tax revenues would then be donated to the Italian government (monetary authority) where they would be spent, resulting in an increase in Italian demand and a reduction in Italian unemployment. The use of fiscal policy does not correct for the imbalances in the Italian and Swedish current accounts but, under monetary union, they would be less visible (a fuller discussion of the use of fiscal policy within a monetary union will be given in chapter 5).[12]

There is one further point to consider when examining the costs of joining a monetary union – the loss of seignorage revenue. Seignorage is usually taken to be the command over real resources which the government can obtain by printing money.[13] The seignorage derived from note issue can be an important source of revenue for countries, especially in times of war or in other crises, when revenue from taxes or bond issues is difficult or impossible to raise.[14] In addition, when countries have an inefficient tax system, they find it more beneficial to raise revenue by means of inflation (i.e. seignorage). This is because, for a country with an underdeveloped fiscal system, raising revenue by increasing tax rates is costly (because of such factors as tax collection arrangements and increased bureaucracy). On the other hand, it is less costly to increase government revenue by means of inflation. However, joining a monetary union (with a low inflation commitment) means forfeiting this source of revenue because national monetary authorities are no longer free to institute inflation as a means of creating government income.[15]

So far in this section we have concentrated upon the potential costs of joining a monetary union; it is, however, possible to distinguish several economic advantages of a monetary union of the type envisaged in the Maastricht Treaty. First, joining a monetary union will lead to an increase in efficiency because financial transactions between the Member States will be simpler. Transactions costs result whenever one currency is exchanged for another, and obviously disappear if there is a single currency. Moreover, the more integrated Europe becomes, the larger will be the increase in intra-EU trade and the more savings will be incurred on these transactions costs. This is because the larger the ratio of trade to Gross Domestic Product (GDP), the greater will be the benefits from not having to change from one currency to another. In addition, the elimination of transactions costs will be particularly beneficial for those countries that have a less efficient national system for foreign exchange transactions (the less efficient the system, the higher the transactions costs).[16] The elimination of transactions costs should also reduce price discrimination (if one agrees with the argument that price differentials exist between countries because of the presence of transactions costs). The EC Commission estimated that the possible gains from the elimination of transactions costs are up to 20 billion ECUs.[17]

Second, there are gains to be made from joining a monetary union, arising from the fact that financial risk, largely due to exchange rate uncertainty, will be eliminated. Because exchange rates are irrevocably fixed (or because a single currency exists) in a monetary union, there is no longer any need for individuals or states to take part in arbitrage activities in order to secure the highest gain from currency conversion. Firms, too, will be able to quote prices for their products and not have to worry that subsequent changes in exchange rates will put them at a disadvantage. In addition, the removal of exchange rate uncertainty is likely to help firms in making decisions about where to locate their operations. Under a regime of exchange rate uncertainty, firms may 'scatter' their plants across a number of countries in order to hedge against exchange rate risk. By removing this uncertainty, firms are now much more able to locate according to considerations of economies of scale which, in the long run, will lead to a more efficient allocation of resources.[18]

Another consequence of exchange rate uncertainty is that it may reduce the volume of foreign trade and overseas investment. It may be argued that the expected return in terms of the home currency is uncertain because of exchange rate fluctuation. Given that economic agents are risk averse, this will reduce the volume of foreign trade and overseas investment. An additional consequence of exchange rate uncertainty is that the expected (home currency) return of investment in foreign financial assets is uncertain. Therefore economic agents would require an additional 'risk premium' in compensation. This increases the real interest rate. Moreover, in a riskier economic environment, economic agents will increase the rate at which they discount future returns. In these terms, exchange rate uncertainty which leads to this type of increased systemic risk will also increase the long-term real interest rate.

For example, an increase in the interest rate changes the incentives which the borrower has, making it more advantageous to increase the riskiness of the investment projects undertaken. This is due to the fact that there is an asymmetry of expected profits and losses: if the investment is successful then the extra profits go to the borrower; if, however, the investment project is unsuccessful, and the borrower goes bankrupt, the loss is limited to the borrower's equity share in the project. The higher the interest rate, the more acute this so-called 'moral hazard problem' becomes, as this asymmetry gives the borrower the incentive to select more risky projects. On average, therefore, investment projects will become riskier as the real interest rate increases. Moreover, the problem is intensified as lenders attempt to defend themselves by requiring an additional risk premium.[19, 20]

In addition, as the interest rate increases, those who supply low-risk investment projects will tend to drop out of the credit market. This 'adverse selection problem' is a result of the fact that it is less attractive to borrow at high interest rates for projects which do not represent a high risk. On average, therefore, the riskiness of investment projects will increase as the interest rate increases – that is, in both moral hazard and adverse selection more risky investment projects are selected. Eliminating that risk by moving towards a common currency therefore reduces the amount of risky projects which are selected by the market.

The final benefit of joining a monetary union is that it gives the Member States the chance to re-establish European control over European monetary conditions. There is a feeling that Europe will be more insulated from changes in international exchange rate conditions, because she is in control of her own monetary destiny, and thus the individual Member States are less likely to be affected by changes in international monetary conditions in the way that they were in the 1960s and 1970s. Moreover, it can be argued that Europe, as a whole, would have more of a say in international economic negotiations with the introduction of a single currency, because negotiations on behalf of the European countries can take place with all of the interests of the European countries in mind.

These, then, are the basic economic costs and benefits of European monetary integration, but what of the international political economy perspective?

THE IPE OF EMU: SOME BASIC ISSUES

There are three basic (and related) issues which must be considered when we examine the contemporary international political economy. All three can, in some form or other, be applied to the issue of monetary integration in Europe.[21] First, there is the obvious relationship between the economic and political domains. The design and operation of the international economic system are, to a large degree, determined by the design and operation of the international political system. Throughout modern history, production, distribution, and consumption have been affected by diplomatic and strategic factors. As noted by Hettne:[22]

> 'no economic system can exist for long without a stabilising political framework of some sort. Thus the world economy and the international political system cannot be usefully analysed in separation from each other, but must be dealt with within one single theoretical framework, . . .'

This interaction between economic and political factors can clearly be seen in the conduct of European monetary integration. We have already seen the type of economic costs and benefits which EMU may create, but EMU is also a political phenomenon in that the creation of a single currency and a single central monetary authority happens as a result of a political process: dialogue between the Member States; ongoing consultation and co-ordination between various actors; and reconciliation of differing interests and aspirations regarding the future of Europe. In this way, the European Union is both an economic and a political regime; a complex, not always harmonious, relationship between sub-national, national and international concerns. The problem of reconciling such concerns, domestic and international, is the second major issue in contemporary studies of the international political economy.

For Europe, this translates into the question of how the structures and policies of domestic political and economic life in the Member States interact with the supranational political and economic structures and policies of the European Union, and how they in turn operate within the wider international system. The process of European monetary integration is both intergovernmental and supranational. Each Member State cannot divorce national and domestic interests from their context within the wider European framework.[23] Any set of national interests formulated by an individual Member State must take account of how their policies will fit with those agreed within the context of the wider European Union. We have seen this process of inter-state bargaining throughout the lifetime of the European integration process. For example, the history of the Community consists, to a considerable extent, of the bargains and agreements negotiated among the original six Member States. In more recent times, the relationship that these original six Member States have had with new members of the European Community (EC) has been a pivotal factor in the development of the European Union.[24]

Finally, we must consider the nature of the state and what exactly its role is in the interaction between domestic and international decision-making. It is the state which is the pivotal actor in the relationship between the economic and political domains and the domestic and international domains. For Europe, as the process of economic integration continues so does that of political integration, and it will be upon the support of or opposition to this process by the nation state that this process will ultimately be judged. It must never be forgotten that the six founding members of the European Community signed a treaty and not a constitution.[25] It is thus the individual Member States that control the degree to which Europe integrates. As Sbragia notes: 'the very framework within which the Commission was established, that is, the Treaty of Rome, was destined to undergird the power of national governments as decision-makers.'[26] Moreover, the issue of the role of the state is of importance when we consider the process of international financial globalisation which has been so major a part of the transformation of the post-World War II international political economy.

The globalisation thesis basically states that there has been a change in the nature of social activities in the very recent past, part of which is the emergence of a global financial market.[27] The amount of currency trading which now takes place in global financial markets goes far beyond the amount of resources which any individual government has at its disposal for the purpose of defending its national currency should it get into difficulty. In this way, it could be argued that the globalisation of financial markets subordinates national economies to international markets. From this perspective, the increase in the power held by global financial markets is welcome because it increases the ability of the market to allocate capital efficiently. However, in theories of economic policy which include the state as an actor, it raises the issue of how much power the state retains over domestic economic policy.[28] Helleiner argues that the re-emergence of global finance over the past thirty years was not a product merely of market and technological developments but also of state behaviour and political choices.[29] The European Union is part of this increasingly globalised international system and must consider its future role in the light of this. Before examining such issues further, however, it is useful to consider whether or not history can provide us with any lessons at all on the experience of monetary integration.[30]

EARLY ATTEMPTS AT MONETARY INTEGRATION

The notion of monetary integration goes back at least as far as the mid-fourteenth century. Then, a commercial organisation known as the Hanseatic League was formed among towns in Northern Germany, its aim being to protect and control trade.[31] At that time, there were a number of different currencies in use in Northern Germany. This was because from the thirteenth century onwards, as a result of the region's princes being granted the right to mint, appreciable variations became obvious in the value of the pfennig (the only minted currency of the period) in the various regions of Northern Germany.[32] This was seen to hamper Hanseatic commerce (because of such factors as increased transaction costs), and with this difficulty in mind, a monetary union of the so-called 'Wendish' towns – notably Lübeck, Hamburg, Wismar and Lüneburg – was formed in 1379.

The influence of this embryonic monetary union was felt over a large area, including almost the whole of Scandinavia, but was related only to coins and did not include any changes to the credit arrangements which were already in place between the participating towns.[33] However, although monetary integration was limited in this way, the monetary arrangements of the Hanseatic League were a precursor to those later international arrangements which were aimed at securing a regional foundation for monetary co-operation and co-ordination. Indeed, members of the Hanseatic monetary union did their best to maintain

the monetary standard which had been agreed upon by the participants; attempted to control currency circulation within the union (including the supervision of the mints); and attempted to maintain the
monopoly which the Wendish towns had over the buying and selling
of precious metal, all elements which were to serve as precursors to
later attempts at European monetary integration in the nineteenth century.[34]

In comparison to the association of towns practised in the Hanseatic
monetary union, these nineteenth-century experiments in monetary union
were much more ambitious and sought to establish a common system
of coinage and currency for several clearly distinct nation states.[35] The
impetus for these moves resulted from the highly fragmentary nature
of European banking and monetary systems in the nineteenth century
(for example, the Rhineland had at least seventy types of foreign coins
in circulation in 1816).[36] With these difficulties in mind, the Austro-
German monetary union of 1857, formed between Austria and the
members of the German *Zollverein* (or customs union) was one of the
first significant attempts to construct an international monetary union.[37]

The *Zollverein* began in 1818 with the unification of the Prussian
tariff. Previous to that, within Prussia there were sixty-seven different
tariffs and thirteen non-Prussian enclaves, each with a different fiscal
system. With this in mind, 1818 therefore saw the abolition of internal
customs duties in Prussia. Following this, one of the Prussian enclaves
was induced by the Prussian Foreign Minister, Motz, to hand over its
customs administration in 1819, and six other small states followed
suit in 1822. Other German states, perceiving the economic strength
that was accruing to Prussia, formed unions (northern, central and southern
groups) of their own in 1828, but as the resources of the Prussian
union were greater, they too were forced into the *Zollverein* by the
end of 1833.

The initial treaty provided for the payment of customs duties in the
gold or silver coins of any of the members (an arrangement which
served to maintain monetary sovereignty), but regarded a uniform system of weights, measures and coinage as the ultimate goal. The first
step with regard to coinage was, however, only a partial one when a
group of southern members entered into a treaty in Munich in 1837,
establishing the gulden, or florin, as the common monetary unit.[38] The
northern group responded in July 1838 with a monetary agreement
which fixed on the existing Prussian thaler (fourteen to the Cologne
mark of silver). This was followed by the Dresden Convention between the north and the south which set the exchange rate at four
Prussian thalers to seven gulden. The Convention also provided for

the minting of a new coin, the *Vereinsmünze*, which was equal to two thalers or three and a half gulden.

The Dresden Convention remained in force until, roughly two decades later, Austria began its contention with Prussia for leadership of the German states. Austria was badly in need of currency reform: the Austrian National Bank had suspended convertibility in the revolutionary troubles of 1848, and in 1854, with the gold discoveries in California and Australia, it suggested that it and the *Zollverein* states move to a new monetary system which would be based on gold. This was rejected and in 1856 Austria yielded to Prussian insistence that currency negotiations be limited to an improvement of the Dresden Convention. The result of this was the *Münzverein*, or Union of Coinage, which abandoned the Cologne mark of silver for the so-called *Zollpfund* (customs union pound) of 500 grams divided metrically (as part of the general system towards the metric system in mid-century). There would be a simplified exchange rate structure of one thaler, equal to $1^3/_4$ south German florins or $1^1/_2$ Austrian florins, and a new gold coin, the crown, was to be minted for international use.[39] In addition, this Austro-German monetary union was the only international monetary agreement of the time which touched on the issue of paper money with Austria agreeing to return to bank-note convertibility into silver. This it did in September 1858, only to suspend convertibility once again in April 1859 when war broke out in Italy. Further to this, war between Austria and Prussia in 1866 led Austria to withdraw from the *Münzverein*, with its bank notes still inconvertible.[40] Political expediency had curtailed this early monetary arrangement.

Another, and one of the most well-documented, of the nineteenth-century monetary arrangements was the Latin Monetary Union. This was created on 23 December 1865 between France, Belgium, Switzerland and Italy. Later in the same year, the Papal States were admitted, followed by Greece and Rumania in 1867. Eventually, the Latin Monetary Union had a membership of eighteen countries.

The initiative for such a Union dates back to 1793, when the French revolutionary government reformed France's currency on a decimal basis. Two years later, the franc was substituted for the lire, and the value of the franc was fixed at 4.5g of pure silver. Later, in 1803, gold coins were introduced, and the value of gold was fixed at 15.5 times that of silver. This 'bimetallic' system was extended throughout Napoleon's empire and by 1850 had also been adopted in Belgium, Lombardy, the Veneto and Switzerland.

In the 1850s, the relative value of the two metals began to shift with silver becoming relatively more expensive. The different states took different measures to correct this, making the confusion worse. In particular, the immediate impetus for the Latin Monetary Union was the decision by France, Italy and Switzerland to reduce the fineness of their five-franc pieces in order to limit their disappearance because of mint undervaluation. France and Italy chose to move from a standard of 0.9 fine to 0.835 fine. Switzerland, however, happened to choose 0.8, which threatened to lead to the displacement of French and Italian silver coins by Swiss ones. At this stage, Belgium saw the wisdom of making its fineness conform to that of its neighbouring states using the franc (as Belgium was too small to have an independent currency) and on its initiative the conference began to discuss the creation of a monetary arrangement between Belgium, France, Italy and Switzerland which, took place in Paris in 1865.[41]

In the initial union, the four countries agreed upon an exchange rate between gold and silver, to mint identical gold and silver coins and to make each other's currency legal tender (the treaty concluded fixing the five-franc [lira] silver coin at 0.9 fine, but lesser coins at 0.835). This meant that their currencies could circulate freely throughout the union. A date was set for the withdrawal of the old coinage and the money supply was to be strictly regulated, with a limit set upon the minting of lesser coins because of their substantial seignorage. Without such a limit (fixed at six francs of lesser coin per inhabitant of each country), one state might earn revenue from overminting and then introducing the excess coinage into neighbouring markets.

For France, the Latin Monetary Union was seen as a way of maintaining her supremacy in monetary affairs. Emperor Napoleon III thought that French influence abroad would increase if the French monetary unit and French monetary policies could become the basis of a wider European arrangement. For Belgium, Switzerland and Italy, there was therefore great interest in discussing the issue of amending the basic monetary standard. In the end, however, the treaty which resulted was basically a reiteration of the prevailing position, with France taking the lead in setting the monetary agenda.[42]

Events, however, were soon to overtake the spirit of the Latin Monetary Union and, indeed, France's ambitions for monetary predominance. An exchange crisis in Italy in 1866 led to an outflow of currency, particularly silver, and after France lost the Franco-Prussian war of 1870–1, the silver content of the smaller coins was reduced. With the formation of the Reich and the founding of the Reichsbank, Germany became the leader in monetary affairs and shifted from bimetallism to the gold standard. To ensure that it was not in any way associated with France and French history, the gold basis which was adopted was totally different from and incompatible with the French system, making a European monetary union out of the question.[43] Ultimately, then, the Latin Monetary Union was a failure. The last quarter of the nineteenth century saw a steady rise in the value of gold, the pace of which was slackened, but not halted, by the discovery of gold in South Africa. This gave rise to further instability within the Latin Union, but other countries (Finland, Bulgaria, Russia) continued to adopt similar systems. The system was also, of course, extended to the colonies of participating states. However, the suspension of silver coinage was agreed upon by the entire Union in 1878, and this heralded the de facto end of the enterprise. Not until the First World War shifted the balance decisively in favour of paper money though, did the Union break down. It was formally dissolved in March 1927.

As Bartel has noted, the Latin Monetary Union arrangement was significant because of the importance of its members and because of its role in stimulating international action towards monetary collaboration in the latter half of the nineteenth century.[44] In addition, the Latin Monetary Union did stimulate monetary integration, of a form, in other areas. One endeavour, in part inspired by such previous initiatives, was the Scandinavian Monetary Union which Sweden and Denmark formally initiated in 1873, with Norway joining in 1875.

The Scandinavian Monetary Union was a much looser arrangement than the Latin Monetary Union and did not employ the standard unit of any other country or monetary system. Instead, it instituted its own currency unit based on the Scandinavian krone (sub-divided into 100 öre) which circulated in all three countries. On the whole, the Scandinavian Monetary Union went far beyond the Latin Union in facilitating international payments. Indeed, the Scandinavian Monetary Union can be considered to be the most successful of the pre-World War II monetary unions, because it not only provided for the intercirculation of metallic money and subsidiary coinage but also encouraged the intercirculation of bank note money. The three central banks accepted each other's coins and notes as part of a clearing system: effectively there was a pooling of reserves, with the central banks opening credit lines for each other. The fact that the Scandinavian Monetary Union was considerably more advanced technically than the Latin Monetary Union was as a result of the stability of exchange rates among the participating nations and the political will which existed among its members to cooperate in such a way.[45] However, in 1905 Sweden cancelled its membership, following the separation of Norway from Sweden, only to resume the same form of co-operation with Denmark. With the onset of World War I, the Union was put under strain by disruption to the respective exchange values of the three currencies in addition to the different degree of involvement in the war which each of the members had, and the enterprise eventually came to an end in 1917.[46]

These early attempts at European monetary integration are not only a historical curiosity but also provide interesting comparisons to latter-day monetary arrangements. Perlman noted that the major concerns faced by all of these monetary arrangements were the difficulties of introducing a common currency (whether alongside the existing national currencies or in place of them); the use of transitional arrangements (arrangements aimed at smoothing and facilitating the move towards monetary integration); and the importance of both domestic and international factors in the decision about whether a country takes part in a monetary integration effort.[47] In addition, any notion of a central institutional structure which could be used to affirm the role of the common interests of the states party to these monetary agreements was lacking: when negotiations took place, it was without the supranationality which was required for such a high degree of cooperation.

More than this, however, these early attempts at monetary integration undoubtedly demonstrate the variety of motives which result in such arrangements. For example, whereas both the Hanseatic League and the Austro-German monetary union were formed largely for economic reasons, the motives behind the Latin Monetary Union were far more political with one economically dominant country (France) on a quest to achieve wider political ambitions. Similarly the Scandinavian Monetary Union was comparatively successful because of political expediency – the political will existed among its members to co-operate in such a way. In addition in both the Latin and Scandinavian monetary unions the policy leaders found it important to create monetary unions consisting of members who were politically sympathetic to one another. In an increasingly interdependent nineteenth-century economic system, this was one way in which these countries could maintain control over external events.[48]

Despite the historical interest which such early attempts at monetary integration provide, however, the contemporary process of economic and monetary union in Europe differs in a number of crucial respects: in none of the earlier cases did states with a long history of control over the conduct of their own national monetary affairs relinquish that control to a central monetary authority with the power to regulate their national monetary policies, including the ability to issue a common currency.[49] It is with these thoughts in mind that we turn to an examination of the factors which led to the creation of the European Economic Community.

THE MOOD FOR CHANGE

By the end of World War II, much of Europe had endured the experience of defeat and enemy occupation, a shared ordeal which had established the idea of Europe having some kind of common destiny. Some of the strongest proponents of this view were those who had taken part in wartime Resistance movements. Indeed, Resistance leaders met in secret in Switzerland in 1944 and there voiced their strong support for a post-war European federation. The initial movement towards European union, then, started with three basic motives.[50]

First was the theory that a united Europe would be better able to resist the threat from Soviet Russia.[51] With the end of World War II marking the beginning of the Cold War it was thought that, for the countries of Europe, the creation of a third force in the world would counterbalance the threat of the United States and the Soviet Union. For Joseph Stalin, confronted in August 1945 with the evidence of Hiroshima and Nagasaki, the outstanding fact was that the Soviet Union possessed no strategic air force and could not deliver an attack on the United States. The best, then, that Stalin could do was to pose a threat to Western Europe which might deter the Americans from attacking the Soviet Union. Western European countries recognised this threat and were anxious to counter it.

Second, and importantly, a European union would prevent further European wars by ending the sovereign independence of national states (in particular German sovereign independence), a fact which was noted in Winston Churchill's famous speech of 1946:[52]

'Germany must be deprived of the power to rearm and make another aggressive war. But when all this has been done, as it will be done, as it is being done, there must be an end to retribution. . . . If Europe is to be saved from infinite misery, and indeed from final doom, there must be an act of faith in the European family and an act of oblivion against all the crimes and follies of the past.'[53]

Finally, European integration would allow full use to be made of European economic and military resources by organising them on a continental, as opposed to a national, basis. Although, by the end of the war, Western European governments (or more usually national representatives, because governments on the Continent were not properly restored until 1945–46) had agreed to the founding of a new international economic order, in the form of the arrangements made at Bretton Woods, there was still a notion that a more West European-based economic initiative would offer more stability in the long term.

The first stage in this had come earlier, in 1944, when the governments of Belgium, the Netherlands, and Luxembourg (all still in exile in London) met in order to sign a Customs Convention, under which a customs union would be set up, beginning on January 1, 1948, to be known as Benelux.[54] This union actually came into operation in June 1948, when customs duties were withdrawn within the Benelux Union and common external tariffs were adopted, with the intention of eventually extending the customs union into a full economic union with a merger of the fiscal and monetary systems of the member countries. The Benelux customs union as such was a great success. There was a rapid expansion in international trade, an expansion even more rapid than trade with countries outside Benelux. The customs union also appeared to encourage reforms in the structure of Benelux industry. The competitive pressures accompanying the expansion of the market stimulated rationalisation, specialisation and industrial renewal. This phenomenon ensured, within the Benelux area, a new international division of labour not so much between as within industrial sectors. Finally, and importantly, the Benelux formula stimulated other European countries to promote economic integration.[55] This notion had been given further credence with the large balance of payments and dollar shortage of 1947–48. The United States stepped in with Marshall Aid, on condition that those states helped out of financial difficulty would attempt to foster enhanced economic cooperation between themselves. As a result of this, the first major post-war Western European organisation, the Organisation for European Economic Cooperation (OEEC), was founded in April 1948.[56]

Moreover, an improvement in the European economic climate in 1949 altered the way in which the majority of European countries viewed further progress towards trade convertibility and trade liberalisation. As a result, the European Co-operation Administration proposed a strategy for a European Clearing Union to the OEEC in December 1949, which led to the creation of the European Payments Union (EPU) the following year.[57] It can be said that monetary cooperation in Europe really began with the EPU. It was designed to tackle the removal of trade and exchange restrictions in Western Europe and to provide a framework within which to achieve European currency convertibility. It would do this by setting up a multilateral system of intra-European payments. It was also hoped that countries could be prevailed upon to change domestic policies in order to address growing intra-European trade imbalances and hence eventually to reduce their dependence upon credit facilities. It was intended that the EPU only last until 30 June 1951, but it actually continued, with amendments in 1954 and 1955, until the introduction of a workable policy of currency convertibility in 1958. From the viewpoint of European monetary integration, one of the major achievements of the Union was the drive which it engendered towards subsequent monetary cooperation in Europe.

THE EUROPEAN COAL AND STEEL COMMUNITY

One of the most significant milestones in the movement towards European integration was the foundation of the European Coal and Steel Community (ECSC). At the end of the war, France was incapable of imposing any control over Germany and was dubious of the capacity of her allies to do so for long. The French government wanted a weak German state, disarmed and disabled by internal political fragmentation. However, what France also wanted was coal for her own reconstruction plans. When the American and British governments decided to rebuild the West German economy, there were feelings of mistrust within the economies of Europe.[58] The then French foreign minister, Robert Schuman, sought to allay these feelings whilst at the same time attempting to address French reconstruction by promoting a positive attitude of co-operation. He thus set out, in a speech on 9 May 1950, a plan developed by Jean Monnet to pool the resources of the French and German coal and steel industries. The sentiments that Schuman put forward were that: 'The coming together of the nations of Europe requires the elimination of the age-old opposition of France and Germany. Any action taken must in the first place concern these two countries.'[59] Schuman's sentiments were recognised as making sense, with the result that, in addition to France and Germany, Italy and the Benelux countries expressed a desire to take part in a common market for coal and steel.

But there were other reasons for the participation of states other than France and Germany, reasons which parallel those of countries who were to sympathise with integration efforts later. The Benelux countries were not big European powers. If they were going to exercise any kind of influence in international affairs, particularly if Europe was beginning a process of integration, they needed to be part of that process. Not only that, but a unification effort by France and Germany could jeopardise their own economic initiatives. All in all, joining a European initiative was easier, both economically and politically, that not joining one.[60]

The original six founding members of the European Economic Community, then, formed the European Coal and Steel Community and on 18 April 1951, the Treaty of Paris was signed, according to which the ECSC was set into operation from 25 July, 1952. Its aim was to increase efficiency, and hence productivity, in the coal and steel industries. All import duties and quota restrictions on coal, iron ore, steel, and scrap were eliminated on intra-Community trade. The treaty also provided for the control of restrictive practices and mergers which were considered contrary to the maintenance of free competition.

Overall executive responsibility was entrusted to a supranational organ, the High Authority (of which Monnet was the first President), staffed by independent members assigned by the countries involved, which had power to raise finance by means of a levy on coal and steel production in the Community. This income financed a readaptation fund that gave assistance to redundant or redeployed workers (the first signs of a future European social policy). The authority could make loans for capital investment, and could also, at the request of a Special Council of Ministers, fix price levels and production and trade quotas. Discussion and decision-making were further facilitated by a Common Assembly, composed of 78 members from legislatures in the signatory states, to which the High Authority was politically responsible. The Treaty thus established the institutional framework that was later used for the more ambitious European Economic Community: The ECSC's High Authority was the prototype for the Commission, and the Common Assembly developed into the European Parliament.

The European Coal and Steel Community proved to be very successful. Production increased and trade in coal and steel products within the Community rose very rapidly throughout the 1950s. Under these circumstances it was felt desirable to expand to include free competition in all industries in order to achieve comprehensive economic integration. It was also felt that further progress towards European unification should be made.

In 1954, the Assembly of the ECSC urged the Community to widen its activities, and in June 1955 the Benelux countries, under the auspices of the ECSC, launched the Beyen Plan, first introduced in 1952–53 by the Dutch Minister of Foreign Affairs, Johan W. Beyen, to promote the economic unification of Europe. The plan was accepted during a meeting at Messina on 1–2 June 1955, when the Foreign Ministers of the Six decided to extend European integration to all branches of the economy and a committee of experts was nominated under the chairmanship of Paul-Henri Spaak to prepare concrete proposals. Britain was invited to participate but withdrew in November 1955. The British delegates could not reconcile themselves to the options formulated by the other countries. They were of the opinion that to realise the Beyen Plan, no particular institutions were needed, and the creation of a simple free trade area within the OEEC was more than sufficient.[62] The British also had objections to the intention of giving special protection to European agriculture and were mistrustful of the idea of supranational organs with real decision-making power.

The Spaak Report, presented to the Foreign Ministers of the Six in Venice in May 1956, was concerned with three issues: the creation of a common market; common organisation of the development of nuclear energy; and the priority sectors requiring urgent action (including non-nuclear energy, transport and telecommunications). In Spaak's view, the creation of the Common Market was to be attained in three successive stages. First, a real fusion of the six national markets was to be brought about – that is, a full customs union which implied not only the abolition of all tariffs among the six countries but also the lifting of all quantitative restrictions and other non-tariff barriers to trade within the group. In the second stage, a common policy would be developed on agriculture and transport, and legislation on all other matters would be harmonised. In the third stage, the free movement of labour, capital, and services within the Six would be instituted. To manage all this, four specific institutions were envisaged in an institutional model which was broadly similar to that already established for the European Coal and Steel Community: a Council of national ministers, an independent Commission, a Parliament, and a Court of Justice.

Discussion of the Spaak Report, however, led to serious conflict within the Six. France requested special transition measures and resisted the low external tariff that was suggested by the Benelux countries. In addition, France demanded of its partners a promise to share its financial responsibility for overseas territories, to which the other five countries gave way. Against the background of the Suez crisis and the abortive Hungarian uprising, the Six were determined to move ahead as rapidly as possible, and on 25 March 1957 the Treaty of Rome was signed, according to which a European Economic Community (EEC) and a European Community for Atomic Energy (Euratom) came into force from 1 January 1958.

THE FOUNDATIONS OF AN EVER CLOSER UNION

With the beginning of the EEC, France, Italy, West Germany, and the three Benelux countries agreed that trade barriers, in the form of tariffs and quotas, should gradually be removed. Article 2 of the Treaty of Rome indicates a desire for economic policy integration by setting the goal of 'establishing a common market and progressively approximating the economic policies of Member States'.[63] Indeed, the objective of establishing a common market was the primary concern of the Six.

However, although it could be argued that the creation of a true 'common market' logically implies the introduction of a common currency or its equivalent, the Treaty of Rome does not commit the signatory governments to the maintenance of fixed exchange rates. Article 107 does specify that 'each Member State [shall] treat its policy with regard to rates of exchange as a matter of common concern',[64] but it also allows for parity changes if needed 'to ensure the equilibrium of its overall balance of payments and to maintain confidence in its currency, while taking care to ensure a high level of employment and a stable level of prices'.[65] Because these are the usual reasons for alterations in the exchange rate and because the management of economic affairs remains by implication the preserve of national authorities, it is clear that nothing in the Treaty of Rome can be construed as imposing constraints on the member states' exchange rate policies or indicating that such limitations are a necessary part of the creation of a common market.

The Treaty of Rome, then, carefully avoids any commitment to the creation of a monetary union. This omission reflects the nature of European political relations at that time when sovereignty over the exchange rate instrument was still of paramount importance. Losing the exchange rate instrument was, at that time, still too large a step to take. Thus, although Article 3(g) of the Treaty calls for '. . . the application of procedures by which the economic policies of the Member States can be coordinated and disequilibria in their balances of payments remedied',[66] the particular kind of procedures and the measures taken by the EC Commission to attain this are sketched only loosely in

Chapter 2, which suggests 'the setting up of a Monetary Committee with advisory status to keep under review the monetary/financial conditions of the member states, and to report to the Commission and the Council'.[67] This Monetary Committee was, indeed, established on 18 March 1958 as an official-level advisory body to the Council of Ministers in the economic and financial field. In addition, a short-term economic policy committee was created on 9 March 1960 to monitor the demand management policies of the six Member States as the share of intra-Community trade in their Gross National Product (GNP) figures steadily increased. Otherwise, economic and monetary affairs were generally neglected.

As early as 1962, however, the need for progress on the issue of monetary integration was evident (to strengthen the growing customs union) and was explicitly recognised in the Commission's Action Programme for the Second Stage. However, the only achievement of this 1962 initiative was the creation of a Committee of Central Bank Governors which was set up in 1964 (but which only really developed a formal role in the 1970s). Besides this, the only other progress on monetary unification during the first ten years of the Community's existence was the creation of the medium-term Economic Policy Committee on 15 April 1964.[68] Although it was acknowledged, in theory, that the imperatives of European integration required progress towards monetary integration, in practice the Community institutions were so busy implementing the specific provisions of the Treaty of Rome that they could not have considered proposals for action in the field of monetary affairs before 1963. The establishment of a customs union and the introduction of the Common Agricultural Policy (CAP) took precedence over other endeavours and demanded the virtually exclusive attention of the Commission and the Council. Quite simply, the establishment of a customs union and the introduction of the CAP were seen as the most important policy objectives at that time and demanded the virtually exclusive attention of the Commission and the Council.[69] In fact, the first significant initiatives for European monetary integration did not take place until the 1960s, when international monetary conditions underwent intensive changes.

NOTES

1. 'Preamble' to the *Treaty on European Union* (1992), Office for Official Publications of the European Communities.
2. Address by J. Delors, President of the Commission of the European Communities, Bruges, 17 October 1989.
3. R. Gilpin, *The Political Economy of International Relations* (Princeton University Press, 1987).
4. This section draws on the work of P. Macmillan and A. M. S. Watson, 'Economic and Monetary Union' in P. Barbour (ed.), *The European Union Handbook* (Fitzroy Dearborn: London, 1996), pp. 145–58.
5. Committee for the Study of Economic and Monetary Union, *Report on Economic and Monetary Union in the European Community* (known as the 'Delors Report'), (Office for Official Publications of the European Communities, 1989), paragraph 16.
6. E. Leigh, *An Essay upon Credit* (London, 1715).
7. The creation of a single European currency also, of course, has an important symbolic value. The fact that the European consumer will be using a European currency in a future Economic and Monetary Union could go a long way in the creation of a people's Europe; a process which began in 1985 with the publication of the Adonnino Report, commissioned by the Fountainebleau European Council.
8. R. Mundell, 'A Theory of Optimal Currency Areas', *American Economic Review*, 51 (1961). Mundell's original analysis considered a system of irrevocably fixed exchange rates. Most of the following discussion applies to both a single currency and irrevocably fixed exchange rates.
9. See P. De Grauwe, *The Economics of Monetary Integration*, 2nd edition (Oxford University Press, 1994), for a more detailed analysis of these considerations.
10. Assuming that countries can trade off inflation against unemployment (see chapter 4).
11. B. Eichengreen, 'Is Europe an Optimal Currency Area?', *CEPR Discussion Paper*, 478 (1990).
12. P. Masson and J. Melitz, 'Fiscal Policy Independence in a European Monetary Union', *CEPR Discussion Paper*, 414 (1990).
13. D. Gros and G. Vandille, 'Seigniorage and EMU: The Fiscal Implications of Price Stability and Financial Market Integration', *Journal of Common Market Studies*, 33 (1995), p. 176.
14. C. A. E. Goodhart, 'The Political Economy of Monetary Union' in C. A. E. Goodhart, *The Central Bank and the Financial System* (London: Macmillan, 1995), p. 162.
15. In addition, these countries will have to develop their fiscal systems to the same level of efficiency as every other country in the union, a point to which the analysis will return in Chapter 5.
16. M. Artis, 'European Monetary Union', in M. Artis and N. Lee (eds), *The Economics of the European Union* (Oxford University Press, 1994), p. 349.
17. EC Commission, 'One Market, One Money', *European Economy*, 44 (1990).
18. M. Artis, *op. cit.* (1994), p. 349.

19. The moral hazard problem may, in the end, result in the lender applying credit ceilings as a way of limiting the amount of risk.
20. J. Stiglitz and A. Weiss, 'Credit Rationing in Markets with Imperfect Information', *American Economic Review*, 71: 393–410 (1981).
21. G. R. D. Underhill, 'Introduction: Conceptualising the Changing Global Order', in R. Stubbs and G. R. D. Underhill (eds), *Political Economy and the Changing Global Order* (London: Macmillan, 1994), pp. 34–35.
22. B. Hettne, 'Introduction: The International Political Economy of Transformation', in *International Political Economy – Understanding Global Disorder*, ed. B. Hettne (London: Zed Books, 1995), p. 2.
23. W. Sandholtz, 'Choosing Union: Monetary Politics and Maastricht', in B. F. Nelsen and A. C–G. Stubb (eds), *The European Union* (Colorado: Lynne Rienner, 1994).
24. D. R. Cameron, 'The 1992 Initiative: Causes and Consequences', in A. M. Sbragia (ed.), *Euro-politics* (The Brookings Institution, 1992).
25. A. M. Sbragia, 'Thinking About The European Future: The Uses of Comparison', in A. M. Sbragia (ed.), *op. cit.* (1992), p. 271.
26. *Ibid.*, p. 272.
27. A. Amin, B. Gills, R. Palan and P. Taylor, 'Editorial: Forum for Heterodox International Political Economy', *Review of International Political Economy*, 1 (1994), p. 2.
28. L. Harris, 'International Financial Markets and National Transmission Mechanisms', in J. Michie and J. G. Smith (eds), *Managing the Global Economy* (Oxford University Press, 1995), p. 200.
29. E. Helleiner, 'Explaining the globalization of financial markets: bringing states back in', *Review of International Political Economy*, 2 (1995), pp. 315–41.
30. A. Amin, B. Gills, R. Palan and P. Taylor, *op. cit.* (1994), p. 4.
31. P. Dollinger, *The German Hansa* (1964), translated by D. S. Ault and S. H. Steinberg (London: Macmillan, 1970).
32. *Ibid.*, pp. 206–207.
33. *Ibid.*, pp. 206–209; C. P. Kindleberger, *A Financial History of Western Europe* (London: George Allen and Unwin, 1984), p. 44.
34. P. Dollinger, *op. cit.* (1964), p. 208.
35. R. J. Bartel, 'International Monetary Unions: The 19th Century Experience', *Journal of European Economic History*, 3 (1974), p. 689.
36. R. H. Tilly, *Financial Institutions and Industrialization in the Rhineland, 1815–1870* (Madison, Wisconsin: University of Wisconsin Press, 1966), p. 20.
37. The *Zollverein* began in 1818 with the unification of the Prussian tariff and among the German states in 1828 with the establishment of northern, central and southern groups which were joined into one in 1833. The initial treaty made arrangements for the payment of customs duties in the gold or silver coins of any of the members, thus preserving monetary sovereignty, but contemplated an ultimate uniform system of weights, measures and coinage (C. P. Kindleberger, *op. cit.* (1984), p. 119).
38. This minted $24^1/_2$ out of a Cologne mark of fine silver (233.855 grammes).
39. K-L. Holtfrerich, 'The monetary unification process in 19th-century Germany: relevance and lessons for Europe today', in M. de Cecco and

A. Giovannini (eds), *A European Central Bank?* (Cambridge University Press, 1989), p. 223.

40. C. P Kindleberger, *op. cit.* (1985), pp. 119–20.
41. In economic terms, by the early 1860s France, Belgium, Italy and Switzerland were already de facto in a currency union based upon French coinage. The French franc was a metric coin on a bimetallic base. When Belgium achieved its independence, its franc was modelled on the French franc, as was the reform of Swiss coinage in 1850. Piedmont had retained the franc (named the lira) from the Napoleonic occupation and, thus, Italy followed suit.
42. R. J. Bartel, *op. cit.* (1974), pp. 695–96.
43. M. Perlman, 'In Search of Monetary Union', London School of Economics Financial Markets Group, (Special Paper, No 39, 1991).
44. R. Bartel, *op. cit.* (1974), pp. 689–704.
45. *Ibid.*, (1974), p. 701.
46. *Ibid.*, p. 702.
47. M. Perlman, *op. cit.* (1991).
48. K. Dyson, *Elusive Union: The Process of Economic and Monetary Union in Europe* (London: Longman, 1994), p. 29.
49. Barry Eichengreen, 'European Monetary Unification', *Journal of Economic Literature*, Vol. 31 (1993), pp. 13–22.
50. For a more in-depth analysis of the historical origins of European integration, see: C. Archer, *Organizing Western Europe* (London: Edward Arnold, 1990); E. Haas, *The Uniting of Europe: Political, social, and economic forces, 1950–57* (Stanford: Stanford University Press, 1958); A. S. Milward, *The Reconstruction of Western Europe 1945–51* (London: Methuen, 1987); R. Morgan, *West European Politics since 1945: the shaping of the European Community* (London: Batsford, 1972); Derek Urwin, *The Community of Europe: a history of European integration since 1945* (Harlow: Longman, 1991); D. Weigal and P. Stirk (eds), *The Origins and Development of the European Community* (London: Leicester University Press, 1992).
51. General Marshall, for example, had become convinced, after visiting Moscow in April 1947, that the Soviet Union was intent on increasing its influence in Western Europe.
52. R. R. James (ed.), *Winston S. Churchill: His Complete Speeches, 1897–1963*, Vol. VII, 1943–49 (1974).
53. The Europeans were also encouraged by the support of Churchill who, in a speech to the University of Zurich, called for a kind of 'United States of Europe'. Almost immediately after this speech, however, the British and the Scandinavians, who had suffered least from occupation and destruction, were in the end unwilling to submit to any real loss of sovereignty – even Churchill refused later, in 1951, to lead his country into a European federation.
54. The Benelux Customs Union complemented the economic union already existing between Belgium and Luxembourg, known as the BLEU (Belgo-Luxembourg Economic Union). BLEU was set up under a convention signed in 1921, and frontier controls between the two countries were effectively removed on 1 May 1922. BLEU still exists within Benelux. The two

countries hold their gold and foreign exchange reserves in common, the Belgian and Luxembourg francs are maintained at parity, and each country's currency is legal tender in the other. Although in recent years there has been talk of the Luxembourg franc breaking its ties with the (less reliable) Belgian franc, on the whole the relationship has been a successful one.

55. P. Coffey and J. R. Presley, *European Monetary Integration* (London: Macmillan, 1971). For example, in March 1948, France and Italy set up a customs union known as Francital which was fully attained in 1955, and proposals were put forward for a Fritalux Union including France, Italy and the Benelux countries. This was opposed by the Netherlands, however, on the grounds that it might disrupt the progress towards further European integration which was then beginning to be made.

56. The OEEC subsequently became the organisation for Economic Cooperation and Development (OECD).

57. Subsequent to this, in 1947, an agreement was reached on multilateral monetary compensations between Belgium, France, Italy, Luxembourg and the Netherlands. Although this agreement was largely unsuccessful, it did pave the way for this later initiative.

58. France and the Benelux countries were very distrustful of this decision and demanded that international control be established over the development of German heavy industry, and that deliveries of coal from the Ruhr area to their own basic industries be guaranteed. This was guaranteed when the International Control Authority for the Ruhr was set up at the Conference of London in March 1948, its members being the United States, Britain, France, West Germany and the Benelux countries. West Germany, in turn, was frustrated at this decision, feeling itself placed under guardianship at precisely the time that the recovery of its economy and the restoration of its political sovereignty seemed assured.

59. *Europe – A Fresh Start: The Schuman Declaration, 1950–90*, Office for Official Publications of the European Communities (1990).

60. N. Nugent, *The Government and Politics of the European Union* (London, Macmillan, 1994), p. 25.

61. The six countries of the ECSC accepted a French plan (the Meyer plan) that a European army should be established and to this end, on 27 May 1952, signed the treaty of the European Defence Community (EDC). This form of integrated defence implied a common foreign policy and, in the long term, full political integration. In recognition of this, a European Political Community (EPC) was also proposed: a combination of the supranational organs of the ECSC and the European Defence Community. No further progress was made, however, on this political initiative because on 30 August, 1954, the French parliament refused to ratify the European Defence Community.

62. The OEEC was set up as a result of a conference held in Paris in July, 1947, as a way of co-ordinating the economic recovery programme of Western Europe (the member countries were Austria, Belgium, Denmark, France, Greece, Iceland, the Republic of Ireland, Italy, Luxembourg, the Netherlands, Norway, Portugal, Sweden, Switzerland, Turkey and the UK). The OEEC opened negotiations for the setting up of a European Free

Trade Area (EFTA) linking the EEC with the other member countries of the Organization, but this proved abortive in the face of opposition from the EEC. In 1961, the OEEC was replaced by the OECD which included Canada and the US as full members.

63. S. Nelson (ed.) with D. Pollard and A. Wheeler, *The Convoluted Treaties, Volume II, Rome 1957, Treaty Establishing the European Economic Community* (London: Nelson and Pollard Publishing, 1993), p. 2.
64. *ibid.*, p. 20.
65. *ibid.*, p. 20.
66. *ibid.*, p. 2.
67. T, Hitiris and A. Zervoyianni, 'Monetary Integration in the European Community, in J. Lodge (ed.), *Institutions and Policies of the European Union* (London: Frances Pinter, 1983), p. 131.
68. D. C. Kruse, *Monetary Integration in Western Europe: EMU, EMS and Beyond* (London: Butterworths, 1980), p. 15.
69. *ibid.*, pp. 16–17.

2 European Monetary Integration: A New Initiative

As a rule, there is nothing that offends us more than a new type of money.

Robert Lynd, *The Pleasures of Ignorance*, 1921

INTRODUCTION

Problems began in the international monetary system in the mid-1960s, principally as a result of a change in economic policy in the United States.[1] Under President Kennedy, economic growth had become an important aim for the United States economy, with the result that the American government was more willing to actively intervene in the economy in order that production would stay as close as possible to the country's capacity.[2] Nevertheless, it was only in February 1964 that tax cuts, aimed at helping to promote this policy, became a reality with the signing of the Revenue Act by President Lyndon Johnson. As a result of this, the gap between potential and actual production visibly diminished and the American economy began to move more in line with the other Western growth economies, a fact witnessed by an acceleration in the American growth rate.

This American policy of growth was given further impetus by the Vietnam War in July 1965. Typically, one would expect that the expensive effects of increased military expenditure would be neutralised in three possible ways: by imposing higher taxes; by reducing non-military spending; and/or by extreme caution when considering an expansion of the money supply. However, none of these measures were taken because Johnson was unwilling to sacrifice the social benefits of his so-called 'Great Society' programme of increased growth. Instead, the government attempted to mitigate increases in prices and wages entirely through direct contacts with management and the unions. This policy, however, proved to be inadequate in coping with the growing problems in the US economy. The result was new inflation in 1965–66 and an increasing American balance of payments deficit, events which understandably caused alarm both within the United States and abroad, for they were regarded (correctly) as an assault on the foundations of the Bretton Woods system which required a strong dollar for its operation.[3] Moreover, at around the same time, a major European currency was caught by speculative pressures, the devaluation of the pound by 14.3 per cent in November 1967 ending a period of almost seven years during which there had been no changes in the parities of the major world currencies (although the UK was at that time not a member of the European Community and so this event did not affect the Community directly).[4]

The general unease about the ability of the US to continue to manage the international monetary system and maintain the dollar exchange rate intensified after sterling's devaluation. In addition, there was increasing concern in Europe that the Americans were deriving seignorage benefits from the role played by their currency and institutions in the Bretton Woods system of macroeconomic management.[5] This whole situation intensified pressure on the US dollar. The US official gold stock had fallen from $17.8 billion in 1960 to $10.9 billion in 1968, so foreign central banks could not demand payment for US foreign exchange transactions in gold, nor could they continue to absorb the amount of dollar reserves that they were being faced with. This glut of dollars and the presumption that eventually the dollar would have to be devalued led to a lack of confidence in the dollar as an asset. The disintegration of the Bretton Woods system was evident.

Moreover, from May 1968, the French franc and the German mark became the second and third European currencies to be caught by speculative pressures. Although they resisted these difficulties initially by the adoption of foreign exchange controls, as the tide continued the French authorities were forced to devalue the franc by 11.1 per cent in August 1969, and the Germans to revalue the mark by 9.3 per cent in September 1969. Both of these events were major tests for the Community. The operation of the customs union was not altered, fundamentally, by these exchange rate changes, but the Common Agricultural Policy (CAP) required attention owing to the movement in intra-European Community (EC) exchange rates. This was because the prices of many agricultural products were fixed in a standard unit (then called the European Unit of Account or EUA, later to become the European Currency Unit – the ECU, and defined as the gold content of one US dollar, which was the international monetary standard at the time) representing a basket of national currencies. Thus, changes in currency values changed the composition of the basket.[6] Because the French and German governments did not adopt the changes in price which would have resulted from the exchange rate changes, the only solution was to allow the common agricultural market to break up and instead maintain separate prices for agricultural products in different countries.[7] In practice, therefore, exchange rate changes and uncertainty over the strength of the US dollar threatened the then centrepiece of the Community, the Common Agricultural Policy.

It was against this background that the Commission launched its first major initiative in the field of monetary affairs since the adoption of the proposals in the Action Programme almost four years earlier. The 1969 Barre Plan 'on the Co-ordination of Economic Policies and Monetary Co-operation within the Community' (better known as the Barre Report) was the Community's first attempt at formulating an efficient and consistent approach towards monetary integration in Europe. It called for more consultation and coordination of monetary and economic policies in general within the EEC, and proposed the creation of a short- and medium-term financial assistance programme to enhance the Member States' existing credit facilities. The Barre Plan was limited, however, in that it was directed less towards the goal of further integration and more towards the need for monetary cooperation in order to safeguard the accomplishments of the previous decade, namely the Customs Union and the Common Agricultural Policy.[8]

Nevertheless, following discussions in Council, the European Community leaders' summit in The Hague on 1 and 2 December of that year called for the establishment of an Economic and Monetary Union (EMU), in three stages, based on the Barre proposals. The issuing of this statement was a critical event in the life of the European Community. Monetary co-operation and the possible creation of a European Reserve Fund (with a portion of German foreign exchange reserves at its disposal) figured highly on the list of priorities during the discussions which took place between the 'Six', and in Article 8 of the final communiqué they formally expressed the Community's intention of proceeding towards a monetary union, the details of which were to be worked out during the course of 1970.

However, although all Member States agreed to the principle of economic and monetary union, they disagreed over what those steps would involve. Indeed, it soon became apparent that contrasting national positions might obstruct the agreement on a definition of economic and monetary union. France, for example, preferred a policy whereby exchange rates would be rapidly frozen as a means of promoting the economic convergence necessary for the final adoption of a single currency. On the other hand, Germany argued that convergence was necessary prior to the freezing of exchange rates, a policy which was designed to counteract the inflationary consequences of a premature move towards economic and monetary union. Drawing up 'a plan by stages' as mandated by the Hague Summit thus seemed likely to be a lengthy and difficult endeavour. Nevertheless, monetary integration had been explicitly adopted as a European Community aim and work began in the Ecofin Council (the Council of Economics and Finance Ministers of the European Union) on designing the appropriate transitional arrangements for the goal of economic and monetary union.

PROGRESS TOWARDS ECONOMIC AND MONETARY UNION

The decision to move towards the goal of economic and monetary union was made as part of a larger commitment to a united Europe. The EMU plan would be based on a Report containing an analysis of the different suggestions, making it possible to identify the basic issues for a realisation of EMU. This Report would be drafted by a committee composed of the chairmen of the Central Bank Governors, Short- and Medium-Term Economic Policy, Monetary, and Budgetary Policy Committees, along with a representative of the Commission, and would be conducted under the chairmanship of the Luxembourg Prime Minister and Finance Minister, Pierre Werner, a well-known proponent of monetary integration.[9] The Werner Committee presented an interim report to the Ecofin Council in June 1970, with the final report being delivered in October.[10]

The Werner Committee proposed establishing economic and monetary union, in stages, by 1980. These stages involved rigid fixing of exchange rates, irreversible interconvertibility of EC currencies, and the introduction of an EC system of central banks, modelled on the US Federal Reserve System, which would take over the conduct of monetary policy and of intervention on the foreign exchange market. This policy effectively implied the creation of a single currency. With this in mind, a common monetary policy would be devised whereby interest rates, the growth of the money supply and credit conditions would be determined at the Community level. The six currencies would move as a bloc against third currencies, exchange reserves would be pooled, and the Six would act as a unit in international monetary affairs.[11] The national governments were further in agreement that economic and monetary union entailed the co-ordination of economic policies. With this in mind, the size of the EC budget would be dramatically increased, there would be a certain amount of harmonisation in tax systems, particularly in the area of indirect taxation, a single European capital market, and a European regional policy.[12]

The Werner Committee, however, was divided over the means and methods for achieving these lofty aims. For example, the co-ordination of economic policies was, to the German government, the central element of EMU. The introduction of a common currency was of secondary importance, a necessary but not sufficient step for the free movement of goods, services and the factors of production.

At first, it would seem that the Werner Committee was an impartial body; a group of independent experts who would examine the various alternatives for creating an economic and monetary union of Europe and recommend the best strategy. However, the Werner Committee actually included one senior official from every country, in addition to the Commission's Director-General for Economic Affairs. Thus, the Committee was not a body of independent experts, but a group of national officials who, although not formally representing their governments, nonetheless did put forward their national positions. From the outset it was clear that the Werner Committee was attempting to assess the feasibility of various alternatives with these national positions in mind.[13]

Under these circumstances, it was not surprising that disagreements over the nature of economic and monetary union soon became obvious. Central to their final report was the principle of 'parallelism'[14], where, for EMU to be realised, parallel progress had to be made in both the economic and the monetary dimensions. The notion of parallelism was really a compromise to the debate between monetarists and economists about how best to proceed towards economic and monetary union.[15]

The debate between monetarists and economists hinges on the issue of how effective the exchange rate instrument is when used as a corrective tool for the effects of different national demand and cost developments.[16] On the one hand, the 'monetarist' view maintains that changes in exchange rates are ineffective when used as instruments to correct for different demand and cost developments between countries. Moreover, even if they were effective, the use of national exchange rate policies would typically make countries worse off. In this 'monetarist' view, then, countries would benefit from relinquishing their national currencies and joining a monetary union.

On the other hand, there was the 'economist' view (represented by the original Mundell model) that the world is full of rigidities (rigid wages and prices, for instance, or immobile labour), and thus the exchange rate is a powerful instrument in eliminating disequilibria. From this perspective, relatively few countries would find it in their interest to join a monetary union. (It also follows from this view that many large countries that now have one currency would be better off (economically) splitting the country into different monetary zones.)[17]

In addition to the compromises made in the Werner Report to this debate between 'monetarists' and 'economists', the Report basically betrayed the degree of German policy control: both on the long-term ambitions for political union (with which the French government was uncomfortable) and on the provisions for Stage 1 with regard to the co-ordination of economic policies and the specific steps towards monetary union.[18] Thus, the final plan, adopted in a lengthy resolution by the Council in March 1971, was a compromise: only the details of the first stage were outlined, but there was no binding commitment about how and when they should proceed to economic and monetary union.[19, 20]

The European Council resolution identified a series of future Council decisions needed to bolster macroeconomic co-ordination over the medium term. Mechanisms for closer co-operation between central banks were agreed. Most importantly, the Member States committed themselves 'from the beginning of the first stage and on an experimental basis' to intervene in order to stabilise their currencies. Hence, elements of the Werner Report were implemented in March 1972, when exchange rate fluctuations were reduced by limiting the swings in bilateral exchange rates to a 2.25 per cent band. This arrangement was known as the 'snake in the tunnel' because it made the participating currencies move up and down together within the wider 4.5 per cent band established for the dollar by the Smithsonian agreement of 1971.

THE 'SNAKE IN THE TUNNEL'

The objective of this arrangement was to maintain bilateral exchange rates within relatively narrow margins. To this end, the agreement included an intervention mechanism and a monetary support scheme for participating countries. National governments reserved the right to withdraw from the 'snake' whenever they deemed it necessary. At the same time as the 'snake' came into operation, rules for joint intervention were instigated in the exchange market and provision was made for very short-term credit between central banks in order to finance these interventions. As part of the strategy of parallelism, a steering committee was also set up for the more effective co-ordination of economic policies.[21]

However, despite the member countries' best intentions, the 'snake' soon came under pressure and within a year, the currencies of four countries (the United Kingdom, Ireland, Denmark and Italy) had withdrawn from the system. Increasingly, the arrangement had proved to be incapable of delivering the exchange rate stability which it had been largely designed to create.[22] In fact, the attack on sterling that developed in early June 1972 can be traced back to the Smithsonian arrangement, following which the pound, like the franc, held its parity against gold and subsequently appreciated around 8 per cent against the dollar.[23] Signs of trouble in the British balance of payments grew throughout April and May and, as funds began to leave the country, the pound was allowed to float against the other currencies, a fact which necessarily entailed its withdrawal from the snake. When the Bretton Woods system effectively collapsed, any hopes of continuing the movement towards economic and monetary union in Europe seemed lost – one of the biggest weaknesses of the European strategy being that, despite these moves towards economic and monetary union, there remained a tacit reliance on the Bretton Woods system which was collapsing at exactly the time the first stages of the Werner plan were supposed to be implemented.[24] Nevertheless, the meeting of heads of government in Paris in October 1972 – in which the United Kingdom took part for the first time – strongly reaffirmed the Community's EMU objective, formally committing the Member States to its full realisation by 1980. In the interim, 'fixed but adjustable parities' would be pursued. Already, however, the integrity of the whole exercise had been fatally prejudiced. When the European Commission duly proposed in April 1973 that the Community move to the second stage of EMU on schedule in 1974, there was no agreement in the Ecofin Council.

By the time that the heads of government met again in Paris two years later they could note only that internal and international difficulties had prevented, in 1973 and 1974, the accomplishment of expected progress on the road to EMU. Chief of these international difficulties was the oil crisis of 1973–74, which had a number of effects on the signatory governments. Those governments that were in charge of the badly hit countries, their populations facing unemployment, increased their money supply more than the preservation of exchange rate margins permitted. Soon, a considerable divergence in inflation rates between the participating countries appeared. Some European currencies were devalued, others were revalued, forcing the member governments to leave the 'snake' at various times. The arrangements finally degenerated in March 1976, after France's second withdrawal. Only countries with tight trade relations with West Germany stayed in and it became little more than a 'Deutschmark zone'[25] Thus, the EC's first steps towards monetary integration failed. The 'snake' proved unable to survive the destabilising forces of the period, and an EC Committee, set up in 1975 to evaluate the situation, found no point in advancing to Stage 2. Thus, the EC Member States allowed their exchange rates to fluctuate against each other – except for the Benelux countries and the Federal Republic of Germany, whose bilateral exchange rates remained stable (Denmark could remain in the arrangement only with continual devaluations) and work on the EMU project was put to one side.

Formal EC interpretation characterised the inadequacy of the 'snake' as the consequence of the demanding external pressures released in the EC by the decline of the Bretton Woods international monetary system and the first oil-price shock of 1973. Nevertheless, a different explanation put forward by some academic economists[26] placed the burden for the failure on the allegedly poor conception of the 'snake' (which had been designed to protect the EC against external pressures, even if pressures of quite such magnitude had not been foreseen).[27] As Tsoukalis noted: '[w]ith the benefit of hindsight, it can be argued that the ambitious initiative, originally intended to transform radically the economic and political map of Western Europe, had been taken at the highest level without much thought of its wider implications.'[28]

In the end, the only concrete achievements of the Werner Report, in addition to a March 1971 decision on strengthening co-operation among central banks, were the creation of the European Monetary Cooperation Fund (EMCF) in 1973, along broadly the lines foreseen in the Report (and in advance of the latter's timetable) and a February 1974 Council Decision 'on the attainment of a high degree of convergence of the economic policies of the Member States'. Although the importance of the Werner Report as an early blueprint for economic and monetary union in Europe should not be underestimated, it can be argued that the Werner Plan was ill-conceived.[29] There was no enforcement mechanism built into the plan which could provide a discipline for those states which did not meet the guidelines towards convergence; and, also, there was no distinct division of responsibility between the various institutions that would be implementing the policy aims. In addition, the views upon how well the Member States would do in achieving the required convergence with the available instruments was, it could be argued, unrealistically optimistic, particularly given the fact that the impetus to move through the stages towards economic and monetary union seemed sadly lacking.

However, several important lessons had been learnt about the economic and political difficulties of moving towards EMU. A sustained record of stable currency management was an indispensable precondition for any serious attempt to adopt a single currency. The absence of stable currencies would render the goal of a single currency meaningless, and governments needed to undertake legally binding commitments, confirmed in the Treaty, if that objective were to stand much chance of being realised. Vague commitments in principle, without a firm timetable fixed in advance, were no good. No lasting progress towards EMU could be achieved without appropriate institutional reforms guaranteeing a transfer of responsibility in the macroeconomic field from national to European level. If this were not done old habits, governed by domestic imperatives, would reassert themselves, allowing little by way of a concerted reaction to international economic circumstances.

In addition to this, the 'snake' had one particularly interesting consequence: it marked the emergence of an increasingly vocal grouping of economists who visualised EMU as being the basis for a strategy of sustained growth in Europe (the Commission helped in this by setting up various study groups of economists). Evidence of this development, and its relevance, is contained in the Commission's report on 'European Union' of 26 June 1975 and in the so-called 'All Saints' Day Manifesto' of November 1975. This was prepared as a contribution to the Tindemans Report, which had been commissioned at the Paris summit of December 1974 as the basis for agreeing an overall concept of European Union.[30] The Report basically advanced the argument that creating an economic and monetary union was an essential component of the establishment of a united Europe (although it recognised that, for the time being, differences among the Member States ruled out common monetary or fiscal policies). The spotlight was focused upon making improvements to existing arrangements rather than on introducing major innovations that would require the Community countries to make the 'qualitative leap' they were not yet prepared to make.[31] It was against this background that the European Community took its second concrete step towards establishing a stable monetary bloc.

On 6–7 July 1978, at a meeting of the European Council in Bremen,

France and the Federal Republic of Germany presented a scheme for closer monetary cooperation – the European Monetary System (EMS) – to replace the currency 'snake'. This proposal followed the impetus provided in Roy Jenkins's famous speech in his first year as President of the European Commission. The EMS was modest by the standards of the earlier Werner initiative. Indeed, in contrast to the Werner plan, full-scale monetary union was not mentioned. It seems that the EC leaders of the day were reluctant to accept the significant institutional changes which a monetary union required.[32] Thus, the Commission drew up a plan for a European Monetary System with far more limited objectives for the immediate future than a monetary union (although the plan did not preclude its future evolution into a monetary union). The EMS, then, was initially designed to stabilise exchange rates without at the same time requiring that international policy divergences be eliminated, either through the elimination of fiscal and monetary rules or by empowering the Community to coordinate national policies.

In many ways, given the events of the previous couple of years, it was surprising that a major new initiative to relaunch monetary integration would be instigated. The Member States at that time had very different economic performances and exchange-rate regimes (ranging from independent floating to 'pivot rates' and a 'two-tier market'). Some countries had achieved a degree of success in keeping inflation at moderate levels and maintaining their commitment to the 'snake', while others had not.[33] Under these circumstances a new regime for European monetary co-operation and co-ordination appeared to be an unlikely venture; but it must be remembered that the reasons behind the establishment of the EMS were not only economic. Indeed, it can be argued that the initiative for the EMS came largely from political aspirations.

A POLITICAL DREAM VERSUS ECONOMIC NECESSITY

There were basically three political considerations behind the EMS initiative.[34] The first reason was the strengthening of the domestic political position of the two initiators of the EMS, Valéry Giscard d'Estaing and Helmut Schmidt, during the winter of 1977–78. Of these, the most easily recognisable change took place in France, with the national parliamentary elections of March 1978.

In the run-up to the elections, it had been widely forecast that the centre-right coalition would lose its majority in the National Assembly.

Even those who were more optimistic agreed that the influence of the French President and Raymond Barre (his Prime Minister, and a member of the centrist party) would weaken within the coalition. In the end, however, neither of these events took place: the centre-right majority was comfortably maintained (indeed, it was increased) while that of its Gaullist rival was reduced. This strengthened position gave Giscard d'Estaing the political authority to follow up the long-term stabilisation of the French economy, introduced with the Barre plan eighteen months earlier, by reentering into an exchange rate commitment with West Germany. The election results at the same time gave West Germany some assurance that French economic policy would be directed towards stability. Raymond Barre's confirmation as Prime Minister was a positive sign that France would not only pursue a non-Gaullist, pro-European foreign policy but also implement domestic policies that would give France more chance of success in a European monetary arrangement than she had previously had.[35]

West Germany also underwent political change during this time. After a difficult period in the shadow of his predecessor Willy Brandt, Helmut Schmidt's popularity within his own party increased, in addition to the then growing support for the coalition of the Social Democrats and the Liberals. A crucial factor in this change of attitude was the success of the operation against the hijackers of a Lufthansa jet at Mogadishu in October 1977.[36] The confidence which his increased popularity gave him, along with growing evidence of a difficult relationship with the United States, prompted Chancellor Schmidt to seek a firmer and wider alliance within the European Community.

The second political consideration in renewing European monetary integration efforts was a concern, voiced most explicitly by Helmut Schmidt, that political events in Italy were taking a turn for the worse. The rising strength of the Italian Communist party persuaded the leaders of the Christian Democrats, Giulio Andreotti and Aldo Moro, to bring the Communists into the government parliamentary majority. The efforts towards what was termed, this 'historical compromise' persuaded Helmut Schmidt of the need to give Italy, which had left the 'snake' within a year of its inception, the opportunity of a more stable European framework for its policies.[37]

The third political consideration arose from a wish, particularly on the part of West Germany, to have more independence from the United States. The latter point is particularly important for this current analysis. Schmidt had been openly critical of the Carter administration's inability to control inflation. The persistent weakening of the US dollar from 1977 onwards brought fears of large shifts towards the Deutschmark, which was Europe's major international currency, and the only one whose flows of capital were unregulated at that time. The reasoning behind increased monetary cooperation was that if Germany was more fully linked to the other major EC countries this would give it a form of protection from the effects of the US dollar. Closer monetary integration in Europe would also increase the influence of Europe on policy-making internationally. This was important as it seemed to offer a satisfactory, coordinated, response to the influence exerted by the US in the world economic summits and the Organisation for Economic Cooperation and Development. In this way Europe would assume more responsibility for growth in the international economy. Not all of the European Community countries, however, were so sure of the validity of this new initiative; in particular, the UK was dubious about its usefulness. The UK's views at this time may be summed up in the following statement:[38]

'While still accepting the goal of greater monetary stability, the Treasury remains sceptical to the point of contempt at most of the detailed content of the France-German scheme.'

The UK was, then, not satisfied with the Plan and remained outside the Agreement.

The EMS was established in a Resolution adopted by the European Council in Brussels in 1978 and came into existence on March 13, 1979. The System was seen as 'a fundamental component of a more comprehensive strategy aimed at lasting growth and stability, a progressive return to full employment, the harmonisation of living standards and the lessening of regional disparities'. In addition, it was intended to 'create a zone of monetary stability in Europe' and to strengthen cooperation between Member States with respect to monetary policy. All EC members, apart from the United Kingdom, linked their currencies to the System's Exchange Rate Mechanism (ERM), which was basically an 'adjustable peg' system and allowed for a 2.25 per cent band among the majority of currencies and a larger band of fluctuation (+6 per cent and –6 per cent) for Italy (until 1990, when it decided to use the narrower band) within which the exchange rates were free to fluctuate.[39] In the case that a currency reached the limits of these bands, the central banks of the countries involved intervened in order to maintain the exchange rate within the band. Realignments were to be allowed within the EMS, although they were expected to be infrequent. This was in line with the prevailing view at the time which was one of great concern about the effects of exchange rate movements on macroeconomic stability. As noted by Duisenberg in 1976 (i.e. before the EMS' inception):

> 'We are worried about the exchange rate developments in the Community. There is at present no effective Community framework for the co-ordination of policies in this area among all members, while recent developments have surely indicated the need for common action.'[40]

In addition to the ERM, financing facilities were provided for countries attempting to hold their exchange rates stable in the face of temporary balance of payments shock. The central bank of the currency facing difficulty was permitted to draw upon the very short-term financing facility (VSTF) to receive unlimited quantities of intervention currencies as required (subject to the agreement of the other central bank concerned).

Unlike previous monetary arrangements, the EMS had a special 'money' – the European Currency Unit (ECU) – which was defined as a basket of currencies of the countries that were members of the European Monetary System (a larger group of countries than the ERM members, because it included all the EC countries) and by an institution to control the issue of money – the European Monetary Fund (EMF).

The founding fathers of the EMS had high hopes about the role of the ECU in the EMS. They wanted it to be used as an instrument which would bring more symmetry into the system of interventions in the exchange market. Therefore an indicator of divergence was defined which was based upon the ECU. When a currency's ECU rate diverged by more than 75 per cent of its permitted band of fluctuation, the country in question was supposed to undertake measures to correct the divergence. This indicator of divergence was supposed to work symmetrically – that is, it would indicate which currency was on average becoming weaker or stronger against the other currencies. This instrument did not, however, work very efficiently, and as a result was quickly abandoned.[41]

Although much less ambitious than the Werner Plan, many analysts saw the European Monetary System as a distinct step towards economic and monetary union through its twin objectives of economic convergence and monetary control. Moreover, the experience of the 1970s led to a general alteration in approach to macroeconomic policy objectives, with an emphasis on monetary control primarily aimed at controlling inflation, and a rejection of the traditional (Keynesian) policies of fiscal expansion to counter high unemployment. Thus, an emphasis on joint monetary action had become the prime tool, with fiscal policy as its necessary adjunct.[42]

However, at the EMS's inception, the general consensus among economists appeared to be that the arrangement was unlikely to be successful. There were large variations in the inflation rates of member countries (threatening exchange rate stability) which led to reservations over how useful the EMS would be at strengthening a European commitment to low inflation. In time, however, analysts began to argue that the EMS had indeed achieved its aim of creating a zone of monetary stability in Europe. For example, various studies argued that there had indeed been a reduction in exchange rate variation, as well as some evidence of a reduction in the volatility of interest rates for ERM members.[43, 44]

One area of concern, however, was over the position of the Deutschmark as the dominant currency in the system. The main proponents of this idea were Giavazzi and Giovannini, who argued that, despite original intentions to the contrary, the EMS functioned asymmetrically – i.e. the burden of adjustment had been shared unequally between West Germany and the other members.[45] They argued that this was because the divergence indicator (which was designed to impose symmetry) had never really been used in this way. Indeed, out of all the members of the EMS, Germany had played the most negligible role in these intervention operations, a fact which suggested that it was the other members in the Mechanism who targeted intra-EMS exchange rates whilst Germany provided the nominal anchor in the arrangement.[46]

The strongest opposition to this view of EMS domination may be seen in the work of Fratianni and von Hagen.[47] They stated that Germany was totally independent of the rest of the EMS countries, in the light of the high degree of economic interdependence between Germany and the other Member States. They also argued that any proposition of German dominance in the EMS implied that the non-German Member States in the mechanism totally relinquished their monetary independence and allowed the Bundesbank to dictate their monetary policy for them, a view which was not upheld by the available evidence. Fratianni and von Hagen were, however, testing only a very extreme form of the German leadership hypothesis, and most of the existing empirical evidence is consistent with the proposition that

Germany was the dominant country in the EMS over the 1980s, in the sense that its monetary policy was the most influential in the system as a whole.

If the effect on exchange rate variation of ERM membership and the role of Germany are two of the issues on which economists focused when assessing the performance of the Exchange Rate Mechanism during its first ten years, others concentrated on the changing nature of the Mechanism itself. Goodhart, for example, noted that throughout the EMS's existence it had been an evolving institution, proceeding through several different stages.[48] The period up until March 1983 proved difficult for the System, both because of policy difficulties within the Member States and because of changes in the external economic environment. During this time, there were frequent realignments and it was far from clear that the EMS was actually making any real change to the conduct of national policies. The turning point was the strategic decision by the French Socialist government in March 1983 to renounce a policy of attempted independent domestic expansion in favour of giving priority to reducing inflation, the credibility of which could be enhanced by holding firmly to the EMS arrangement. With this change in policy, the EMS entered a period of more stability than at any time since its foundation. Although there was a realignment at that point, there were no further realignments for over two years and when one finally did come, only one currency was involved. The emphasis was increasingly on nominal convergence and co-ordination of monetary policies to underpin exchange-rate stability.[49] In fact, the System was virtually transformed into a fixed exchange rate regime as the members firmly committed themselves to fixed exchange rates, using this stance as the rationale for pursuing domestic policies aimed at combating inflation.

This second stage really marked a change in regime, involving an implicit division between West Germany (which was concerned with setting domestic monetary policy so as to maintain internal price stability) and the peripheral countries of the Exchange Rate Mechanism (which were striving to maintain their fixed nominal peg, in order to converge onto a low inflation path). Mastropasqua, Micossi and Rinaldi ascribed this change in resolve to two things: the progress which most of the Member States were managing to make in reducing their inflation rates and stabilising their balance of payments positions; and the realignment of March 1983, which succeeded, to a degree, in restoring the competitive positions of the Member States.[50] They also emphasised the role of the Bundesbank, in influencing the exchange rates of the ERM currencies with regard to the dollar, and that of the

Deutschmark, in its position as the anchor currency within the Exchange Rate Mechanism. During this period, however, there remained doubts among agents in the private sector about the willingness and capacity of the peripheral governments to take the low inflation route. Accordingly, there continued to be periods of speculative trade flows, testing the authorities' resolve (indeed, the authorities in many of these countries – e.g. France, Italy, Belgium – still relied heavily from time to time on exchange controls when speculation about possible realignments appeared). Indeed, although Goodhart argued that the third stage in the development of the ERM began in January 1987, and was characterised by a period of relative calm, doubts remained and, as Mastropasqua, Micossi and Rinaldi argued, that there were still changes which could be made to make the system more stable.[51]

The EMS, then, was viewed by its creators as an intermediate step towards European monetary unification. This 'transitional' role of the EMS is apparent in the features that represented institutional novelties over the experiments that preceded it: the Bretton Woods system and the 'snake'. In addition to this, the perceived success of the EMS appeared to stimulate, and be reinforced by, wider progress on European integration and, despite the doubts of some analysts, the EMS did develop into a very stable system. Changes in the rules of the system made it easier to defend the currency parities and to elicit co-operation from the participating Member States' central banks, in addition to the banks of the countries whose currencies were at risk. At the same time, in the initial period of the EMS's existence there was a large degree of convergence among the Member States, which made the task of defending existing exchange rate parities much easier. Together these provided many of the ingredients for the possible success of moves towards an economic and monetary union of Europe much easier. More significantly, however, and in addition, it may be argued that the proposals for a Single European Market (SEM) would not have been forthcoming were it not for the progress made by the European Monetary System, but that once proposals for a SEM were made it would not be long before discussion of monetary union in Europe became more vocal. It is with this in mind that we continue our analysis of the history of monetary integration in Chapter 3.

NOTES

1. There had, however, been a sign of the possible problems to come much earlier. In 1960, the first run on the US currency occurred when international speculators began to exchange dollars for gold on the London market.
2. A. M. Okun, *The Political Economy of Prosperity* (Washington: The Brookings Institution, 1970), p. 70.
3. H. Van Der Wee, *Prosperity and Upheaval: The World Economy 1945–1980* (London: Penguin, 1986), p. 69.
4. D. Gros and N. Thygesen, *European Monetary Integration, From the European Monetary System to European Monetary Union* (London: Longman, 1992), p. 11.
5. M. Panic, 'The Bretton Woods System: Concept and Practice' in J. Michie and J. Grieve Smith (eds) *Managing the Global Economy* (Oxford: Oxford University Press, 1995), p. 49.
6. As a result of the breakdown of the Bretton Woods system, a method for converting CAP prices into the national currencies in which farmers were actually paid ('green rates') was introduced, together with monetary compensation amounts (MCAs) to be paid or levied on Member States' trade in agricultural products to prevent any exploitation of the difference between market rates and green rates.
7. D. Gros and N. Thygesen, *op. cit.* (1992), p. 11.
8. D. C. Kruse, *op. cit.* (1980), p. 23.
9. *Ibid.*, p. 58.
10. The text of this report can be found in Monetary Committee of the European Communities, *Compendium of community monetary texts*, (Luxembourg: Office of Official Publications of the European Communities, 1986).
11. The Report was not clear, however, on whether there would be an actual single currency or merely a de facto one based on the locked exchange rates.
12. D. C. Kruse, *op. cit.* (1980), p. 59.
13. *Ibid.*, p. 59.
14. Council-Commission of the EC, Report to the Council and the Commission on the Realization by Stages of Economic and Monetary Union in the Community – 'Werner Report', Supplement to the *Bulletin* 11–1970 (Brussels, 1970).
15. K. Dyson, *op. cit.* (1994), p. 80.
16. P. de Grauwe, *op. cit.* (1995), p. 81.
17. *Ibid.*, p. 82.
18. K. Dyson, *op. cit.* (1994), p. 81.
19. The first stage involved the gradual narrowing of exchange rate fluctuation margins, a two billion dollars increase in credit facilities available to member states, an attempt to co-ordinate national economic policies, and a feasibility study on the creation of a European Monetary Fund (EMF).
20. Moreover, Germany insisted, successfully, that unless agreement was reached on the second, and more substantive stage, of EMU by January 1976, the monetary co-operation measures begun during the first stage would be discontinued.
21. L. Tsoukalis, *The New European Economy*, 2nd ed. (Oxford: Oxford University Press, 1993), p. 181.

22. Niels Thygesen, 'International Co-ordination of Monetary Policies with Special Reference to the European Community', in John E. Wadsworth and Francois Leonard de Juvigny (eds), *New Approaches to Monetary Policy*, (Alpen aan der Rijn: Sijthoff and Noordhoff, 1979), pp. 205–24.

23. Sterling's effective appreciation, however, was less that 1 per cent, which, as the Bank of England observed, was more than balanced by the abolition of the American import surtax. Thus, although the pound's new dollar parity was slightly higher than its floating level, the market accepted it and the performance of sterling broadly paralleled that of other European currencies in early 1972, with a slight outflow of capital being followed by upward pressure on the exchange rate during January and February.

24. L. Tsoukalis, *op. cit.* (1993), p. 180.

25. D. Cobham, 'Strategies for Monetary Integration Revisited', *Journal of Common Market Studies*, XXVII (1989), p. 203.

26. Notably: R. Vaubel, 'Real Exchange-rate Changes in the European Community – a new approach to the determination of optimal currency areas', *Journal of International Economics*, 8 (1978); and T. Peeters, 'EMU: Prospects and Retrospect', in M. T. Sumner and G. Zis (eds), *European Monetary Union* (London: Macmillan, 1982).

27. D. Cobham, *op. cit.* (1989), p. 204.

28. L. Tsoukalis, *op. cit.* (1993), p. 182.

29. See: G. D. Baer and T. Padoa-Schioppa, 'The Werner Report revisited', in *Report on Economic and Monetary Union in the Community* ('Delors Report'), (1989), pp. 53–60.

30. K. Dyson, *op. cit.* (1994), p. 87.

31. D. C. Kruse, *op. cit.* (1980), p. 239.

32. For example, at the time of the Werner Report, Giscard d'Estaing indicated that his government would have difficulty in accepting any institutional formula which made explicit the transfer of monetary sovereignty from national to European level.

33. D. Gros and N. Thygesen, *op. cit.* (1992), p. 35.

34. For a fuller explanation, see: D. Gros and N. Thygesen, *op. cit.* (1992).

35. P. Ludlow, *The Making of the European Monetary System* (London: Butterworths, 1982), pp. 84–5.

36. *Ibid.*, p. 79.

37. D. Gros and N. Thygesen, *op. cit.* (1992), p. 36.

38. *The Times*, 11 July, 1978.

39. Although all Member States participated in the EMS, they were not required to join the Exchange Rate Mechanism as part of that participation, hence the British position.

40. D. Gros and N. Thygesen, *op. cit.* (1992), p. 39.

41. P. de Grauwe, *op. cit.* (1995), pp. 99–103.

42. A. Britton and D. Mayes, *Achieving Monetary Union in Europe* (London: Sage, 1992), pp. 8–9.

43. There have been many studies of this particular issue. C. A. E. Goodhart ('Economists' Perspectives on the EMS: A review essay', *Journal of Monetary Economics*, 26 (1990) 471–87) notes at least two problems in the existing studies, over and above the major problem in all EMS studies of attempting to examine a counter-factual – i.e. how would these countries

have fared in the absence of the EMS? The first of these additional problems is that if the growth rate of unit labour costs/domestic inflation does not converge between countries maintaining a fixed nominal exchange rate, real exchange rates will vary much more over the medium and longer term than nominal rates. Secondly, the time frame, or frequency, over which such volatility/stability is tested is important. Unless there are frequent and/or large realignments within the data set, any pegged rate system should exhibit less nominal volatility (and also less real volatility unless inflation rates among the members are very dissimilar) when tested over short periods or high frequencies, e.g. days, weeks, months. While such short-run stability has undoubted advantages (e.g. in the running of the EEC, to businessmen and tourists), the more important issue is whether the EMS managed to reduce the longer-term instability of real exchange rates, as measured over quarters and years.

44. M. J. Artis and M. P. Taylor, 'Exchange Rates, Interest Rates, Capital Controls and the European Monetary System', in F. Giavazzi, S Micossi and M. Miller (eds), *The European Monetary System* (Cambridge: Cambridge University Press, 1988).

45. F. Giavazzi and A. Giavannini, *Limiting Exchange Rate Flexibility: The European Monetary System* (Cambridge, Mass: MIT Press, 1989).

46. C. Mastropasqua, S. Micossi and R. Rinaldi, 'Interventions, Sterilisation and Monetary Policy in the EMS Countries (1979–87)', in F. Giavazzi et. al., *op. cit.* (1988), pp. 252–87.

47. M. Fratianni and J. von Hagen, 'German Dominance in the EMS: The Empirical Evidence', *Open Economies Review*, 1 (1990), pp. 86–7.

48. C. A. E. Goodhart, *op. cit.* (1990).

49. *Ibid.*, p. 83.

50. C. Mastropasqua, S. Micossi and R. Rinaldi, 'Interventions, Sterilisation and Monetary Policy in European Monetary System Countries, 1979–87', in F. Giavazzi, S. Micossi and M. Miller (eds), *The European Monetary System* (Cambridge: Cambridge University Press, 1988), pp. 252–87.

51. C. Mastropasqua, S. Micossi and R. Rinaldi, *op. cit.* (1988).

3 The Maastricht Treaty and Beyond

Europe has always been the continent of doubt and questioning, seeking a humanism appropriate to its time, the cradle of ideas which ultimately encircle the globe. The time has come to return to ideals, to let them penetrate our lives.

Jacques Delors, 1989

INTRODUCTION

Until well into the 1980s a true common market in which national borders no longer interfered with economic activity between the member states of the European Community remained an unfulfilled promise.[1] The realisation, however, that the European Monetary System arrangement was capable of creating a 'zone of monetary stability' was both encouraged by, and encouraged progress on, European integration. In 1985, the new Commission, chaired by Jacques Delors, published a White Paper which made it clear that there had been too many delays in the process of European integration, and that too many barriers still stood in the way of the creation of the kind of economic growth area which a market of over 300 million consumers could represent. Delors aimed at securing the completion of a Single European Market (SEM) by the end of 1992, and set out a specific catalogue of measures to do so. However, to have any realistic prospect of succeeding in only seven years needed more than a mere declaration of political intent. At the European Council meeting in Milan in June 1985, a decision was reached (against opposition from Britain, Denmark and Greece) to convene an intergovernmental conference (IGC) for the purpose of preparing a revision of the existing treaties. The apparent division between the six original members of the Community, and the latecomers (with Ireland in a more neutral position) was centred around the issues of institutional reform (which included the extension of majority voting in the Council of Ministers) the possible extension of the powers of the European Parliament, and the role of European Political Co-operation.[2] This division had become apparent earlier within the Dooge

Committee, which had been asked to prepare a report on institutional reform. Further, the countries which had a more minimalist view of the Community's role naturally did not welcome the idea of a fresh constitutional debate on Europe. This whole issue was of major political importance, and a decision made by the Italian European Council presidency to go ahead on a majority vote was both unexpected and without precedent. It thus became clear that the majority of Member States were determined to continue with institutional reform and the relaunching of the integration process. So it was that the Single European Act (SEA) was signed by representatives of all twelve member countries in February 1986. On 1 July 1987, after referenda were held in Denmark and Ireland, the Single European Act came into force.

The SEA added a new Article 8a to the EEC Treaty (now Article 7a of the EC Treaty) which stated that:[3]

'the Community shall adopt measures with the aim of progressively establishing the internal market over a period expiring on 31 December 1992 . . . [comprising] an area without frontiers in which the free movement of goods, persons, services and capital is ensured.'

Thus, the White Paper had not really increased the extent of the European Communities' ambitions; rather, it set out what needed to be achieved in keeping with the earlier Treaty of Rome. In these terms, the contribution of the White Paper was really in the degree of progress in integration to which it aspired, and the speed in which it hoped to achieve this progress.[4]

Agreement on the policies of economic integration was, and is, very much a political process, but their achievement very much depends upon market conditions. Thus, the speed in which the Single European Act was negotiated reflected a number of factors. For example, by 1985 the process of legislative integration in Europe was lagging behind the degree to which European firms were taking part in the global marketplace. This latter process had become highly developed and European firms discovered that they were losing their share of the market to their, particularly, American and Japanese competitors. This was due to the fact that different rules on the registration of products and on product standards applied to firms registering in different Member States; therefore European firms faced a 'home' (i.e. European) market that was smaller and of a higher cost structure than that of their Japanese or American counterparts.[5]

For this reason, it was important for firms (as could be seen from

the positive reaction of the European Round Table of businesspeople
to such moves) that restrictions and quantitative barriers to trade be
removed. However, it was not enough simply to have increased levels
of microeconomic integration. Macroeconomic integration was also
required. Macroeconomic co-ordination and co-operation, monetary
control and closer exchange rate realignment would help create conditions which encouraged integration at the level of the firm and of the
market players. The 1992 programme therefore created an initiative
which met microeconomic considerations, and began to meet
macroeconomic ones as well.[6] Given these background conditions, the
prospects for monetary union were thus very much different for the
period after the Single European Act was negotiated compared to what
they were in 1970 at the time of the Werner Plan, or even in 1979
when the European Monetary System was established.[7]

Encouraged by the positive reaction to the Single Market programme,
in 1988 the Heads of State or Government set the Community on course
for economic and monetary union. The thinking behind this initiative
was that business and the ordinary citizen would not feel the full benefits of the emerging Single Market until they could also rely on fixed
exchange rates or even a common European currency. The strongest
statement of this view was made later on in the Commission's statement of the case for EMU, 'One Market, One Money'.[8] In addition,
most of the barriers to the free movement of money and capital were
due to disappear under the Single Market by July 1990. As banks and
insurance companies began to operate increasingly across national frontiers, capital flows were steadily growing. Indeed, this greatly reduced
the member states' scope for independent national monetary policies.
This consideration was voiced most strongly by Padoa-Schioppa who
advised against following what he called an 'inconsistent quartet' of
policy objectives, in the form of full capital mobility, fixed exchange
rates, free trade and independent national monetary policies, arguing
that '[i]n the long run, the only solution to the inconsistency is to
complement the internal market with a monetary union'.[9] Thus, as the
Single Market neared completion, the pressure for closer monetary co-
operation and for a faster pace on the road to economic and monetary
union was steadily increasing.

As well as these economic considerations, there were political reasons
for a launch of a new initiative on economic and monetary union –
particularly on the part of France, Italy and West Germany. In a 1988
memorandum to Ecofin, dated 8 January, the French Finance Minister,
Edouard Balladur, made it obvious that French recommendations on

the monetary future of Europe went beyond a mere reform of the European Monetary System. In particular, French officials were uneasy about the asymmetrical nature of the system and the seemingly pivotal role of the Bundesbank. Indeed, Balladur argued that the 'rapid pursuit of the monetary construction of Europe [was] the only possible solution'.[10] Similarly, in a memorandum from the Italian Minister of the Treasury, Guiliano Amato, the feeling was that 'a minimum degree of convergence in the sectors of taxation, supervision and other forms of regulation' was required.[11] Both countries, then, seemed to advocate a fundamental reform of Europe's monetary arrangements. More important yet, however, was the willingness of the German government, signalled by a memorandum from the Foreign Minister, Hans Dietrich Genscher, to take part in this debate.[12]

There were really two major reasons why the French and Italian memoranda were instrumental in eliciting a German response.[13] First of all, the memoranda were rather vague about the institutional implications of moving towards monetary union and of much closer economic policy co-ordination. This therefore left Germany with some room to be assertive over the design of the new initiative. It also had the effect of raising the debate on monetary unification well beyond the realm of purely technical issues to a more general political level.

The second reason why a genuine dialogue could begin on the future of economic and monetary co-operation and co-ordination at this time can be found in a second memorandum, again to Ecofin, this time from the German Finance Minister, Gerhard Stoltenberg. Stoltenburg, who was President of Ecofin at this time, was anxious to see progress on the directive for capital liberalisation put forward by the Commission two years earlier. Once this directive had been adopted, the German government would be prepared to consider the wide-ranging political and institutional reorganisation necessary for the Community to create an economic and monetary union.

It was against this background, then, that the European Council meeting in Hanover in June 1988 convened, and the participating heads of state or government restated the objective of economic and monetary union. At their request, a committee was set up to investigate the prospects for further monetary integration.[14] The committee would be chaired by Jacques Delors and would be composed of the governors of the EC national central banks and three independent experts with 'the task of studying and proposing concrete stages leading towards EMU'. The Committee was asked to complete its work sufficiently well ahead of the meeting of the European Council scheduled to be held Madrid at the end of June 1989 to allow Ecofin to examine its results.[15]

THE DELORS REPORT

The Delors Committee met eight times between September 1988 and the submission of its Report in 1989.[16, 17] The Report consisted of three chapters: the first was a brief overview of the past record of economic and monetary integration in the Community, making the case for EMU as an essential complement to the Single Market; the second contained a more detailed analysis of the implications for the final stage of EMU (including institutional arrangements in the form of a European Monetary Institute – EMI – which would be the precursor to the creation of a European Central Bank – ECB); and the third contained proposals which set out in detail the conditions that had to be met in order to establish economic and monetary union. Paralleling the earlier Werner Plan, it recommended a three-stage plan for its achievement (in 'discrete but evolutionary steps'), this time with the first stage set to begin on 1 July 1990, when the capital liberalisation directive was to come into force.[18] Although the Report suggested that there should be a clear indication of the timing of the third stage, it added that the setting of deadlines, in particular for the move to irrevocably fixed exchange rates, was not advisable. As the Report noted: '[t]he conditions for moving from stage to stage cannot be defined precisely in advance; nor is it possible to foresee today when these conditions will be realised'.[19] Instead, during the first stage the Member States would draw up programmes aimed at converging and improving economic performance, which in turn would make it possible to establish fixed exchange rates. The 'single most important condition' for attaining monetary union in Europe was seen to be the irrevocable locking of exchange rates, after which a single currency would replace the myriad of national currencies which were present within the existing European monetary arrangements. Indeed, in contrast to the Werner Plan, the Delors Report was insistent upon the *early* introduction of a single currency to ensure 'the irreversibility of the move to monetary union'.

In addition to the three-stage plan, the Delors Report made some important recommendations with regard to the institutional framework which should be present in a future European economic and monetary union. With regard to fiscal policy, for example, it proposed to give Ecofin, in cooperation with the European Parliament, the authority to apply binding rules in the form of upper limits to national budget deficits. Indeed, like the Werner Report, the Delors Report highlighted the need for fiscal harmonisation. In particular, the Report states that:[20]

'In the budgetary field, binding rules are required that would: firstly, impose effective upper limits on budget deficits of individual member countries of the Community, although ... the situation of each member country might have to be taken into consideration; secondly, exclude access to direct access to central bank credit and other forms of monetary financing while, however, permitting open market operations in government securities; thirdly, limit recourse to external borrowing in non-Community currencies.'

At its Madrid meeting in June 1989, the European Council agreed that the Delors Committee's report defined a process that might lead to economic and monetary union, but that 'full and adequate preparations' had to precede the setting of dates for the beginning of Stages 2 and 3.[21] The latter qualification was the result of the position of the British government vis-à-vis the EMU proposals. The then British Prime Minister, Margaret Thatcher, was unwilling to allow sterling to enter the ERM under Stage 1 of EMU and did not want the decision to embark upon Stage 1 of the Delors Report to be interpreted as a commitment to economic and monetary union in Europe. Such a commitment was seen as having repercussions for national sovereignty which were too great to be accepted at such an early stage in negotiations. Under pressure, however, from her then Chancellor of the Exchequer, Nigel Lawson, and her then Foreign Secretary, Geoffrey Howe, Thatcher announced her acceptance of Stage 1 on condition that Stages 2 and 3 be left open and no intergovernmental conference convened.

This compromise in the face of British objections was, however, unsatisfactory to most of the Member States, and following an Ecofin meeting in September the French Presidency put together a high-level group of officials from the Member States' Ministries of Finance and Foreign Affairs to prepare the questions for such a conference. This group was presided over by Mme Elisabeth Guigou and produced a report – 'the Guigou Report' – in October, which raised (in the form of questions) a variety of issues to be considered on the agenda of a future intergovernmental conference. In hindsight, it may seem unclear what the reasons for the Guigou Report were, when the Delors Report had already gone such a long way in framing the issues which would be on any IGC agenda. The Delors Report, however, largely involved central bankers or others who had no national political responsibilities. In contrast to this, the framework of the Guigou group allowed for an immediate rehearsal of the important themes among those national governmental decision-makers who would subsequently be participating should a conference be convened.[22] With this in mind, at the Strasbourg meeting of the European Council in December 1989, on a proposal from President Mitterand and against a lone objection from the British government, it was decided to convene an Intergovernmental Conference on economic and monetary union the following year, its purpose being to amend the Treaty of Rome in order that the second and third stages of EMU could be implemented.

The above discussion of the Delors Report may be enough to demonstrate that the drive to put the recommendations of the Delors Report into place was really generated in the first eighteen months after its publication. The political support for the EMU process proved initially to be stronger than the authors of the Delors Report, including the President of the EC Commission, could have anticipated. This became clear both from the setting of dates for the IGC and the efforts to provide a timetable for the stages.

Two developments may have expedited the higher political priority given to the single currency. The first was the strong interest expressed by major European industrial enterprises in a single currency, as well as the drive of the EC Commission. As noted in the Delors Report:[23]

'The adoption of a *single currency*, while not strictly necessary for the creation of a monetary union, might be seen – for economic as well as psychological and political reasons – as a natural and desirable further development of the monetary union. A single currency would clearly demonstrate the irreversibility of the ... union, considerably facilitate the monetary management of the Community and avoid the transactions costs of converting currencies.'

Moreover, there was a growing acceptance by policy-makers, in countries other than West Germany, that the long-term institutional arrangements of EMU provided a solid foundation for success. By defining the final stage clearly and achieving widespread political support for EMU, a constructive feedback was assured on managing the transition from the level of monetary co-ordination in the European Monetary System to the level required by a single central monetary authority in EMU.[24]

However, in addition to these changes in political priorities, there were other political developments taking place at this time which would prove to have a dramatic impact on the future of European integration.

THE COLLAPSE OF COMMUNISM AND THE POSITION OF GERMANY

The year 1989 was one of the most striking in the process of political change in central and eastern Europe, its climax being the fall of the Berlin Wall on 11 November. The key to understanding this process of political change undoubtedly lies in the fundamental transformation of government policy which occurred in the Soviet Union after Soviet President Mikhail Gorbachev came to power. Although ultimately his aim to transform the Soviet economy failed, the policies which he instituted effectively freed Eastern Europe from communism. Although unpredictable in their timing and form, the events of 1989 were almost inevitable once the East Europeans realised that the foundation of Soviet support had been withdrawn from their own discredited regimes. It can be argued, then, that a combination of internal decay and the removal of external support provides the explanation for the speed and lack of violence with which communism in Eastern Europe collapsed – few thought that the system was worth fighting to defend. Moreover, the process of change in central and eastern Europe may be said to reflect a desire by policy-makers in these countries to move towards the West. Indeed, intellectuals and reformers have tended to view the process as a 'return to Europe', where Europe is viewed as their natural, cultural, and spiritual homeland.[25]

This policy transformation in central and eastern Europe persuaded the Community of the need to become a more significant actor on the international scene. In particular, the possibility of a reunified Germany persuaded many that a strengthened Community was needed, one which would provide a firm anchoring for such a state.[26] West Germany, too, wanted reunification to take place without unduly alarming its Community partners. The best way to do this was to emphasise her European credentials and its willingness to operate in partnership with the other Member States. France was particularly anxious to retain its special relationship, fearing that the latter might well 'turn eastwards', seeking new economic ties and political co-operation in that direction.

For the reunified Germany in an enlarged Europe, its post-Cold War state brought further, unexpected, problems. Her geographic position and economic strength meant that she began to receive large numbers of refugees from eastern and central Europe, a situation which grew worse as the conflict in the former Yugoslavia raged on. In addition, although the former East Germany was economically the most advanced of the COMECON states, it was very backward by comparison with the former West Germany. This meant that a reunified Germany now had both the richest and the poorest regions in the European Union. Levels of pollution in the GDR were particularly high, and the whole fabric of the country was in a poor state of repair, demanding huge resources for many years to come. Rapidly growing public expenditure in the new Länder led to high budget deficits in Germany and the acceleration of inflation. The burden of stabilisation efforts fell almost entirely on monetary policy, and this led to higher interest rates in Germany and also indirectly in the other countries of the ERM.[27] Moreover, these events forced EC governments to ask whether the further development of the Community (EC 'deepening') should take place before any possible enlargement of Community membership (EC 'widening').

On 1 July 1990, the starting date of the wider EMU project, West and East Germany instituted a monetary union. On that day the Ostmark, which had been the currency of the German Democratic Republic (GDR) was taken out of circulation and was replaced by the West German Deutschmark (DM).[28] However, even as domestic debate over German Economic and Monetary Union (GEMU) rumbled on, steps were being taken to advance European monetary integration one stage further. In June 1990, at the European Council meeting in Dublin, deepening was chosen before widening, and the decision was taken to convene two intergovernmental conferences – one on economic and monetary union, the other on political union – the work for which was to be completed by the end of 1992, the deadline for the completion of a Single European Market.

THE MAASTRICHT TREATY

In official terms the Maastricht Summit was a meeting of the European Council, those twice-yearly events which have been so crucial in the history of post-war European integration. From it came a major document – the Maastricht Treaty, formally known as the Treaty on European Union (TEU). Officially signed on 7 February 1992, the Maastricht Treaty was the result of the two aforementioned IGCs, conducted in parallel.

In terms of economic and monetary union the Maastricht Treaty builds on the work of the earlier Delors Report, setting out in very great detail the procedures to be followed for the realisation of EMU. As in the Delors Report, these procedures would take place in three stages. However, whereas the Delors Report framed the transitional terms in a rather schematic manner, the Maastricht Treaty was very specific about what each stage towards EMU should entail. Indeed, by the time the Treaty was signed the first stage of EMU was already well under way, with the capital liberalisation directive already in force.[29]

The second stage, basically a transitional period before the attainment of EMU, began on 1 January 1994. The principal goal in the second stage was to secure broad convergence between the economic policies of the Member States. To this end the European Council formulated economic policy guidelines and the Member States were required to submit 'medium-term convergence programmes' setting out all the economic policy measures which they planned in order to ensure their full participation in the final stage of EMU, with the main focus being price stability and sound public finances. Member States whose economic policies jeopardised the prospects of achieving economic and monetary union could be placed under pressure to fall back into line through recommendations issued by the Council of Ministers. Since the final stage involves the establishment of an independent European Central Bank, Member States were required under Articles 107 and 108 of the Maastricht Treaty to begin preparing the way for legislation to guarantee the independence of their monetary authorities during the second stage. (France, for example, began this process at the start of 1994.) In addition, at the start of the second stage the European Monetary Institute (EMI) was established as a forerunner of the European Central Bank, with its seat in Frankfurt-on-Main. This Institute, charged with helping to create the conditions for the transition to the third stage, only operates during the second stage. Its tasks involve strengthening the co-ordination of monetary policy (including consultation between national central banks on technical matters related to monetary union) and ensuring price stability, preparing for the establishment of a European System of Central Banks (ESCB), preparing for a single currency in the third stage and supervising the development of the ECU. The European System of Central Banks is the means whereby the governors of the participating states' central banks play a role alongside the ECB in the overall direction of EMU, its main objective being to ensure price stability, and its main functions to include the operation of monetary policy and payments systems, the conduct of foreign exchange operations, and the holding of the official reserves of participating countries. The role of the European Central Bank is close to that of the Federal Reserve System in the US. It heads the European System of Central Banks and its non-executive members consist of the governors of members' central banks (who have equal voting rights on most issues).

Before embarking upon the third stage, the Member States face the test of determining which of them fulfil the very strict conditions laid down for participation in a single currency. The Commission and the EMI report to Ecofin on the progress made in the fulfilment by the Member States of their obligations regarding the achievement of economic and monetary union. These reports include an examination of the compatibility between each Member State's national legislation, including the statutes of its national central bank, with the Maastricht Treaty and the statute of the ECB. The reports also examine whether a high degree of sustainable economic convergence among EU states has been achieved with reference to the fulfilment of the so-called convergence criteria laid down in Article 109j of the Maastricht Treaty. If the Council of (Finance) Ministers decides (by qualified majority, where each state's vote is weighted by its size) that a majority of Member States meet these criteria, then it may recommend that the European Council vote (again by qualified majority) on whether to initiate Stage III which will establish the European Central Bank to which the responsibility for the conduct of the monetary policy of the Member States will be transferred. To preclude the situation of Stage II continuing indefinitely, the Treaty required that the Heads of State or Government meet no later than 31 December 1996 in order to consider whether a majority of EC Member States satisfy the conditions for monetary union. If they did, then EMU may proceed. If they did not, and no date has been set for EMU by the end of 1997, then Stage III will begin on 1 January 1999. In this case, Stage Three may be instituted with the participation of only a *minority* of EC Member States. Upon the inauguration of Stage III, exchange rates will be irrevocably fixed. The EMI will be succeeded by the European Central Bank and the Council of Ministers will decide when their national currencies will be replaced with the single European currency. This may be on the first day of Stage III or, alternatively, the ECB may simply instruct the Member States' national central banks to convert their national currencies into one another at par until these are replaced by the single currency. Not all states were happy with these arrangements, however. In particular, during the Maastricht negotiations, in July 1991, it had become obvious that a crucial issue remained over the interpretation of the so-called 'no coercion' principle. This principle could be formulated such that even if states signed and ratified the Treaty, this would still not imply an undertaking to move to the third stage. On the other hand, it could allow a specific exception to be made for those states who wanted it – notably the UK (which had long opposed the notion of irreversibility that EMU seemed to imply) and possibly Denmark – whilst at the same time committing, at the time of ratification, all the other Member States to move to the third stage.[30] The latter was indeed what happened, with the final version of the Maastricht Treaty including two specific protocols which granted the United Kingdom and Denmark broad opt-out clauses.

At the time that the Maastricht Treaty negotiations were taking place, there was grave concern felt by those who strongly believed in the spirit of EMU that requirements such as these, made by member states who were not so in favour of a broad, European-wide accession to EMU, would in the end weaken the document itself. It was therefore with much relief that the TEU was signed in February 1992. Ratification did not seem far away. However, before the year was out, events had already conspired to place the entire process of economic and monetary union in Europe in jeopardy.

CRISIS IN THE SYSTEM

Since the Maastricht Treaty was signed, a combination of economic recession, unstable currency markets (arising partly from Germany's high interest rates, maintained as a consequence of German reunification) and national political attitudes towards the European integration process have cast doubt on whether or not EMU is attainable, and on which Member States might be in a position to participate in the Third Stage.

Most notable of the events which have occurred subsequent to the Maastricht Treaty, and which have threatened the progress of EMU, was the turbulence in the Exchange Rate Mechanism of the European Monetary System. The Danish rejection of the Treaty on European Union in their national referendum of 2 June 1992 acted as a stimulus for those who opposed the Maastricht Treaty in other Member States (notably in Britain, but also in France and Germany) leading to a series of crises which fundamentally altered the operation of the ERM as a framework for monetary policy co-ordination within the European Union.

In particular, in August of that year tensions began to develop within the EMS, focused largely on the lira. These intensified early in September, when public opinion polls began to suggest that French voters might also reject the Maastricht Treaty in their referendum of 20 September. Although this did not in fact happen (though the vote was indeed very close), by that time it was too late. The real crises had occurred a few days earlier, with the withdrawal of the British and Italian currencies from the arrangement after a series of politically embarrassing and large-scale currency realignments. In addition, the peseta had been devalued and other EMS currencies had come under attack. Moreover, in November the peseta and escudo were devalued, and the punt was devalued in January 1993 (although the fates of the franc and the krone were also in doubt for some time they were, in the end, successfully defended). In addition, although the crisis seemed to abate in the early months of 1993, tension re-emerged in April. The peseta and escudo were devalued once more in May, and the French franc came under sustained attack during July. On 1 August, the ERM band was widened from 2.25 per cent to fifteen per cent and the whole future of economic and monetary union in Europe seemed in doubt.[31]

Although precipitated by concerns over the future course of European integration which had been laid down in the Maastricht Treaty, these difficulties within the Mechanism may actually be traced back to the late 1980s when the growing political momentum towards economic and monetary union transformed the ERM from a 'fixed but adjustable' mechanism into one where any adjustments were politically costly. Unfortunately this transformation took place just as Germany was adapting to her changing economic and political needs after unification (with the concomitant increases in German interest rates, which then spread to the rest of the Member States); and the cost competitiveness of certain EC countries, particularly Italy and Spain, but also Britain, was undergoing an apparent deterioration. As an International Monetary Fund report of the crisis noted:[32]

'One important factor that contributed to market pressures against some currencies was the apparent deterioration of international cost competitiveness. In the years preceding the crisis, limited adjustments of parities and a lack of full convergence of inflation rates resulted in significant real appreciations of the lira, the escudo, and the peseta, as well as of the Swedish krone, which was unilaterally pegged to the ECU.'

In addition, the weakness of the dollar in the late 1980s both emphasised and exacerbated the then weak competitive position of countries competing directly with the United States in international markets (such as the United Kingdom). Moreover, what the latter also served to highlight was that even though the European countries aspired to act as a single bloc, they were in fact highly vulnerable (collectively as well as individually) to the vagaries of the international marketplace. Indeed, this notion was emphasised by reports that the speculative crises of 1992–93 were, in fact, self-fulfilling in character. Speculators observed that, due to prevailing economic conditions, some of the authorities involved had an incentive to change their policies. Inflation rates, for example, in some Member States remained higher than in others; whilst in several Member States serious budgetary imbalances were not tackled.[33] The only way in which the Member States could tackle these difficulties, in the eyes of foreign exchange traders, was to drop out of the Exchange Rate Mechanism.[34] Because they then expected such an event to take place, foreign exchange traders began a speculation which, in the end, actually forced the authorities to drop out of the system. This feature had been analysed in theoretical models, and should not have come as a surprise.[35] It has, however, led many people to think that the speculators are to blame for the collapse of the EMS,[36] a fact which has prompted some economists to propose the reintroduction of capital controls, thereby reducing the amount of funds that can be mobilised by speculators.[37] It may be argued, however, that, although the absence of capital controls affected the timing and the dynamics of the disintegration of the EMS, it did not fundamentally alter its instability, which resulted from the credibility and the liquidity problems of rigidly fixed exchange rate systems.[38] It does, however, raise the issue of what the prospects for economic and monetary union actually are, when the existing monetary arrangements seemed to so easily fall foul of the international marketplace. The European Commission appears confident that any such difficulties can be overcome. Indeed, the opening lines of the Green Paper on the Practical Arrangements for the Introduction of the Single Currency are testament to the Commission's beliefs over the viability of the EMU project:[39]

'By the end of the century, Europe will have a single currency. It will be strong and stable. This is the wish of the leaders and peoples in signing and then ratifying the Treaty on European Union.'

However, whether or not such confidence is actually misplaced will be evident soon when the Member States face the test of whether or not a high degree of sustainable economic convergence among the EU states has been achieved with reference to the fulfilment of the convergence criteria. It is to a full examination of these convergence criteria – their explanation, their aims, and their possible achievement – that this analysis now turns.

NOTES

1. K-D. Borchardt, *European Integration, The origins and growth of the European Union*, 4th ed. (Luxembourg: Office for Official Publications of the European Communities, 1995), p. 31.
2. See: M. W. J. Lak, 'Interaction between European Political Cooperation and the European Community: existing rules and challenges', *Common Market Law Review*, vol. 26, no. 2 (1989); Renaud Dehousse, 'European Political Cooperation', *European Journal of International Law*, vol. 1, no. 1/2 (1990); and Lionel Barber, 'Europe's Political Cooperation: An American Perspective on European Union', *Europe*, December, no. 302 (1990).
3. *Completing the Internal Market. White Paper from the Commission to the European Council* (Luxembourg: Office for Official Publications of the European Communities, 1985).
4. A. Britton and D. Mayes, *op. cit.* (1992), pp. 12–13.
5. *Ibid.*, p. 13.
6. For a fuller description of the negotiations leading to the Single European Act, see: A. Moravscik, 'Negotiating the Single European Act', in R. Keohane and S. Hoffman (eds), *The New European Community: Decisionmaking and Institutional Change* (San Francisco: Boulder, Oxford: Westview Press, 1991); N. Colchester and D. Buchan, *Europe Relaunched: Truths and Illusions on the Way to 1992* (London: The Economist Books/ Hutchinson, 1990); P. Taylor, 'The new dynamics of EC integration in the 1980s', in J. Lodge (ed.), *The European Community and the Challenge of the Future* (London: Pinter, 1989).
7. A. Britton and D. Mayes *op. cit.* (1992), p. 13.
8. Commission of the European Communities, 'One Market, One Money', *European Economy* (1990), p. 44.
9. T. Padoa-Schioppa, 'The European Monetary System: A Long-Term View' in F. Giavazzi, S. Micossi and M. Miller (eds.), *The European Monetary System* (Cambridge: Cambridge University Press, 1988), p. 376.
10. For a more wide-ranging discussion of the Balladur memorandum, see D. Gros and N. Thygesen, *op. cit.* (1992), pp. 312–15.
11. G. Amato (1988). The Italian memorandum to ECOFIN, dated 23 February, was published under the title 'Un motore per lo SME' in the Italian business paper *Il Sole 24 Ore* two days later. Reprint of the Memorandum to ECOFIN Council, 23 February.

12. D. M. Harrison, *The Organisation of Europe – Developing A Continental Market Order* (London: Routledge, 1995), pp. 108–109.
13. Germany held the Presidency in the EC in the first half of 1988, so it was perhaps natural that the Presidents of the General Affairs Council and the Ecofin Council should both want to put Europe's monetary construction on their agenda.
14. B. Eichengreen and J. A. Frieden (1994), 'The Political Economy of European Monetary Unification: An Analytical Introduction', in J. A. Frieden and D. A. Lake (eds), 3rd ed., *International Political Economy, Perspectives on Global Power and Wealth* (London: Routledge, 1995), p. 267.
15. D. Gros and N. Thygesen, *op. cit.* (1992), pp. 311–317.
16. There was immediate publication of the Report itself in April. A volume including the Collected Papers contributed by members and rapporteurs was published in August. This and other chapters refer to this fuller version, Committee for the Study of Economic and Monetary Union (1989).
17. D. Gros and N. Thygesen, *op. cit.* (1992), p. 317.
18. *Ibid.*, (1992), p. 317.
19. The 'Delors' Report, *op. cit.* (1989), paragraph 43.
20. The 'Delors' Report, *op. cit.* (1989), paragraph 30.
21. The United Kingdom insisted that the Conclusions be framed in this rather vague way basically because this left scope for considerable delay, and hence a more gradualist approach.
22. D. R. Cameron, *op. cit.* (1992), p. 71.
23. The 'Delors' Report, *op. cit.* (1989), paragraph 23.
24. *Ibid.*, (1992), p. 324.
25. T. Mazowiecki, 'Returning to Europe', *European Affairs*, 4, 46 (Spring 1990), pp. 41–43.
26. Although there were also those who saw the situation from a different perspective: that the break-up of the Eastern bloc should not be met by a strengthening of the existing Community, but rather by greater collaboration and participation in decision-making throughout Europe.
27. L. Tsoukalis, *op. cit.* (1993), pp. 203–204.
28. P. de Grauwe, *op. cit.* (1995), p. 151.
29. The Delors Report had, of course, been accepted by the Member State governments at the Madrid Summit in June of 1989. There they decided upon the date for initiating Stage I.
30. Lorenzo Bini-Smaghi, Tommaso Padoa-Scioppa and Francesco Papadia, 'The Transition to EMU in the Maastricht Treaty', *Princeton Essays in International Finance*, No. 194, Nov. (1994), p. 17.
31. For a much fuller account of these crises, see: *International Monetary Fund, World Economic Outlook: October 1993*, (Washington: International Monetary Fund, 1993); and, B. Eichengreen and C. Wyplosz, *op. cit.* (1993).
32. International Monetary Fund, *op. cit.* (1993), p. 30.
33. European Economy (1993), Part B – Report on progress with regard to economic and monetary divergence, p. 66.
34. This notion is backed up by the work of Eichengreen and Wyplosz, who surveyed the attitudes of foreign exchange traders to the EMS crises. When asked when they had begun to believe that changes in Member States' exchange rates were imminent (i.e that devaluations would take place)

22 per cent of foreign exchange traders said 'before the Danish referendum'. However, 59 per cent said that they believed exchange rate changes would take place either in the light of the result of the Danish referendum, or in the light of public attitudes to the Treaty in France. When questioned over the currency weaknesses of 1992, and whether or not these had led to the expectation that other currencies would follow suit, 90 per cent of foreign exchange traders said yes, whilst 77 per cent of those explained that the markets had 'tasted blood'. See: B. Eichengreen and C. Wyplosz, *op. cit.* (1993).

35. M. Obstfeld, 'Rational and Self-Fulfilling Balance of Payments Crises', *American Economic Review*, 76 (1986), pp. 72–81.
36. P. de Grauwe, *op. cit.* (1995), p. 125.
37. An example of such a proposal is given in: B. Eichengreen and C. Wyplosz, 'The Unstable EMS', CEPR Discussion Paper, No. 817, 1993.
38. P. de Grauwe, *op. cit.* (1995), p. 125.
39. *Green Paper on the Practical Arrangements for the Introduction of the Single Currency*, Office for Official Publications of the European Communities (1995).

Part 2
The Notion of Convergence

THE NOTION OF CONVERGENCE

*to 'converge': 1. to move or cause to move towards the same point
2. to meet or join.'*

The Maastricht Treaty sets out the economic convergence criteria which a country must satisfy in order to be eligible for membership of the economic and monetary union. These criteria can be analysed under four main headings: inflation rate convergence; fiscal performance convergence; exchange rate convergence; and interest rate convergence.

According to the inflation rate convergence criterion, the prospective members of EMU must maintain a high degree of price stability. For the preceding year the average rate of inflation (as measured by the consumer price index (CPI)) must not exceed that of the three best performing states by more than 1.5 per cent.[1]

The fiscal criteria require that the government financial position be sustainable. Countries can proceed towards economic and monetary union if the ratio of the government budget deficit to gross domestic product (GDP) is less than 3 per cent, and if the ratio of the stock of outstanding government debt to GDP is less than 60 per cent. There are, however, fiscal criteria 'escape clauses' built into the Maastricht Treaty. Even if they have exceeded the convergence values, a country may still be deemed to have qualified for EMU under the fiscal criteria if this excess is believed to be temporary and exceptional, or if it has been falling substantially and continually in the time prior to that country's performance being examined. On the other hand, even if both of the fiscal criteria have been met, the Commission can still prepare a report opposing EMU membership for any particular Member State if it believes there is a risk of future fiscal excesses.

The exchange rate criterion states that the 'normal' fluctuation margins of the ERM must have been observed, 'without tension' for at least two years without a devaluation.[2]

Finally, the interest rate convergence criterion states that for the preceding year the average nominal long-term rate of interest must not exceed that of the three best Member States (in terms of low inflation), by more than two percentage points with interest rates being measured on the basis of long-term government bonds or other comparable securities.

The question of what convergence conditions it would be necessary for states to meet before their final passage to the third stage of EMU occupied a central place in the intergovernmental negotiations leading to Maastricht. In the end, the Maastricht Treaty basically embodied two principles: first, that the transition to monetary union be gradual: a long transition period is required in order that states attempt to meet these convergence conditions; second, that not all EC countries had to join a monetary union at the same time, their accession to the union having been made dependent on satisfying the criteria.[3]

In many ways, these criteria were built on the EMS notion of convergence, implying a narrowing of international differences in the development of those economic variables that have a direct impact on exchange rate stability.[4] The point of these criteria, in general, is to ensure that the constraints on policy implied by participation in the EMU are likely to prove acceptable within the country concerned. Whether or not a country proceeds with economic and monetary union cannot just be left for the government of that country to decide, owing to the consequences implied for other members of the union of a bad judgment. For example, once exchange rates are fixed, as in a monetary union, any country whose prices rise substantially faster than the rest will lose competitiveness and market share. It therefore makes sense for a country to maintain a low-inflation target.

However, in addition to economic factors such as these, there are institutional and individual Member State reasons for the nature of the convergence criteria. As Dyson notes, it is:[5]

'essential to remember that . . . the influence of the German Finance Ministry and the Bundesbank was decisively brought to bear on the final shape and content of [the] treaty provisions . . . on [the convergence criteria. . . .]'

Negotiations of the criteria were delegated to the EC Monetary Committee where there was a high degree of conflict between the Member States' positions. The lead in negotiations was taken by German and Dutch officials, with Spanish backing. Spain had a preference for tough convergence criteria because of its desire to place itself in a straitjacket that would facilitate and legitimise difficult fiscal decisions at home. On the other hand, the German policy position was facilitated by the fact that the German economy would suffer if it entered into a monetary union which was without a firm monetary policy stance. It was, therefore, within Germany's national economic interest to ensure that the potential members of an economic and monetary union were committed to a low-inflation stance before entering. This German stance was not however totally intransigent, the reason being that Germany was determined to achieve closer political integration in Europe and thus was willing, at times, to make concessions on EMU.[6] As a result of this, many German economists and bankers believed that the convergence criteria were too weak, and that the planned structures of the ECB and ESCB were such that EMU could increase inflation in Germany. Other countries, however, were not so sure that tough convergence criteria were the way in which EMU would best progress. The Italian government, for example, suspected that tough convergence criteria were a way of reducing the prospects for Italian eligibility in the light of their unstable domestic political position.

What is important in this present analysis is that the convergence criteria have a dual role: they are both an important indication of sound economic management, as well as being the objective basis upon which the political decision to advance to economic and monetary union will be made. What this present analysis argues is that the individual convergence criteria themselves have deep-rooted implications, not just for Europe, but for the contemporary international political economy as a whole. In order to understand their full meaning we must, therefore, not only examine the kind of arguments already featured; we must also examine the rationale of, and the prospects for, economic convergence in Europe, given the nature of the prevailing international economic system. Only once we have done this can we begin to understand the fundamental importance of the convergence criteria to the process of economic and political integration in Europe. It is to a more detailed analysis of these criteria that we now turn.

NOTES

1. It is usually assumed that an arithmetical average will be taken of these three rates; however, it is possible that members' inflation rates will be compared to the worst of the three best.
2. At the time that the Maastricht Treaty was signed 'normal' basically meant the 2.5 per cent band which was usual in the Exchange Rate Mechanism. However, following the speculative crises in the ERM of 1992 and 1993, the bands were widened. Convergence would thus be facilitated if these wider bands were defined as 'normal'. See: M. Artis, *op. cit.* (1994).
3. Although not all economists agree that the process for achieving economic and monetary union in Europe as laid down at Maastricht is appropriate. Dornbusch, for example, argued for an immediate move to monetary union led by France and Germany, on the basis that a two-speed EMU was better than no EMU at all – as might be the case if a firmer date for Stage III

was not set. See: R. Dornbusch, 'Two-Track EMU, Now!', in *Britain and EMU*, (London: Centre for Economic Performance, 1990).

4. H. Ungerer, O. Evans, T. Mayer and P. Young, 'The European Monetary System: Recent Developments', *IMF Occasional Papers*, No. 48, 1986.

5. K. Dyson, *op. cit.* (1995).

6. P. Jacquet, 'The Politics of EMU: A Selective Overview', in *The Monetary Future of Europe* (London: Centre for Economic Policy Research, 1993).

4 The Convergence Criteria: Price Stability

Much money makes a country poor, for it sets a dearer price on every thing.

George Herbert, *Jacula prudentum*, 1640

INTRODUCTION

The behaviour of prices is a fundamental indicator of the health of an economy. In any competitive economy with a large degree of freedom from government intervention (a decentralised or market economy), the forces of supply and demand are co-ordinated and made consistent with each other by movements in prices. If prices are stable, which for the purposes of this present study implies not only an average inflation rate which is close to zero but also that prices remain predictable (i.e. inflation should not vary around an average value of zero),[1] then the economy is likely to be in good condition because resources are being allocated efficiently.

Although this form of decentralisation in an economy results on the whole in a more efficient allocation of resources, the market mechanism is not perfect, and there are times when price instability, particularly in the form of inflation, can cause major problems. The effects of this are not easy to quantify. As Fischer argued:[2]

'It is well known that the costs of inflation depend on the sources of inflation, on whether and when the inflation was anticipated, and on the institutional structure of the economy. There is, therefore, no short answer to the costs of inflation.'

Nevertheless, it is easy to see some of the problems which inflation may cause. For example, it may discourage saving, because the real value of the sum saved (the value after the change in the price level is taken into account) falls through time. Although the interest rate will tend to rise in order to compensate for this – and many types of saving exist which are designed to offset, or hedge, against inflation – savers

73

are still faced with a high degree of uncertainty, leading to changes in money holdings. Firms, too, may experience problems arising from the incidence of inflation: they will not properly be able to make decisions on production and manufacturing and enter into long-term contracts because they will not be able to predict their future costs and, hence, set the price for their product. In addition, in an economy in which the exchange rate is fixed and domestic firms engage in a large amount of international trade, inflation may cause domestic prices to rise relative to those of other countries. This variability in relative prices in turn will cause exports to fall and imports to rise leading to lower investment and production and the possible development of balance of payments deficits.[3] On the other hand, if the exchange rate was floating, the changes in the balance of imports and exports as a result of differential rates of inflation will result in changes in exchange rates. Other things being equal, we would expect that the currency of that country with a higher rate of inflation than other countries will suffer a decline in the value of their currency – in other words, a depreciation.

Since the end of the Second World War, many of the Western economies have suffered price instability in the form of inflation. This phenomenon has been viewed by economists as completely different from the high levels of inflation experienced in industrial economies before World War II. This is because, in contrast to the pre-World War II years, inflation is now regarded as an inherent part of the economic experience of mixed economies, namely economies where a mixture of public and privates enterprises exist.[4] Some analysts, however, have argued that it is surprising that governments have allowed inflation in the post-World War II period to exist to such an extent. For example, Glasner argued that high inflation rates should be far more prevalent during wartime because a state could use the price level to fund the increase in government expenditure which is necessary in times of war. In other words, the fact that the state has a monopoly over money 'was founded on security considerations . . . [playing the role of] an instrument of wartime finance'.[5] Thus in times of war states would print money, deriving seignorage revenue in the process.[6] This income was then used to finance the war effort. In the light of these arguments, one would therefore expect that the fact that the last World War ended over fifty years ago would have made the period since WWII one of low inflation levels when, in fact, the opposite has been the case. Goodhart, however, explained this post-World War II inflation phenomenon by arguing that '[p]erhaps a nuclear-age war is considered so remote, or so apocalyptic, that the need to hold monetary finance in reserve for such an occurrence is perceived as much reduced or even pointless.'[7]

Whatever the reasons for the continued presence of inflation over the last fifty years, the emphasis on policies which will tackle this price instability has strengthened considerably given the rapid acceleration in inflation rates (partly as a result of the oil price rises) in most, if not all, of the OECD countries in the 1970s and 1980s.[8] For example, average consumer prices in the OECD countries rose by 7.8 per cent in 1977, 6.8 per cent in 1978 and 8 per cent in 1979.[9] Moreover, when we concentrate on European inflation rates, we can see that the average rate of inflation in the EC during this time was 8.2 per cent a year and in every year the average price level rose. The peak was in 1974 when the European average inflation rate was over 14 per cent. Since then, no Member State, on average, achieved price stability (as defined earlier) or, indeed, came anywhere close to achieving it. The best performance, unsurprisingly, was in West Germany, with a peak of over 7 per cent.[10] Because of figures like these, low inflation was among the most important of the policy targets pursued by Member State governments during the 1980s and early 1990s, a pursuit which was given deeper significance by the convergence requirement laid down in the Maastricht Treaty over the low inflation levels which states had to meet before their accession to EMU.[11]

This chapter analyses the price stability and inflation convergence criterion of the Maastricht Treaty. At all times it is the intention of this study to marry the economic rationale of a particular convergence criterion with the political reasoning behind it, and this we do in the third and fourth sections of this present analysis. However, before this can be done we must consider the wider theoretical implications of price stability and inflation within the international political economy. Thus, in this present chapter we must examine the ways in which inflation incidence can be explained by factors in the political environment, such as labour market institutions or electoral preferences. Only by setting up such a framework can we be clear as to what effect such influences have had on the European policy-making environment.

THE INTERNATIONAL POLITICAL ECONOMY OF PRICES

Price instability and inflation are not simply an economic problem: their causes and consequences have long impinged upon the political domain as well. Whether we are considering the inflationary pressures caused by wars and their aftermath, when governments place added burdens on already stretched economies in order to increase their production capacity and to purchase much-needed arms and other equipment, or the measures taken by governments to prevent price rises in an attempt to stabilise their economies and their political position in the eyes of the electorate, the importance of the inflation phenomenon to the contemporary international political economy is obvious.

The Domestic Perspective

To understand the reasons for the continued presence of inflation over the last fifty years, and hence to construct a political theory of inflation in the contemporary international political economy, demands an explanation of the precise mechanisms through which political variables contribute to increases in the price level.[12] One way of doing this is by using a public choice approach, sometimes known as the 'economic theory of politics'. This:[13]

> 'provides, on the one hand, an explicit positive approach to the workings of political institutions and to the behavior of governments, parties, voters, interest groups, and (public) bureaucracies; and it seeks, on the other, normatively to establish the most desirable and effective political institutions.'

With regard to constructing a political theory of inflation, there are two areas which are of particular concern. The first is to consider the wage-setting environment in which policymakers operate; the second, linked to the first, is to consider the issue of an unemployment-inflation trade-off.

In studies of the advanced industrial states, cross-national variations in inflation have been traced to differences in wage-setting institutions and relations between business, organised labour and government.[14] Some countries may have stronger trade union movements than others, and trade unions with more power are more likely to exert upward pressure upon wage levels, independently of market conditions.[15] On the other hand, other analysts have argued that it is not just the strength of union power which is important, but also the level of centralisation of that union power. Bruno and Sachs, for example, examine the differences between centralised and decentralised wage bargaining in an economy.[16] When wage bargaining is centralised, trade unions realise that extravagant wage claims will lead to inflation. An increase in the level of prices in the wake of higher wage settlements means, in the end, that real wages will not actually increase. In such a wage-setting environment, the rate of inflation will therefore tend to be lower. On the other hand, in a country which has a more decentralised trade union system, individual unions that bargain for higher wages realise that the effect of these wage increases on the economy-wide price level would be small, due to the fact that these unions only represent a small fraction of the labour force. Therefore, each union has an interest in increasing the nominal wage of its members because, if it does not do this, the real wage of its members will decline, given that all of the other unions are likely to increase the nominal wages for their members. However, no individual union has an incentive to take the first step in reducing its nominal wage claim because it risks that the others will not follow, so that the real wage level of its members will decline. In circumstances such as these, the inflation rate therefore remains high.

This can be demonstrated more clearly with reference to the oft-quoted analogy of spectators at a football ground.[17] When all of the spectators are seated, any individual spectator has an incentive to stand up. That way he or she will have a much better view of the pitch. However, if all of the spectators do this, they will be less comfortable (because they are not seated) and none of them will see any better. However, once a spectator has stood up, it is just as difficult to persuade him or her to sit down again. The only way this will happen is if all the other spectators sit down as well, but because the football ground is so big, and those who sit down cannot be clearly seen, most of the spectators will not even notice that one spectator has done this, let alone follow the same course.

In an extension of this type of analysis, Calmfors and Driffill argued that the relationship between the centralisation of wage bargaining and the expected outcome is not a linear one.[18] In particular, the more decentralised the wage-bargaining process, the more direct the impact that wage claims will have upon the competitiveness of any individual firm, and hence on the employment prospects of individual union members.[19] In this case, extravagant wage claims by an individual union will lead to a definite increase in unemployment for the members of that union. For this reason, when faced with a supply shock (such as the oil price rises), unions in such a highly decentralised system may demonstrate a considerable degree of restraint on their claims for higher wages.

This, and the previous analysis by Bruno and Sachs, then leads to the conclusion that countries with either strong centralisation or strong decentralisation of wage bargaining are better equipped to face supply shocks – because of their greater wage moderation – than countries with an intermediate degree of decentralisation. As a result, the countries with extreme centralisation or decentralisation tend to fare better, in terms of inflation, following supply shocks than the others.

Analysts have, however, criticised the usefulness of viewing inflation and price instability from the standpoint of social group interaction, such as the above wage bargaining arrangements between employers and workers. Albert Hirschman, for example, has pointed out that 'the explanation of inflation in terms of social conflict between groups, each aspiring to a greater share of the social product, has become the sociologist's monotonous equivalent of the economist's untiring stress on the money supply'.[20]

A lot of the economic reasoning behind this societal explanation of inflation can be traced back to the work of A. W. Phillips who investigated the relationship between the change in money wages (later, inflation) and the rate of unemployment.[21] Basically, Phillips, using UK data over the period 1861–1957, concluded that there was a stable (non-linear) negative relationship between these two variables. The main implication of this is that, because a particular level of unemployment in the economy implies a particular rate of increase in wages, the aims of low unemployment and a low rate of inflation may be inconsistent. This is because a low level of unemployment implies that there will be a high degree of demand for labour, which in turn implies a large rate of increase in money wages, and thus a high level of inflation. The government must then choose between the feasible combinations of unemployment and inflation (taking into consideration the wage-setting environment) as shown by the Phillips curve.[22]

From this conclusion, analysts proposed that countries could base their policy decisions about the suitable level of inflation and unemployment for their economies upon this relationship. Thus, an economy where the preferred policy priority was low inflation (achieved by the intervention of the government in monetary and fiscal policy) would have higher unemployment than an economy for which low unemployment was the highest policy priority. What this also suggests is that governments have a high level of control over achieving their policy priorities.

In public choice terms, this suggestion of a high level of government control is important when we are considering how political variables contribute to increases in the price level. This is because such a degree of authority over the price mechanism could actually lead the government to manipulate inflation and unemployment levels in order to improve their popularity;[23] an assumption which underlies the hypothesis that governments can create a political business cycle aimed at improving their re-election chances.[24]

The first contribution to a public choice theory of political business cycles was by William D. Nordhaus, who noted that:[25]

'The typical cycle will run as follows: immediately after an election the victor will raise unemployment to some relatively high level in order to combat inflation. As elections approach, the unemployment rate will be lowered until, on election eve, the unemployment rate will be lowered to the purely myopic point.'

Following on from this, Barro and Gordon noted that there are advantages for the government, in the short run, in creating surprise inflation.[26] In this case, what the government is doing is playing a game, the outcome of which is dependent on the interaction between the goals of the incumbent government and upon the expectations which the public holds on these goals. For example, Kirchgassner examined the popularity of various parties in the UK and Germany in the post-World War II period.[27] He discovered that there was a strong statistical relationship between unemployment and inflation rates in these countries and the popularity of the governing parties. In addition, Allan Meltzer and Marc Vellrath, examining a similar relationship for the United States, discovered that unemployment and inflation rates were the key explanatory variables in explaining the votes, by state, in four presidential elections.[28]

Nordhaus argued that it is so-called 'voter myopia' which makes the electorate support parties who offer current, low unemployment levels, without regard to the fact that such unemployment levels will (later) produce unwanted inflation.[29] This is due to the fact that voting behaviour will be heavily influenced by the state of the economy in the run-up to the election and that, consequently, the level of unemployment will be the variable whose recent performance determines votes. Glasner argues that this idea is acutely bound up with the political conditions and aspirations which the incumbent government face: 'government decision makers have a limited tenure in office and have no transferable property rights in the assets ... they create while in office.'[30] For Glasner, the assets that a government creates are the ·

expectations fostered in the electorate regarding the magnitude of key economic variables, such as the level of inflation. In keeping with the spirit of Nordhaus' analysis, The short-sightedness of the electorate, coupled with the government's overriding goal of winning the next election, then leads to an optimal government strategy of raising unemployment levels (thereby reducing inflation) in the politically safe post-election-victory period, and then reducing unemployment going into the election, with the resulting inflation not becoming apparent until after the election results are in. In other words, '[i]ncumbent politicians desire re-election and they believe that a booming pre-election economy will help to achieve it'.[31] Moreover, in addition to 'voter myopia', the inflation process is assumed to be sufficiently misunderstood by the electorate that politicians can avoid the blame for inflation more easily than they can in the case of unemployment, i.e., '[a]t any moment of time the inflation is blamed on events which are not under the control of the political party in power, but ideally on the political party previously in power'.[32] As a result, advocates of the public-choice view argue that elected officials will respond to inflation with restrictive policies but will respond to unemployment with expansionary policies, implying that the fiscal policy process will have an inflationary bias (a point to which we will return in our next chapter).

There is, however, one important consideration to be made by any government attempting to influence the level of key economic variables for electoral gain: when policymakers make decisions as to the nature of their future policy conduct, they must take into consideration how credible that conduct is in the eyes of their electorate. If the electorate is accustomed to the government behaving in such a manner as will influence voting patterns, then the government's professed commitment to a policy (e.g. low inflation) will command little credibility – the manipulation of the economy by the government for its own aims will be expected and private firms and the electorate will thus readjust their expectations up to a point where the government no longer has an incentive to manipulate the economy for electoral gain. Voters can no longer be seen as myopic. With regard to inflation, this would result in an ever increasing price level as the electorate shift their expectations upwards because, in order to attempt to surprise the electorate, the government has to raise inflation above the level of the electorate's expectations. The latter policy,is thus said to be *time-inconsistent*. In other words, a government must maintain a consistent policy over time for the policy to be believed – it must build up a reputation for adhering to a particular policy, rather than engaging in an obvious policy cycle designed for electoral advantage.[33]

However, this whole idea that incumbent governments attempt to affect their probability of re-election by manipulating macroeconomic variables has been challenged by a number of analysts. George Stigler, for example, argued that the unemployed were too few in number and uninfluential to be a major target of government policies, and that rising real income per capita was the basic goal of all political parties. Indeed, he postulated that 'the economic bases for party affiliation must be sought in [the] area of income redistribution'.[34] This view was backed up by Wright, who discovered that the amount of income redistribution which took place in Roosevelt's New Deal government did well in explaining party support at the polls.[35]

Moreover, by the late 1970s the basis for these studies of unemployment and inflation trade-offs, i.e. the Phillips curve, had fallen into disrepute.[36] Analysts argued that the problem of inflation at that time was an international one, afflicting a wide variety of countries, with very different socio-political backgrounds, simultaneously. In such circumstances, factors such as national union and voter behaviour did not appear to offer the solution to this dilemma. Not only that, but a number of countries experienced rising unemployment and increasing inflation. It therefore seemed as if it was impossible for national monetary authorities to be able to choose the trade-off which they desired between inflation and unemployment. Instead attention turned to the dynamics of the international economy in the hope that this would provide some explanation as to the reasons for the increasing incidence of inflation in the contemporary global system and its explanation in politico-economic terms.

The International Perspective

So far, we have considered a public choice approach to domestic policymaking and how this can be used to examine the level of price stability and inflation in an economy. However, for our present purposes of constructing an international political economy approach, it is important to consider not only the domestic policy-making environment but also the role of international factors, particularly given the increasing international integration of goods, services, and capital markets among the advanced industrial economies in the past few decades. Hence, the nature of the international political economy itself may make any promises made by national policymakers to their electorates regarding future domestic political and/or economic behaviour unbelievable. This is due to the fact that the use of economic policy instruments by national authorities is undoubtedly influenced by conditions in the international economy. Thus, national policy-makers may simply not have the degree of policy control in the contemporary environment which would allow them to manipulate the economy to their own ends and, if this is the case, the previous arguments on the existence of a political business cycle may indeed need rethinking.

The government's desire to engineer a 'surprise' inflation in the domestic economy may be thwarted for two main reasons. First, domestic economic agents will base their expectations of future inflation not only on the domestic but on the international economic environment; and second, a rise in the price of domestic goods will have a negative impact on the balance of payments. Domestic goods will no longer be as attractive to buyers in the international marketplace.

For example, in terms of the international economic environment, monetarist economists believe that the increase in inflation experienced by industrialised economies over the last few decades is as a direct result of the increase in the world supply of money which largely resulted from the problems with the balance of payments deficit in the United States which began in the late 1960s. When a country starts running a balance of payments deficit, it pays out more for its imports than it receives from abroad in payment for its exports. If that country is as economically dominant as the United States, one way of financing this deficit is to issue the domestic currency, in this case dollars, to foreigners. Moreover, because the dollar is the most readily acceptable currency within the Western trading bloc, foreigners will be perfectly willing to accept payments for their exports (i.e. US imports) in dollars. Nevertheless, the impact upon the rest of the world of this continual injection of dollars into their respective economies will be to provoke inflation, for unless it is counteracted by the policies of the individual monetary authorities the effect of the dollar deficit is very similar to domestic credit creation by the central banks of the rest of the world.

On the other hand, a Keynesian economist would argue that if imports are regarded as a withdrawal from the level of demand and exports as an injection, then an increase in the flow of exports over imports resulting from the American balance of payments deficit will lead to a net injection of demand into the economies of the rest of the world. If these economies are at or near full employment, this increase in demand will drive the level of prices upwards for as long as the economies of the rest of the world continue to run a balance of payments surplus with the United States.

Advocates of the monetarist and of the Keynesian approaches both predict the same outcome, namely inflationary pressure generated by a dominant country and disseminated through the rest of the world. In other words, in a highly interdependent world economy, inflationary pressure is no respecter of national boundaries. Keohane and Nye argue that this high level of interdependence between countries changes economic relationships between them and hence creates a new form of political interaction.[37] For example, in such an interdependent environment, national monetary authorities must consider 'what kind of international arrangements should exist on exchange rates . . ., and [the] control of international capital movements, ...'[38]

Hence, whereas in the previous section we examined how a national monetary authority might manipulate the domestic economy for electoral gain, and the resulting effects that such a manipulation would have on an incumbent government's reputation, now we can see that given the nature of the contemporary, globalised, international system the importance of the level of commitment to a policy which a government shows and thus the reputation which a government earns, in economic and in political terms, increases. This is because a change in the domestic economic environment could affect how that country is perceived in the international marketplace. If, for example, a country is known to renege on its commitment to low inflation, then not only will its announcement of a commitment to a low inflation stance not be believed by domestic economic agents (e.g. voters); it will not be believed in the international marketplace either. Thus, the degree of independence which financial markets have makes cheating costly for governments attempting to outwit the forces of supply and demand.[39] In such circumstances the only way that governments can hope to overcome the stigma of their reputation for reneging upon a commitment is by having some mechanism through which their policies gain more credibility. In the contemporary international political economy, this is done by means of international arrangements between national monetary authorities, either informally, in terms of regular meetings to discuss policy stance (such as the G7 summit meetings), or formally, through the creation of an international organisation.[40]

The literature on international organisations is voluminous, and it is not the intention of this present analysis to present a critique of international organisation theory.[41] Any international organisation may perform various services. It may provide public goods and services (such as defence), coordinate the activities of actors in the international system, and/or form an institutional setting for alliances. However, as we have already noted, international organisations may also be used to further private (i.e. domestic) aims, such as the use of the organisation to give a national monetary authority credibility in the eyes of domestic and international economic agents. For this reason, it would be a mistake to assume that every international organisation always maximises the collective welfare of those who are a party to it. For example, in the case of an organisation which provides a public good, the possibility that one or more of the members may 'free ride' means that having a control mechanism built into the organisation's constitution is more of a necessity. A typical method of control is to punish all members of an organisation for an act committed by only one of its members.[42] Another method is to have one member of the organisation as leader. The latter then controls the reward structure of the remaining members, the only precondition being that the leader is motivated enough to take on the role and has the capability of issuing credible and effective enough threats to curtail free riding within the organisation.[43] How, though, do these kinds of issues – and, indeed, the international political economy approach to price stability and inflation just described – apply in the context of price stability and the process of European economic and monetary union?

EUROPEAN PRICE STABILITY

The members of the European Union have long been aware of the political significance of price stability. Although, when the Treaty of Rome was instigated, inflation levels appear to have been quite moderate (averaging 2–3 per cent) the perception among the Western industrialised economies at that time was that inflation was a problem. Indeed, the OEEC devoted a special expert's report in 1961 to 'the problem of rising prices'.[44] It was not surprising, then, that Article 104 of the Treaty of Rome called for each Member State to:[45]

'pursue the economic policy needed to ensure the equilibrium of its overall balance of payments and to maintain confidence in its currency, while taking care to ensure a high level of employment and a stable level of prices.'

By the time that the Delors Committee presented its report, emphasising that proposed arrangements for European monetary union 'would be committed to the objective of price stability',[46] the European countries had been through the experience of rising inflation levels in the 1970s and early 1980s. Price stability was seen as an important priority and a necessary adjunct to the successful creation of a Single European Market and the continued process of integration. It was no surprise, then, that the Maastricht Treaty followed the lead given by the Delors Report, asserting that price stability should be one of the criteria upon which a country's proposed passage to the third stage of economic and monetary union be judged.

The Economic Rationale

The criterion on price stability as laid down in the Maastricht Treaty is very clearly related to the basic rationale for achieving convergence before economic and monetary union in Europe can take place – the need to hand on to the European Central Bank a stable economic situation while at the same time not making it bear the blame for imposing the costs of achieving one.[47]

There are various reasons for believing that inflation rate convergence is necessary in an economic and monetary union, a number of which actually hinge on a relationship between exchange rates and prices originally put forward in the seventeenth century by the mercantilist Gerard de Malynes. He gave an account of an international mechanism for foreign exchange which worked through price levels and gold and silver movements.[48] This work was later formalised by Cassel, who introduced the notion of purchasing power parity (PPP).[49] This concept begins from the premise that the price, in terms of a common currency, of any tradeable commodity in any two markets will differ at most by the cost of transport, tariffs and the differences in retail costs involved in moving goods from one market to another.

For example, let us consider two countries – say, France and Germany – and let us assume that these two countries produce only tradeable goods. We shall also assume that the goods produced by these two countries are homogeneous (e.g. a hairdryer produced in Germany is identical to a hairdryer produced in France), there are no barriers to international trade (for example, transaction costs or tariff barriers), there is full employment, there are no transportation costs, and the price system is efficient at allocating resources. Under these circumstances, the price of a hairdryer in Germany must equal the price of an identical hairdryer in France, multiplied by the spot exchange rate. If these conditions did not hold, it would be profitable for arbitrageurs to trade goods from one market to another. Let us say that French goods were cheaper in this case. It would then be profitable for economic agents in France to buy the good in France, transport it to Germany and sell it at the higher price. In the same way it would be profitable for speculators in Germany to convert their funds into French francs, buy the good in France and transport it to Germany. This process of arbitrage would continue until it was no longer profitable to continue and prices between the two countries were equalised.[50, 51] How, then, does the adjustment take place?

If the exchange rate is fixed (as it would be in a monetary union) then the price of a good will rise in France and fall in Germany as the commodity is arbitraged to Germany. If, on the other hand, the exchange rate is perfectly flexible then the price of a good will stay fixed both in Germany and France, and equilibrium will be restored by a change in exchange rates rather than an adjustment in the price level. If we argue that these conditions hold for all the goods in the economy then we say that 'purchasing power parity' has been achieved.[52] Thus, in a monetary union, where exchange rates are fixed and there is a single currency in operation, purchasing power parity can be used to explain the change in reserves caused by changes in the international exchange of commodities.[53] Indeed, De Grauwe considered the achievement of purchasing power parity to be the equilibrium position for countries within a monetary union.[54] If this were not the case, then if, say, France's rate of inflation were greater than in Germany's, France would have to depreciate its currency to leave the competitiveness of its products in the international marketplace unchanged. If France and Germany then decided to form a monetary union, the exchange rate would be fixed and thus the rates of inflation between the two countries must be equal. If this were not so, and France had higher inflation, then the French economy would find itself in a position of ever-decreasing competitiveness. Hence, inflation rate convergence is necessary in an economic and monetary union. This is supported by the presence of fixed exchange rates which reinforce the effect that having a single currency has on the credibility given to national anti-inflation policies. Fixed exchange rates strengthen the credibility of government economic policy because of the variability which exists in the real exchange rate between realignments of the nominal rates. This variability arises from inflation differentials with the rest of the world which, Giavazzi and Giovannini argue, leads the policy-makers to face politically costly domestic inflation.[55] On the other hand, participating in a monetary union means that member countries effectively relinquish the opportunity of reverting to inflationary policies and thus represents an efficient anti-inflationary commitment technology.[56, 57]

This is in line with another analysis of the importance of the exchange rate–price relationship by Begg, who argued that joining an economic and monetary union with a single currency would engender price stability, because it would increase the speed of adjustment to shocks within that union as one possible part of the adjustment process, namely real exchange rate variation, will be removed.[58] Because exchange rate variation injects uncertainty about the level of future prices into an economy (and manufacturers and other firms base their production decisions on the information that they glean from the price system) this exchange rate variation means that firms will not be able to anticipate price behaviour, and therefore resource allocation will be less efficient. The riskiness of investment projects will be increased, which will in turn mean that investors will want compensation for undertaking investment in such an environment (i.e. a higher risk premium and discount rate), increasing the real interest rate. However, this in itself causes problems, leading to the selection of higher-risk investment projects. Countries in a monetary union, by reducing price uncertainty, reduce the amount of high-risk projects that are chosen in an economy:[59] the price system of resource allocation will work more efficiently because information is more certain. Wage-setters will perceive this and alter their behaviour, thus reinforcing the effect. Hence, joining an economic and monetary union with a single currency will eliminate exchange rate risk, and thus will lead to a more efficient working of the price mechanism.

Another reason for believing that inflation rate convergence is necessary in an economic and monetary union is that with a Single European Market already in place there would be increased competition and specialisation (due to the effect of economies of scale) within the monetary union. This would tend to make the prices of those goods which are traded within the European Union more homogeneous and would gradually reduce the scope for price discrimination between national markets. This basically arises from the fact that the use of a single currency (after economic and monetary union takes place) within the European Union leads to the elimination of information costs and of incentives for price discrimination. It is inconvenient for consumers to have to compare prices in different units, even if the exchange rate is fixed. For firms, substantial savings could be realised by the use of a single currency by keeping accounts, making internal calculations and settlements and designing marketing strategies on the basis of a pricing policy expressed in a single unit. Indeed, it is an integral element of the aims of a Single European Market to approach the state of affairs observed in the United States, where firms quote a national price exclusive of sales taxes in individual states. It is impossible to give an exact estimate of the gains to be made in these respects, as there would probably be some overlap with the gains estimated in the Cecchini Report on the Single European Market, some of which could hardly be realised fully without complete monetary unification. Gros and Thygesen, however, believe that an additional 2 per cent of the European Union's gross domestic product could easily be attained.[60]

Despite these arguments, however, there is at least one problem with the notion of price stability as conceived in the Maastricht Treaty: the choice of an appropriate price index. In order to make the concept of price stability operational, it is necessary to specify what price index is to be stabilised. The Maastricht Treaty states that: 'Inflation shall be measured by means of the consumer price index on a comparable basis, taking into account differences in national definitions'.[61] Although the Maastricht Treaty goes to some lengths to set precise arithmetical targets for convergence, nowhere does it define 'price stability'. In effect the central bankers will be left to define their own objectives. There is no 'anchor' tying down the price level in the long run as there was under the Gold Standard. If, by accident, the price level rises in one year, there is no pressure on the central bankers to bring it back down again. If the shocks to the system are asymmetrical – more often pushing prices up than down – then the price level may tend to drift slowly upwards.[62]

From a theoretical point of view, the appropriate target index is the one that is most closely related to the source of the cost of inflation. For example, if one considers the main cost of inflation to be changes in money holdings, then the appropriate index to use would be the consumer price index (CPI). This has the advantage of being published monthly everywhere, in contrast to wholesale and producer prices which are not always available with this frequency. A further advantage of the CPI is that it is widely understood. However, the goods and services which make up the CPI will be different in different places and will differ from year to year. As well as this, the measurement of quality is notoriously difficult. So, if quality rises from year to year, as it clearly does for some (but not all) items, then indices based on consumer prices may slightly overstate the rate of inflation. In addition, in an area as large as the Community, national price trends measured by consumer price indices may diverge substantially between countries, even over the medium term, because the weight of non-traded goods and services in this index is substantial and price trends for these goods are less directly constrained by the process of market integration.

On the other hand, if the main cost of inflation is taken to derive from the variability in relative prices which leads to lower investment and production, the appropriate price index to stabilise might be the producer price index (PPI). However, there are also problems with PPI as an appropriate index. As noted by Fraser, Taylor and Webster:[63]

'If, for example, industrial structure differs between countries, then in aggregate data this will be reflected in price indices being constructed with different weights.'

In addition, Kravis and Lipsey noted that prices might differ between countries because in some industries firms may be more (or less) responsive to changes in domestic demand as compared to demand in each foreign market.[64] Profit-maximising behaviour would then lead these firms to charge lower prices in those markets that are characterised by more (or less) responsive demand. This possibility of price differences among different exporters from the same or different countries is supported by the existence of product differentiation, both in terms of the physical characteristics of the good, such as appearance and performance, and in terms of various service elements connected with the good, such as the sales service, credit terms, and how quickly the good is delivered to the consumer. It is, therefore, difficult to decide on purely theoretical grounds which price index should be stabilised under economic and monetary union by the European Central Bank. Even in countries where price stability is the main mandate of their national monetary authority, the choice is rarely made explicit.

Moreover, these sorts of structural factors, such as differences in investment or production, or in the amount of non-traded goods in an economy are important too for the politics of European price stability. In our earlier examination of the international political economy of prices, we argued that the issue could be examined from two related perspectives: domestic and international. Within these perspectives we considered that in order to understand the political economy of prices, an explanation was needed as to the exact way in which societal and institutional variables could contribute to increases in the price level. What we must now consider is how these ideas relate to the political rationale behind the European price stability criterion.

THE POLITICAL RATIONALE

When examining the politics of European price stability, what we must first of all consider is how domestic political factors in Europe have contributed to the levels of prices that have been witnessed in Europe in the time since European monetary integration has been part of the policy agenda. This will enable us not only to understand the political desire for a low inflation commitment, but also to consider the feasibility of actually achieving the inflation levels required by the Maastricht Treaty for accession to EMU. In this there are two areas which are of particular concern. The first is the European wage-setting environment; the second, is the resonance of the unemployment-inflation trade-off to European decision-making.

With regard to the wage-setting environment, one factor which is certain is that there are important institutional differences between European countries. Germany, for example, has highly centralised labour unions. An umbrella organisation, known as the Deutsche Gewerkschaftsbund (DGB) and consisting of sixteen constituent industrial unions, acts as the negotiating partner for workers' rights in collective bargaining. Hence, with regard to the arguments in the earlier section on the international political economy of prices, the power of the DGB in Germany would lead it to realise that extravagant wage claims will result in inflation, because there will be an increase in the general price level in the wake of widespread higher wage settlements – which means, in the end, that real wages will not actually increase. In Germany, then, the prevailing institutional structure with regard to labour union organisation is such that low inflation levels are more likely.

On the other hand, the United Kingdom's labour union movement has more intermediate levels of decentralisation. Although the Trades Union Congress (TUC) exists as a central organisation, individual unions, such as the National Union of Teachers (NUT) or the Scottish Prison Officers Association (SPOA), although affiliated to the TUC, are much more likely to negotiate their own wage claims. Therefore individual unions are much more prone to make wage claims in the belief that the effect on economy-wide prices will be limited. Higher inflation levels will result. What is particularly important for this present analysis, however, is that these differences may inject significant costs into the monetary union project, and may indeed preclude some states from actually attaining the inflation rate criterion laid down in the Maastricht Treaty in the first place. The main reason for this is that different wage-setting environments may lead to conflicting wage and price effects, even when countries are facing the same economic disturbance, because labour unions may react to such disturbances differently. Even once membership of a monetary union is achieved, there could still be difficulties: membership would make it difficult to correct for such differences, because the exchange rate is irrevocably fixed and there is a single currency in operation.

With regard to the resonance of the unemployment–inflation trade-off in European decision-making, when the Werner Committee put forward its recommendations on economic and monetary union the idea that inflation might have a societal explanation, as discussed earlier, was very much accepted. The Phillips curve was then very much a prevailing part of economic methodology. Economists believed that a government could make a choice between inflation and unemployment by using monetary and fiscal policy, and the Werner Report very much reflected this view. As Baer and Padoa-Schioppa noted:[65]

'[t]he procedures for policy coordination detailed in the Report implied a very high degree of confidence in the ability of policy instruments to affect policy goals in a known and predictable way.'

Policy-makers were seen to have a high level of control over achieving their policy priorities. However, while monetary and fiscal policy is still important, since the Phillips curve fell into disrepute few academics would be willing to predict precisely the size and speed of the response to a particular policy change.

This fear of unpredictability was evident as far back as when discussions were taking place on the feasibility of a European Monetary System. One of the reasons why economists were dubious about the long-run viability of such a system was that the inflation rates of the participating countries differed too radically for the maintenance of stable exchange rates. For analysts to have confidence in the future of the EMS required some reason to believe that the system itself would support the high inflation countries in their attempts to implement policies which would bring down inflation rates. Analysts, as well as the European electorate, needed to be convinced of the credibility of the low inflation commitment; time consistency in the EMS policy was crucial.

Giavazzi and Pagano argued that the asymmetrical nature of the European Monetary System, with the dominance of the Deutschmark, was a way of doing this.[66] By pegging their exchange rates to the strongest currency in the system, countries with traditionally high rates of inflation would be forced to follow the lead of the Bundesbank and hence would acquire a reputation of commitment to price stability. As De Grauwe notes:[67]

> '[a]ll these factors contribute to raising the perceived political costs of a devaluation. As a result, countries will quite often be reluctant to devalue their currencies, so that their incentive to cheat declines. This then increases the credibility of the fixed exchange rate arrangement.'[68]

In addition, the succession of changes in the internal politics of several of the member countries during the initial stages of the System resulted in a more solid commitment to the Exchange Rate Mechanism. This was particularly the case for France, where the Socialist government, to a large extent, surrendered control of its national monetary policy to the Bundesbank. This substantially increased the credibility of the Socialist government's commitment to the EMS in the eyes of the both the French electorate and other European policymakers. The European Monetary System was seen then to have the political credibility it so desperately needed in order to be successful. So, much of the success of the EMS (or, more strictly the ERM), particularly during its first ten years, was identified with the fact that member countries used it as a counterinflationary framework, aided by the low inflation commitment of the dominant country in the system, Germany.[69] The story, however, is a different one with regard to economic and monetary union.

At the time that the decisions over Maastricht were being made, countries appeared to display different preferences over the level of inflation that they thought should be achieved before the progression to the third stage of EMU took place. The Belgian, Greek and Portuguese delegations at Maastricht, for example, were consistently worried over their ability to achieve the necessary reference values. On the other hand, a more rigid inflation criterion was favoured by Italian[70] and German policy-makers. Each had their own reasons for this. The Italian government wanted to reduce public inflationary expectations, which a strong commitment to rigid criteria on price stability would hopefully achieve. Theirs was very much a policy, then, which was geared to ensuring credible monetary conduct in the eyes both of Italian voters and of the rest of the European marketplace.

On the other hand, German policymakers wanted a rigid price criterion because they wanted some sort of assurance that a European Central Bank would not be persuaded to adopt a more inflationary stance once monetary union had been achieved.[71] Herein lies Germany's dilemma: in economic terms, Germany has nothing to gain from joining a union with high-inflation countries. Rather, all the gains are for the high-inflation countries. In fact, the position is such that it would be in Germany's interests to keep the monetary union small and to prevent high-inflation countries from being part of it. This is because a monetary union implies that a common rate of inflation will have to be selected. If we assume that in the future monetary union the European Central Bank will reflect the preferences of those countries that are members of the union, then the inflation outcome in the union will be determined by the size of the union. Thus if, for example, Germany and France form a union without Italy, this union will be attractive to Germany only if it considers the gains in economic efficiency from joining such a union (less price uncertainty, etc.) to outweigh the loss in welfare caused by the higher rate of inflation which would undoubtedly be engendered in such a union.[72] Such concerns have been evident in the growing debate over monetary union within Germany. Indeed, as far back as the period 1989–90, the leaders of the governing coalition parties – the Christian Democrat Union/Christian Social Union (CDU/CSU) and Free Democrat Party (FDP) – feared that a rapid movement towards monetary union could leave the federal government vulnerable to charges from the nationalist right that it was not putting German interests first but was instead selling out to other countries by giving away the much loved Deutschmark.[73] Why then, given such concerns, would Germany want EMU? The answer lies in the political advantages to be gained from EMU rather than the economic ones, particularly in the light of the collapse of communism in central and eastern Europe.[74] In the run-up to the European Council meeting in Dublin in April 1989, for example, Chancellor Kohl took the initiative in pressing his colleagues 'to construct a European roof over a united Germany' in order both to overcome mistrust of a united Germany and to emphasise the German commitment to a 'European Germany' as opposed to a 'German Europe'.

There is, then, a fundamental dichotomy regarding the level of German political will towards economic and monetary union as an instrument of economic policy; and the level of German political will towards economic and monetary union as a process to achieve the eventual political union of Europe. In the normal course of events, this dichotomy would be immediately perceived as being a threat to the credibility of the policy of EMU. However, the way that the prospective EMU governments have overcome this perception is through the creation of an institutional framework which will provide a solid basis for a credible Europe-wide monetary policy.

The Institutional Dimension

The provisions laid down in the Maastricht Treaty for the creation of the new institutions for economic and monetary union are remarkably consistent, in structure, with those proposed in the Delors report. The explicit mandate of the European Central Bank is to maintain price stability. To this end, the extent to which an ECB will be able to conduct a credible monetary policy geared towards assuring price stability depends upon a number of considerations, the most important of which are the organisational structure of the European Central Bank and the budgetary policies followed by the Member States (to which we turn in our next chapter). With this in mind, two constitutional features of a European Central Bank are of great importance in determining to what extent it pursues a monetary policy which is geared towards the maintenance of price stability – its statutory duty to ensure that price stability and the degree of its political independence. In other words:[75]

'If we are to have a European monetary regime, then it has to be as good as, for example, the Bundesbank's. And a European central bank can only achieve price stability if it is independent in its monetary policies of the EC institutions and governments.'

Indeed, the need for central bank independence has been cited as one of the main advantages of economic and monetary union in Europe because national governments will be forced to grant a level of independence to their own central banks which they have refused to grant previously.[76]

The degree of the European Central Bank's political independence may be gauged in various ways. The ECB should be formally independent in the constitutional sense. As stated in Article 107:[77]

'When exercising the powers and carrying out the tasks and duties conferred upon them by this Treaty and the Statute of the ESCB, neither the ECB, nor a national central bank, nor any member of their decision-making bodies shall seek or take instructions from Community institutions or bodies, from any Government of a Member State or from any other body.'

It is also necessary that the terms of office of the Governor and the Board of Directors should protect these individuals from pressure to deviate from the objective of price stability. If the monetary policy followed within EMU is going to be credible, then the ECB should not be burdened with other duties and obligations that might oblige it to engage in an expensive monetary policy incompatible with the control of inflation. The Governing Council of the European Central Bank (ECB), on which national central bank governors will sit, will enjoy statutory protection from political pressures.[78] For example, national central bank governors will serve long terms in office and will be prohibited from campaigning for reappointment.[79] In addition, the European Central Bank is forbidden to lend to national governments or to Commission organisations and the responsibility for the supervision of banks and financial institutions is placed elsewhere. This is in order that its pursuit of price stability will not be compromised by actions taken in pursuit of these other possible obligations. Similarly, whilst exchange rate policy is not the ECB's direct prerogative, it is afforded considerable influence over any such policy (a point to which we will return in Chapter 6). In addition, the terms of office of the Governor and members of the Board are drawn up in such a way as to remove the possibility that ECB officials might act as if they were 'representatives' of their country under the influence of their country's government.[80, 81] Another important factor is the legal rank of the ECB's statutes. This determines the conditions under which the statutes of the Central Bank can be changed; the more difficult this is, the more secure the Central Bank – and hence the public – could be that its independence is permanent.

What these arrangements do is to ensure that the institutional structure for maintaining price stability is geared towards the maintenance of co-operation within it. In terms of our earlier discussion on the international perspective of the IPE of prices, a European institution made up of the members of an international organisation (i.e. the EU) is giving the national monetary authorities of the Member States credibility in the eyes of domestic and international economic agents. However, notwithstanding the mechanisms already created to ensure the successful running of a European Central Bank, there are a number of other potential difficulties with regard to the scenario for these newly-created European monetary institutions.

First, although price stability is in itself beneficial, it is difficult to say whether it should be ascribed, if achieved, to EMU or to the structural and constitutional foundations of the European Central Bank. In other words, with regard to the objective of price stability as laid down in the Maastricht Treaty, the answer in many ways seems to be to design tougher and more effective monetary controls – presumably via the creation of an independent European Central Bank. If this is done, EMU actually adds very little in terms of improving economic performance and, indeed, may even detract from it in the absence of supporting fiscal policies.[82]

Second, the Member States will have equal representation on the Governing Council of the European Central Bank, regardless of whether their traditional policy stance is a high-inflation one or a low-inflation one. Although, once a country is part of the economic and monetary union it would be politically costly for it to leave the arrangement, it remains to be seen what effect the continued presence of countries with different stances on price stability will have.[83] Not only might there be a clash between the ESCB's pursuit of price stability and the international monetary policy framework which the politicians have decided (because European politicians want to preserve their ability to determine the exchange rate regime and to take the lead in international monetary policy meetings, such as those at the Plaza in 1985 and at the Louvre in 1987), but there also remains a possibility that some elements of fiscal policy, remaining largely under national political control, may be varied in a manner antithetical to the thrust of monetary policy. The governors have sought to meet the problem by insisting that the ESCB should never be required to monetise public sector debt, and that there should be no bailouts of public sector bodies, including national governments, which cannot meet their debt obligations.[84] However, only in Greece, Spain and Italy is there an automatic credit line for governments, and legal prohibitions on automatic financing have not, in the past, prevented central banks from accommodating government deficits (a point to which we will return in our next chapter).

Third, one reason why the proposed constitution of the ECB is so 'hard' is because there is an apprehension that a new institution with no accumulated reputation (i.e. credibility) needs extra advantages to compensate for its lack of history; it needs to get its credibility from somewhere. However, this suggestion reveals a point of difficulty with the constitutional approach. Transplanting a constitution – even a strengthened one – is not the same as transplanting history: it may be that, in countries with low inflation and independent central banks, it is history that makes the actions of the central bank, which must often be harsh ones, acceptable to the public. Thus, the Bundesbank has latitude to make temporarily 'unpopular' decisions; similar actions undertaken by the ECB might not be well received in some of the countries in the EMU – for example, in the inflation-prone economies of Italy, the United Kingdom, or Spain.[85] Moreover, the events in Eastern Europe have complicated this scenario. The economic costs of a single currency union for all of Europe increase as the number of countries (all with different prevailing economic conditions) increases.[86] While these countries struggle towards an improvement in their economies, inflation may result, a fact which would only jeopardise the price stability criterion.

In addition to these difficulties, the (contentious) question remains as to how far national monetary autonomy over fiscal policy should be constrained, in the interest of maintaining price stability.[87] The statutory independence which the ECB has would not be sufficient to guarantee that it is responsible for the common monetary policy in EMU and will always pursue stable prices. For example, its task may become difficult if tensions in the labour market result in excessive increases in nominal wages, i.e. in supply-side shocks (which, as we saw earlier, will, in large part, depend upon the level of centralisation/decentralisation existing in the national wage-setting environments) because the European Central Bank would only be left with the choice of accommodating the inflationary pressure or pursuing a restrictive policy with adverse consequences on employment. The environment in which a European Central Bank operates is therefore an important element in determining to what extent it will be able to attain the goal of price stability. By joining a political institution, such as the ECB, European policy-makers signal their commitment towards fighting inflation. Any proposal to then alter the nature of these political institutions would call into question the credibility of the policy commitment, probably resulting in market-based penalties for the higher inflation rates which would be expected as a result of the loss in credibility.

Yet despite these arguments, the ability of the Member States to achieve the inflation criterion does not so far appear to have been significantly jeopardised. The recent recession has made the inflation criterion relatively easy to meet for a majority of countries, at least for the time being. This process was further facilitated in the early 1990s as inflation increased in Germany as a consequence of unification. In fact, between 1990 and 1992 deviation from the EC average price inflation fell from 3.4 to 2 per cent, with – in 1991 and 1992 – price inflation higher in Germany (4.2 and 3.7 per cent) than in Belgium, Denmark, France, Ireland and Luxembourg.[88] Twelve out of the fifteen Member States, including the UK, are at present forecast to meet the inflation criterion (see Table 4.1).

Table 4.1   The Maastricht Inflation Criterion
% change – consumer price deflator

Austria	3.1	Belgium	2.6
Denmark	2.4	Finland	2.7
France	2.1	Germany	2.4
Greece	9.0	Ireland	2.7
Italy	3.5	Luxembourg	2.7
Netherlands	2.5	Portugal	4.4
Spain	4.4	Sweden	3.1
UK	3.3	Three best	2.3

Source: European Commission 1995 Annual Economic Report

However, before EMU is formed, it may not be thought of as sufficient merely to demonstrate that rates of inflation have been held close together for a few years; it should also be shown that they have been held together without strain. Convergence may, then, be superficial. If so, the strain will show in indices of relative costs, in balance of payments deficits or in unemployment. These may all be signs of an imbalance which will need eventually to be corrected – and one must be confident that they will be corrected within an economic and monetary union.[89]

CONCLUSION

In classical economics price stability is the responsibility of the national monetary authorities, because they control the quantity of money. The price level thus varies with the amount of money in circulation. The idea is straightforward, but its modern application can be troublesome.[90] In Europe, the nature of economic and monetary union takes the maintenance of price stability out of the hands of national policy-makers.

This chapter has analysed the price stability and inflation convergence criterion of the Maastricht Treaty. Following a brief introduction on the nature of inflation and prices, we went on to examine the international political economy of prices from a theoretical perspective. In this regard, we were interested in two issues in particular: first, the domestic setting in which price decisions are made; and second, the international environment. In the case of the former, we examined the importance of the wage-setting environment in which policy-makers operate, i.e. the level of centralisation or decentralisation of the union movement, as well as the issue of an inflation-unemployment trade-off. We concluded that the wage-setting environment was crucial to the level of inflation in an economy, but that to consider that the government would have the degree of control over the domestic economy such that it could trade off this level against unemployment would be problematical, particularly given the contemporary international political environment. This then brought us to our examination of the international environment in which pricing decisions are made, where we considered that the level of interdependence now existing between countries in the world economy would make it difficult for a national monetary authority to have the level of control over the price level which had been posited in the previous section. Any policy commitment made by the national monetary authorities would be subject not only to the scrutiny of the domestic electorate, but also to the scrutiny of other countries' national monetary authorities and speculators in the international marketplace. In order to enhance national policy commitment in such an environment, countries therefore join international organisations. The EU is an example of such an organisation, and with this in mind the analysis then turned to the economic and political rationale of European price stability. After examining the various reasons why price stability and inflation convergence is necess-ary and would take place in an economic and monetary union, we argued that there were various factors (including the use of an appropriate price index) with regard to the structure of the criterion which might make its achievement difficult. In order to understand these factors more fully, it was necessary to examine the political structure of the criterion – in particular, those factors which we had considered in our earlier IPE analysis.

As in our earlier section on IPE, we first of all considered the domestic political environment in which the national monetary authorities made their pricing decisions. It was found that there were indeed important institutional differences with regard to the wage-setting environment of European countries which could account for the differences in the incidence of inflation witnessed by the national monetary authorities. In addition, the posited inflation–unemployment trade-off had been a factor in the consideration of earlier monetary integration efforts, such as the recommendations of the Werner report. However, this policy stance and the posited level of predictability which it gave to policy-makers that went with it had fallen into disrepute by the time that the more recent monetary integration efforts had taken place. In particular, fear of unpredictability had led to such efforts as the Exchange Rate Mechanism of the EMS, with its low-inflation commitment technology designed to enhance policy credibility. Concerns of policy credibility were similarly built into EMU. Echoing our analysis of the IPE of prices from an international perspective, the EU as an organisation has organised EMU, and in particular the constitution of the ECB, in such a way as to enhance its policy reputation. However, the environment in which the ECB operates is crucial, as are the after-effects of the EU's policy on price stability and inflation convergence.[91] Also, monetary policy may be particularly dependent on supporting fiscal policies. Hence, although achievement of the inflation criterion by the Member States so far appears to be encouraging, the proper co-ordination of fiscal policies with monetary policy is essential to EMU. It is to an examination of the Maastricht criterion on fiscal conditions that we now turn.

NOTES

1. European Commission, 1992, p. 96.
2. S. Fischer, 'Towards an understanding of the costs of inflation: II', *Carnegie Rochester Series on Public Policy* (1981), 15, p. 5.
3. Note, however, the importance of the rate of domestic inflation relative to that of other countries. If all countries were inflating at the same rate, there would be no change in relative prices. There would then be a redistribution of world wealth because the real value of the liabilities of debtor nations would fall, as would the real value of assets of the creditor nations.
4. J. A. Trevithik, *Inflation, A Guide to the Crisis in Economics*, 2nd ed. (London: Penguin Books, 1980), p. 11.
5. D. Glasner, *Free Banking and Monetary Reform* (Cambridge: Cambridge University Press, 1989), p. 31.
6. Seigniorage is the process of raising government revenue by increasing inflation.
7. C. A. E. Goodhart, 'The Political Economy of Monetary Union', in C. A. E. Goodhart, *The Central Bank and the Financial System* (London: Macmillan, 1995), p. 163.
8. *Ibid.*, pp. 163–64.
9. *OECD Economic Outlook*, December 1979.
10. A. Britton and D. Mayes, *op. cit.* (1992), p. 40.
11. M. Artis and N. Weaver, *op. cit.* (1994), p. 55.
12. S. Haggard, 'Inflation and Stabilization', in J. A. Frieden and D. A. Lake, *op. cit.* (1991), p. 448.
13. B. S. Frey, 'The Public Choice View of International Political Economy', *International Organization*, 38, 1, Winter (1994), p. 201.
14. See, for example: Dave Turner, 'The Role of Real and Nominal Rigidities

in Macroeconomic Adjustment: A Comparative Study of the G3 Economies', *OECD Economic Studies*, no. 21, Winter (1993).

15. J. A. Trevithik, *op. cit.* (1974), pp. 109–110.
16. M. Bruno and J. Sachs, *Economics of Worldwide Inflation* (Oxford: Basil Blackwell, 1985).
17. Paul de Grauwe, *op. cit.* (1994), p. 22.
18. L. Calmfors and J. Driffill, 'Bargaining Structure, Corporatism and Macroeconomic Performance', *Economic Policy*, 6, pp. 13–61.
19. See: David J. Smyth and Susan Washburn Taylor, 'The Inflation-Unemployment Trade-offs of Union Members', *Journal of Labor Research*, vol. 73, no. 2 (1992).
20. A. O. Hirschman, *Exit, Voice and Loyalty: Responses to Decline in Firms, Organisations and States* (Cambridge: Harvard University Press, 1970).
21. A. W. Phillips, 'The Relation Between Unemployment and the Rate of Change of Money Wage Rates in the United Kingdom, 1861–1957', *Economica*, 22 (1958), pp. 283–99.
22. Alternatively, it may attempt to bring about basic changes in the workings of the economy, e.g. a prices and incomes policy, in order to reduce the rate of inflation consistent with unemployment.
23. See: B. S. Frey and F. Schneider, 'On the Modelling of Politico–Economic Interdependence, *European Journal of Political Research*, Dec. 1975, 3. pp. 339–360; B. S. Frey, 'Politico-Economic Models and Cycles', *Journal of Public Economics*, April 1978, 9, pp. 203–220.
24. On the other hand, of course, the government's actions may simply depend upon its ideology if it considers the chances of re-election to be good.
25. W. D. Nordhaus, 'The Political Business Cycle', *Review of Economic Studies*, 42 (1975), p. 184.
26. R. Barro and D. Gordon, 'Rules, Discretion and Reputation in a Model of Monetary Policy', *Journal of Monetary Economics*, 12 (1983), 101–121. See, also: F. Kydland and E. Prescott, 'Rules Rather than Discretion: The Inconsistency of Optimal Plans', *Journal of Political Economy*, 85, (1977).
27. G. Kirchgassner, 'Ökonometrische Untersuchungen des Einflusses der Wirtschaftlage auf die Popularität der Parteien', *Schweizerische Zeitschrift für Volkswirtschaft und Statistik*, (1974), 110, pp. 409–45.
28. They conclude, however, that these economic variables work to the advantage of the Democrats, in or out of office, and do not systematically affect the fortunes of only the incumbent party.
29. W. D. Nordhaus, 'The Political Business Cycle', *Review of Economic Studies*, 42 (1975), pp. 169–90.
30. D. Glasner, *op. cit.* (1989), p. 39.
31. E. R. Tufte, *Political Control of the Economy* (Princeton, New Jersey: Princeton University Press, 1978), p. 5.
32. M. Perlman, 'Party Politics and Bureaucracy in Economic Policy', in G. Tullock, *The Vote Motive*, (London: Institute for International Affairs, 1976), p. 69.
33. For example, it may be argued that, in the UK, the post-1979 Conservative government built up a reputation for controlling inflation over its first few years in power.

34. G. Stigler, 'General Economic Conditions and National Elections', *American Economic Review*, 63 (1973), p. 167.
35. G. Wright, 'The Political Economy of New Deal Spending: An Econometric Analysis, *Review of Economics and Statistics*, 56, (1974), pp. 30–8.
36. The attack on the Phillips curve really began a decade earlier with Milton Friedman's presidential address to the American Economic Association in 1968. According to Friedman, the Phillips curve was fundamentally misspecified, and should have been cast in terms of the rate of growth of the real wage instead of the rate of growth of the money wage.
37. R. O. Keohane and J. S. Nye, *Power and Interdependence: World Politics in Transition* (New York: Little, Brown, 1977).
38. *Ibid.*, (1977), p. 60.
39. J. Melitz, 'Monetary Discipline and Cooperation in the European Monetary System: A Synthesis', in F. Giavazzi et al. (eds), *op. cit.* (1988).
40. R. Cooper, *op. cit.* (1990), p. 116.
41. See, for example: Inis Claude, *Swords into Ploughshares*, (New York: Random House, 1956); Robert Cox and Harold Jacobson, *The Anatomy of Influence: Decision making in International Organizations* (New Haven, Conn.: Yale University Press, 1983); G. Gallorotti, 'The Limits of International Organization: Systematic Failure in the Management of International Organizations', *International Organization*, 45 (1991), pp. 183–220; Harold K. Jacobsen, William M. Reisinger and Todd Mathers, 'National Entanglements in International Governmental Organizations', *American Political Science Review*, 80 (1986), pp. 141–59; and, F. Kratochwil and John C. Ruggie, 'International Organization: A State of the Art or an Art of the State', *International Organization*, 40 (1986), pp. 754–75.
42. J. Bendor and D. Mukherjee, 'Institutional Structure and the Logic of Ongoing Collective Action', *American Political Science Review*, 81 (1987), pp. 129–54.
43. W. T. Bianco and R. H. Bates, 'Cooperation by Design: Leadership, Structure and Collective Dilemmas', *American Political Science Review*, 84 (1990), pp. 133–47.
44. C. Allsopp, 'Inflation', in A. Boltho (ed.), *The European Economy, Growth and Crisis* (Oxford, Oxford University Press, 1982), pp. 81–82.
45. S. Nelson, *op. cit.* (1993), p. 20.
46. The 'Delors' Report, *op. cit.* (1989), paragraph 32.
47. Peter B. Kenen, *Economic and Monetary Union in Europe – Moving beyond Maastricht* (Cambridge: Cambridge University Press, 1995), p. 129.
48. G. de Malynes, 'A Treatise on the Canker of England's Commonwealth', in R. H. Tawney and E. Power (eds), *Tudor Economic Documents* (New York: Barnes and Noble, 1963).
49. See: G. Cassel, 'The Present Situation of the Foreign Exchanges I', *Economic Journal*, 26 (1916), 62–65; 'The Present Situation of the Foreign Exchanges II', *Economic Journal*, 26 (1916), 319–323; 'Comment', *Economic Journal*, 30 (1920), 44–45; *The World's Monetary Problems* (London: Constable, 1921); *Post-war Monetary Stabilisation*, (New York: Columbia University Press, 1928); *Money and Foreign Exchange after 1919* (London: Macmillan, 1930).

50. See: R. MacDonald, *Floating Exchange Rates, Theories and Evidence* (London: Unwin Hyman, 1988), pp. 23–5.
51. Note that transaction costs would modify this result in the sense that they would create a 'neutral band' within which it was unprofitable to engage in the process of arbitrage.
52. The concept of purchasing power applies to the sum of all goods in the economy. If we are examining price equalisation for one good, we are, strictly speaking, dealing with the 'law of one price'.
53. There are, however, a number of difficulties with the concept of purchasing power parity. The most significant difficulty is that in our definition of PPP only traded goods prices have been included; however, all countries also produce a range of non-traded goods which enter into the calculation of price indices, such as the retail price index (RPI) and the GDP deflator. Under our definition of PPP there is no mechanism for the equalisation of the prices of these non-tradeables.

    In addition, the actual validity of the relationship has not always been upheld, with some critics using a reductio ad absurdum to destroy the theory. For example, Samuelson has the view that:

    'Of course, under perfect competition, free trade without tariffs, quotas or exchange controls, relative prices of one good could not deviate regionally if transport costs were zero. In that case only, each competitive good's international price ratio would have to equal the official free exchange rate exactly, as a result of quick-acting competitive arbitrage; and what is true for each and every good, must be true for the average index number of price.'

    See: P. Samuelson, 'Analytical Notes on International Real-Income Measures', *Economic Journal*, 84 (1974), 595–608.
54. P. de Grauwe, *op. cit.* (1995), p. 15.
55. F. Giavazzi and A. Giavannini, 'The Role of the Exchange-Rate Regime in a Disinflation: Empirical Evidence on the European Monetary System', in F. Giavazzi et al. (eds), *op. cit.* (1988), 85–107.
56. B. Eichengreen and J. A. Frieden, *op. cit.* (1995), p. 271.
57. Although Thomas Willett, for example, has argued that an expansionary economic policy yields more favourable trade-offs between inflation-unemployment in the short run with a system of adjustable pegs (what De Grauwe terms an 'incomplete monetary union') than with a depreciating exchange rate. See: T. D. Willett, 'Some Aspects of the Public Choice Approach to International Economic Relations', and T. D. Willett and J. Mullen, 'The Effects of Alternative International Monetary Systems on Macroeconomic Discipline and Inflationary Biases', both in R. Lombra and W. Witte, eds, *The Political Economy of International and Domestic Monetary Relations* (Ames: Iowa State University Press, 1982). The implication of this is that a system of adjustable pegs may be expected to increase the government's incentive to attempt to gain votes by introducing an expansionary policy (e.g. lowering unemployment) before an election, and devaluing in the aftermath of the election.

58. D. Begg, 'Discussion – Economic Growth and Exchange Rates in the European Monetary System: Their Trade Effects in a Changing External Environment', in F. Giavazzi (et. al.), *op. cit.* (1988), pp. 178–182.
59. P. de Grauwe, *op. cit.* (1995), pp. 67–9.
60. D. Gros and N. Thygesen, *op. cit.* (1990), p. 926.
61. 'Protocol On The Convergence Criteria Referred To In Article 109j Of The Treaty Establishing the European Community', Article 1.
62. A. Britton and D. Mayes, *op. cit.* (1992), p. 40.
63. P. Fraser, M. Taylor and A. Webster, 'An Empirical Analysis of Long-Run Purchasing Power Parity as a Theory of International Commodity Arbitrage', *University of Dundee Discussion Papers in Economics*, 3 (1990), p. 3.
64. I. B. Kravis and R. E. Lipsey, 'Price Behaviour in the Light of Balance of Payments Theories', *Journal of International Economics*, 8 (1978), pp. 193–246.
65. G. D. Baer and T. Padoa-Schioppa, 'The Werner Report Revisited', paper annexed to the *Delors Report* (1989).
66. F. Giavazzi and M. Pagano, 'The Advantage of Tying One's Hands: EMS Discipline and Central Bank Credibility', *European Economic Review*, 32 (1988), pp. 1055–82.
67. P. De Grauwe, *op. cit.* (1992), p. 108.
68. We can see this quite clearly within the context of Britain's entry into the Exchange Rate Mechanism and the subsequent exchange rate crises of 1992–93. When Britain entered the Exchange Rate Mechanism, it was a widely held belief that she had entered at an exchange rate value which was too high to be sustained. German Economic and Monetary Union then took place, which resulted in a large rise in government spending in Germany, leading to the creation of inflationary pressures there. As a result of this, the Bundesbank gave complete priority to combating inflation by a restrictive monetary policy. This was at odds, however, with policy in the UK which, because of the European recession, required a monetary policy which was less restrictive. The UK then pressured the German monetary authorities to relax their monetary policies and reduce interest rates. Speculators, witnessing this developing conflict, realised that the British monetary authorities were tempted to sever their relationship with the Deutschmark in order that they could follow a less restrictive monetary policy, and thus started to speculate against the pound sterling, eventually leading to the currency's withdrawal from the Exchange Rate Mechanism in September 1992. However, the political costs of this devaluation and exit from the ERM (on so-called 'Black Wednesday') for the British monetary authorities and for leading figures within the British cabinet were very significant indeed. Opinion polls taken after the British exit demonstrated that the United Kingdom electorate no longer trusted in the government's ability to handle the economy effectively. In addition, the then Chancellor of the Exchequer, Norman Lamont, was sacked from his position. However, if, on the other hand, speculators had perceived that, despite the growing conflict between the UK and Germany, the British monetary authorities would maintain their commitment to the ERM whatever, then the credibility of the arrangement would have actually

increased. For Britain, however, this would never have happened, as there had been doubts from the start about the level of the UK commitment to the Mechanism, stemming not only from the historic attitudes of Britain towards increasing integration in Europe, but also because at the outset there were doubts as to the feasibility of the UK commitment in view of the level of the exchange rate which had been chosen.

69. Taking this same line of reasoning, it could be argued that the entrance of a country which was seen as not having a credible commitment to the ERM's low inflation stance, i.e. the UK, hastened its demise.

70. In contrast to their views over some of the other criteria, a point to which we will return later in this analysis.

71. W. M. Corden, *op. cit.* (1995), pp. 154–55.

72. P. de Grauwe, *op. cit.* (1995), pp. 160–162.

73. Michael J. Baun, 'The Maastricht Treaty as High Politics', *Political Science Quarterly*, 110, 4 (1995–96), pp. 605–624.

74. P. de Grauwe, *op. cit.* (1995), p. 160.

75. Karl Otto-Pohl, quoted in Wolfgang Munchau, 'Hard Ecu, Harder Problems Says Pohl', *The Times*, 26 June 1990, p. 23.

76. R. C. K. Burdekin, C. Wihlborg and T. D. Willett, 'A Monetary Constitution Case for an Independent European Central Bank', *The World Economy*, March (1992).

77. This appears with slight modifications as Article 8 of the Statute of the European Monetary Institute.

78. *Treaty on European Union*, Article 109.

79. B. Eichengreen and J. A. Frieden, *op. cit.* (1995), p. 271.

80. M. Artis, *op. cit.* (1994), p. 363.

81. The Deutsche Bundesbank had many of these features and in the Maastricht constitution for the ECB we can see many of the same features – typically somewhat strengthened – repeated.

82. For a fuller discussion of this phenomenon, see: A. Hughes-Hallett and D. Vines, 'On the Possible Costs of European Monetary Union', *Manchester School Journal*, 61 (1993), pp. 35–64.

83. B. Eichengreen and J. A. Frieden, *op. cit.* (1995), p. 271.

84. C. A. E. Goodhart, 'A European Central Bank', in C. A. E. Goodhart, *op. cit.* (1995), pp. 323–24.

85. *Ibid.*, p. 364.

86. M. Feldstein, 'Does One Market Require One Money?' in P. King (ed.), *op. cit.* (1995), p. 371.

87. *Ibid.*, pp. 324–25.

88. Committee of Governors of the Central Banks of the Member States of the European Community, *Annual Report 1992*, pp. 11–12 and 34.

89. A. Britton and D. Mayes, *op. cit.* (1992), p. 51.

90. *Ibid.*, p. 39.

91. D. Gros and G. Vandille, *op. cit.* (1995), p. 175.

5 The Convergence Criteria: Budgetary Conditions

So the poor debtor, seeing naught around him,
Yet feels the limits pitiless that bound him;
Grieves at his debt and studies to evade it,
and finds at last he might as well have paid it.

Ambrose Bierce, The Cynic's Word Book, 1906

INTRODUCTION

Government borrowing has traditionally been viewed as a sign of weakness in an economy, a necessary policy that has the object of stimulating economic activity and employment by injecting increased purchasing power into a depressed economic system. If a country is running a budget deficit, this means that government expenditure for that economy is larger than government receipts.

Budget deficits may be financed by increased taxation; by borrowing, usually in the form of the sale of government bonds; by creating new money within the economy or selling foreign exchange reserves; or by selling nationally owned assets, including the privatisation of publicly owned industries. The latter, in particular, is only a short-term solution (a government cannot go on indefinitely selling a nation's assets or increasing taxation), and continuous budget deficits lead to a build-up of debt. As a result of this, government expenditure must be diverted towards the costs of servicing this debt. Governments obviously do not like to find themselves in such a position as their expenditure on public goods and services will go down and tax levels will go up. Their reputation for sound handling of the national economy (if they have one!) will be damaged and this, in turn, may have a very negative impact upon their future electoral fortunes. For this reason, governments aspire to budgetary discipline.

Discipline is an intuitive notion, but not an easy concept to define and quantify. Its most straightforward, and only indisputable, definition relates to the fact that the government has to ensure that it does not become insolvent. This definition is known as the 'sustainability' condition of the debt–deficit path (also known as the 'intertemporal budget constraint').[1] If the interest rate on government debt exceeds the growth rate of the economy, the debt to GDP ratio will continue to increase, eventually leading to an unsustainable domestic economic position urgently in need of correction.

In addition, budgetary sustainability is always a concern for monetary policy because monetary and budgetary policy are interdependent in the long-run: protracted deficits which lead to unsustainable budget positions end up either in debt 'monetisation' or government default (unless, of course, the government is in a position to drastically reduce government expenditure and/or raise taxes, both of which are unattractive options for both the electorate, and an incumbent government seeking re-election). In the first case, monetary authorities give up their autonomy in order to rescue the government. In the second, they stick to their own objectives but force the government to repudiate part of its debt. Moreover, in the latter case, the market may perceive in advance that there is a chance of government defaults. This, in turn means that a risk premium will have to be paid, as the interest rate on the debt will be pushed up and the government's debt position will be even more serious.[2]

Despite the difficulties which government debt causes, government expenditure is now, relatively speaking, much larger than in previous times. This phenomenon can largely be traced back to the Keynesian revolution, wherein budget deficits became the tool by which a 'benign, enlightened government' sought to ensure full employment by increasing government expenditure.[3] Thus, budget deficits became common in industrialised economies and many have a long experience of leniency in the conduct of their fiscal affairs. In Europe, for example, throughout the 1960s, the debt-to-GDP ratio was more than 60 per cent in the United Kingdom and Belgium. This increased further in the period after the second oil price shocks with, for example, the debt-to-GDP ratio in Ireland peaking at 122 per cent in 1987, and in Belgium peaking at 132 per cent in 1988.[4]

This European experience of fiscal leniency is reflected in the budgetary provisions of the Maastricht Treaty which are concerned with preventing 'excessive' fiscal deficits (Article 104c(1)). The Maastricht criteria for judging whether or not fiscal deficits are excessive are that they should not be more than three per cent of gross domestic product, and that general government gross debt should not be more than 60 per cent of gross domestic product. Deficits can exceed three per cent only if 'the ratio has declined substantially and continuously and reached a level that comes close to the reference value, or, alternatively, the excess over the reference value is only exceptional and temporary and the ratio remains close to the reference value'.[5] Further, the debt: gross domestic product ratio can exceed 60 per cent only 'if the ratio is sufficiently diminishing and approaching the reference value at a satisfactory pace'.[6]

This chapter analyses the importance of these budgetary convergence conditions in the Maastricht Treaty to the progress of economic and monetary union in Europe, the objective being to explain the reasons, both economic and political, why the achievement of a budgetary criterion was thought to be necessary for the transition to EMU. With this objective in mind, we begin with an overview of some ways in which debt accumulation may be viewed from an international political economy perspective. In particular, we want to consider in detail why governments in recent times have allowed such high levels of debt accumulation. From this discussion it becomes apparent that the reasons why industrialised states in recent times have followed policies which may be termed fiscally lenient have less to do with economics and rather more to do with political expediency. Such arguments lead us first of all into our examination of the economic reasoning behind the budgetary criterion laid down at Maastricht, where we specifically consider two issues. First, we want to examine the economic rationale behind the budgetary criterion and how it relates to the other convergence criteria; and second, we want to examine the part played by fiscal policy in a monetary union. The latter has proved to be a particularly contentious issue in the EMU debate, a fact reflected in our examination of the political rationale behind the European budgetary conditions, where we consider not only to what degree the European experience of debt accumulation can be explained by our previous discussion of the IPE of the budgetary conditions, but also the important issue of the appropriate level of centralisation of fiscal policy decision making in an economic and monetary union.

THE INTERNATIONAL POLITICAL ECONOMY OF THE BUDGETARY CONDITIONS

In the same way that political theories of inflation require an explanation of the precise ways in which political variables contribute to increases in the price level, political theories of debt require a knowledge of the particular incentives and characteristics of the state and non-state actors involved in the policy process.

The literature on the political economy of debt is very large and dates back to the Italian school of public finance in the nineteenth century.[7] For our present purposes, this literature can be placed within three major frameworks: the public choice approach (including political business cycle models); the strategic public debt choice approach; and the government weakness and decentralised government approach (although there is a degree of overlap between all three).[8] We will now go through these in turn.

The Public Choice Approach

Economists and political scientists who advocate a public choice view (as was seen in the previous chapter) basically argue that macroeconomic policymakers are opportunistic and act to maximise their own welfare or utility rather than for the social good.[9] In the case of elected officials making fiscal policy decisions, then, this approach to policymaking emphasises votes as the central goal variable motivating policymakers. Indeed, some public choice writers argue that in the same way that the money supply can be manipulated in order to engineer a level of inflation which will improve government popularity, public debt may be used in order to improve the government's chances of re-election. In keeping with the idea of 'voter myopia' outlined in the previous chapter, this approach emphasises the notion of 'fiscal delusion' whereby the voters do not understand the intertemporal budget constraint (i.e. the 'sustainability' of the debt-deficit path) which the government faces. They therefore systematically underestimate the level of the tax burden which they will encounter in the future when the incumbent government undertakes a current expenditure programme financed by an increased budget deficit (i.e. taxes must go up in order to pay for the government's pre-election promises). Politicians seeking re-election therefore raise spending more than taxes in order to secure the votes of that portion of the electorate who are 'fiscally deluded' – those who do not understand the mechanics of the budgetary process.[10]

This framework also places some emphasis on the previously mentioned argument that Keynesianism has encouraged the tendency towards excessive deficits and the giving up of responsibility by governments with regard to their budgetary policies. This is because Keynesian stabilisation policies, although advocating the use of budget deficits and budget surpluses as a means of regulating the economy and hence attaining a 'balanced budget', actually were essentially asymmetric in that, in the name of full employment, politicians were always willing to increase expenditure and run deficits in recessions, but were never willing to decrease expenditure in the name of running a budget surplus when recessions were over.[11] Moreover, because the electorate was fiscally deluded, the government was not punished in the voting booths for this kind of behaviour. For example, James Buchanan and Richard Wagner argue that:[12]

'Elected politicians enjoy spending public monies on projects that yield some demonstrable benefit to their constituents. They do not enjoy imposing taxes on the same constituents. The pre-Keynesian norm of budget balance served to constrain spending proclivities so as to keep governmental outlays roughly within the revenue limits generated by taxes. The Keynesian destruction of this norm, without an adequate replacement, effectively removed the constraint. Predictably, politicians responded by increasing spending more than tax revenues, by creating budget deficits as a normal course of events.'

If we accept this public choice characterisation of fiscal policy, how then can this asymmetry in the process be corrected?

Buchanan and Wagner argue that the only way is to restore the 'pre-Keynesian norm of budget balance'.[13] In these terms, the increase in government spending brought on by the Keynesian revolution must be rescinded and all deficit spending avoided. Not only would this eliminate any inflationary effects of deficit spending (for example, because the money supply had been increased due to the creation of new money within the economy to pay for the deficit), but also, the growth of the government sector would be curtailed if deficit spending was reduced in this way, because new or expanded government spending programmes would have to be financed by new taxes in a balanced-budget system. Therefore, in the public choice view, the optimal fiscal policy for a country to follow is not one of designing policies to stabilise the macroeconomy; rather, it is that optimal fiscal policy implies the imposition of rules upon policymakers, the result of which is that the destabilising effects of deficit spending are eliminated.

This public choice characterisation of the incidence of debt accumulation by governments is, however, not completely convincing. In particular, it has been criticised for the weakness of some of its assumptions. For example, the public choice view assumes that private agents (the electorate) systematically underestimate, and are unable to recognise, the motivations of the policy-maker. However, while it is not out of the question that the electorate may misinterpret the information which they receive, it is not obvious why that misinterpretation would always lead to an underestimation of the tax burden relative to the benefits of government expenditure.

On the other hand, if the electorate is seen as naïve in this approach, a further criticism that can be made is that the policymakers are seen as exceptionally cunning, cynically attempting to maximise deficit spending for their own private reasons. Again, such an assumption of systematic selfishness may be far too simplistic.

Despite these difficulties with the public choice approach, however, analysts continue to focus attention upon the proclivities of government and the naïvety of voters in explaining the process of the creation of budget deficits. Indeed, an argument somewhat related to this approach (and, once again, to arguments in the previous chapter) is that put forward in the literature on political business cycles, which stresses the importance of party cycles when examining the electoral motivations of policy-makers. This approach to the examination of debt incidence suggests that fiscal policy may be overly expansionary before elections as a way of gaining electoral advantage. In particular, the political business cycle theory proposed by Nordhaus suggested that office-motivated politicians will tend to follow expansionary fiscal policies before elections in order to maximise their chances of securing re-election.[14] In other words, they try to 'buy' votes, typically in the form of popular tax cuts or promises made immediately before elections, in order to enhance their chances of remaining in office.[15] This implies that excessive government spending, tax reductions, delays in tax increases and therefore fiscal deficits will be observed in electoral years. In other words, the voters reward the politicians without understanding (or, indeed, without learning from their previous behaviour) that expansionary government expenditure in the pre-election period will ultimately be paid for by recession in the post-election years.

This traditional political business cycle theory of a pre-electoral fiscal deficit bias has, however, been criticised for the weakness of some of its assumptions. In particular, and once again, the notion that private agents (the electorate) are unable to recognise the motivations of the policy-makers has proved difficult to substantiate. Macrae, for example, examined whether the US electorate were short-sighted in their voting behaviour, but could find no particular evidence for the existence of a political business cycle.[16] Moreover, as Alt and Chrystal argue:[17]

'No one could read the political business cycle literature without being struck by the lack of supporting evidence. There must be cases where politicians have undertaken electorally motivated interventions. It is difficult to imagine politicians not exploiting some extra information or other resources. But while this clearly happens, and happens particularly clearly in some cases, such cycles may be trivial in comparison with other economic fluctuations. Incumbents may be able to give themselves significant advantages relative to challengers. But the ability to intervene economically is only one of many possible incumbency advantages. The existence of such advantages may not make anything worse overall in the long run.'

In addition, McCallum tested the hypothesis of a political business cycle against an alternative hypothesis suggested by Thomas Sargent and Neil Wallace, but based upon the earlier work of Robert Lucas.[18] The latter hypothesis stated that incumbent governments are unable to produce booms by the end of their terms, even if they wish to, because of the preemptive, i.e. anticipated, behaviour on the part of those concerned.[19] The basis of this proposition is in the hypothesis of rational expectations.

In many ways, the rational expectations hypothesis has become the standard general method of modelling expectations for a wide range of economic variables.[20] In very basic terms, a decision-maker is said to form rational expectations when he uses all the available knowledge and information in an attempt not to make systematic errors. The concept can perhaps most easily be explained by examining a situation of expectations which are not rational, such as the market situation involved in the cobweb theorem.[21] Here, suppliers expect that this period's price will continue to prevail in the next period, despite the fact that in every period they are proved wrong. Any speculator who knew the cobweb theorem could make a profit in the marketplace. However, false expectations cannot persist if there is a profit to be made out of forming correct expectations. Therefore, the usual assumption of rational expectations in economics suggests that expectations which are systematically wrong will be revised, so that in the end expectations will be formed which are on average correct, any errors in expectations will be *randomly distributed* around the correct value. With regard to budget policy under these circumstances, if a government has, in the past, pursued an expansionary fiscal policy before the election, the electorate will take this into account when forming their expectations on future government behaviour. They will therefore expect the government to pursue an expansionary government policy at this time, even if the government declares that it will do otherwise. In other words, the latter change in government policy will have no credibility. McCallum, examining quarterly US data for 1948–1974, discovered that there was unequivocal support for this Lucas-Sargent proposition *against* the hypothesis of a political business cycle. Although McCallum did consider that it was possible that this was for the simple reason that US administrations did not actually attempt to manipulate economic variables for electoral gain, the results did provide an additional strand of information regarding possible difficulties which the assumption of a political business cycle might engender. With this latter result in mind, let us now go on to consider some classes of budget deficit model which are not dependent on the assumed inadequacies of the electorate.

The Strategic Public Debt Choice Approach

The second framework commonly used to examine the incidence of budget deficits is that of strategic public debt choice, often also known as the 'partisan theory' (or 'partisan party') approach. The crucial assumption here is that the level of debt connects past and future policies.[22] Incumbent politicians can thus affect, through the choice of fiscal policy, the economic conditions which their successors will inherit, including the level of debt.

In one of the simplest formulations of these types of model, the relationship between political variables and budget deficits is explained by looking at the role of 'partisan' factors in economic policy-making, where politicians are viewed as ideologically motivated leaders of competing parties.[23, 24] The parties in turn represent different groups of voters with different preferences concerning the composition of public spending. The most common specification of the partisan model examines the relationship between a liberal party and a conservative party. For example, a liberal party might place primary emphasis upon spending for full employment and income redistribution, while a conservative party might place primary emphasis upon defence spending. Let us assume that the party that favours defence spending is in office today (i.e., a conservative party) and the result of the next election is uncertain. A conservative party will then spend on defence and issue debt because that is the primary emphasis of that party's policies. If the conservative party then retains office, its preferred policy position is already in place. If it does not and the liberal party wins the election, the latter will have to forgo the large amount which it would have spent on implementing its policies of full employment and income redistribution in order to service the debt left by the previous (conservative) government. Thus the conservative government has used the level of public debt strategically, with the goal of 'tying the hands' of a future government with different fiscal policy objectives. In this political equilibrium, the level of the budget deficit diverges from the optimal value that would be obtained in the absence of the political distortion (i.e. if instead a benevolent social planner were to take the place of the two political parties).

Arguments such as these have been backed up by empirical analysis. Alesina and Tabellini, for example, revealed that the greater the probability of not being re-elected and the greater the degree of political/ideological polarisation (i.e., the difference in preferences) of the two parties, the larger the budget deficit will be (because governments with differing policy priorities always have to reverse the spending decisions of their predecessors, and hence follow expansionary policies in order to do so). In turn, the greater the level of disagreement over government expenditure, the more unstable the political system will be because of this disagreement.[25, 26, 27] In particular, Alesina and Tabellini considered the effects of such political distortions on external debt and capital flight.[28] They concluded that, in a model in which two types of government with conflicting policy preferences randomly alternate in office, doubts over the type of fiscal policy likely to be pursued by future government generate private capital flight and decreased domestic investment. This environment of political uncertainty also provides the incentives for current governments to over-accumulate external debt.

Similarly, Persson and Svensson argue that a government which is averse to public spending (a 'low-spending' government) finds it advantageous to issue debt in order to force its successors (who, it is assumed, are more keenly disposed to government expenditure – i.e. a 'high-spending' government) to curtail public spending.[29] However, in contrast to previous models in this section, the model by Persson and Svensson is asymmetric in that only one party creates deficits while the other creates surpluses (Alesina and Tabellini, on the other hand, assumed that both parties will issue debt).

In yet another example of this type of analysis, Tabellini and Alesina produce a more explicit illustration of the relationship between deficits and preference polarisation, but this time with regard to individual, rather than party, preferences.[30] They contemplate a political environment where decisions are taken by majority rule and any proposal can be made and voted upon. In these circumstances, the so-called 'median-voter theorem' implies that the adopted policy will be that which is favoured by the median voter.[31] In an uncertain environment, with regard to the preferences of future majorities over spending composition, the current median voter will prefer debt to be issued in such a way as to tilt the future composition of government spending in his favour. Tabellini and Alesina demonstrate that the more concentrated toward the extreme the electorate's preferences are, the larger will be the debt burden – this time because voters will vote in such a way as to reverse the spending decisions of previous governments voted into office by an electorate with a different set of policy priorities.

One of the problems, however, with this analysis (as well as some of the other approaches to the international political economy of the budgetary conditions which we have so far analysed) is that, although the current and future decision makers may differ, at any moment in time a single decision maker is in charge of policy. Nevertheless, this reasoning does not really fit with the facts of contemporary political life. Although policy decisions may look centralised, disagreement among different decision makers may actually result in the postponement of unpopular decisions, such as tax reform.[32] In this sense, a short-sighted policy decision (one which does not take account of the long-term implications of a policy on the level of the debt burden) may not reflect a deliberate choice, but rather an inability to take a collective decision as a result of the fragmentation of power among different decision makers.[33] This weakness in previous models is remedied to some extent in the third framework which can be used to examine the political economy of debt incidence: the government weakness and political instability approach.

The Government Weakness and Political Instability Approach

In this approach to debt incidence, analysts assume that the spending decisions made by 'unstable' forms of government may be a source of sup-optimal fiscal policy behaviour and an important cause of fiscal deficits. Such instability could be caused by any of several decision-making environments, but this present analysis will concentrate on three particular examples: (1) parliamentary democracies; (2) budgetary institutions; and (3) fiscal decentralisation.[34]

Parliamentary democracies
In their analysis of sub-optimal fiscal policy behaviour, Roubini and Sachs, and Grilli, Masciandaro and Tabellini argue that high-public-debt

countries are almost exclusively parliamentary democracies who often have a highly proportional electoral system.[35] This results in a large amount of fragmentation in electoral choice which, in turn, can result in very unstable governments, generally formed by a coalition of parties. Emphasising the effect on budget deficit spending of such multi-party governments, Roubini and Sachs have suggested that short duration multi-party coalition governments lead to fiscal deficits because, in the presence of economic crisis, it is difficult to enforce co-operation upon the parties in a coalition setting. In fact, analysts who advocate a game-theoretic approach suggest that co-operation is more difficult when the number of players is large (e.g. in multi-party coalition governments) and when the horizon of the players is short and not repeated (e.g. in short duration governments). This is because the individual parties in the coalition will each veto spending cuts or tax increases that would impinge upon their narrow constituencies, thereby frustrating that attempts of the executive branch to implement deficit reduction measures.[36]

In another example of the importance of government organisation to debt accumulation, Alesina and Drazen explain delays in fiscal adjustment in the presence of unsustainable fiscal deficits as the result of a 'war of attrition' between two different social classes.[37] Here the conflict is about what social class will bear the tax burden of stabilisation. The model implies that a greater dispersion in the income distribution and a lower degree of political cohesion will cause a delay in the expected rate of stabilisation and will therefore imply a greater and prolonged prestabilisation period of fiscal imbalance and inflation; a conclusion which appears to have been borne out in other empirical analyses (for example, using data for fifteen OECD countries, Roubini and Sachs discovered that a lack of political cohesion does indeed lead to higher real budget deficits).[38, 39] In general, then, the more fragmented the political system, and the more unstable the government, the greater will be the incidence of a significant accumulation of debt.

Budgetary institutions
The notion that debt incidence is related to the decision-making environment in a parliamentary democracy very much ties in with the literature on budgetary institutions wherein the framework in which debt policy is made can potentially explain cross-country variations in deficits and debts. Budgetary institutions are all of the rules and regulations which govern the drafting, approval and implementation of government budgets. These have an effect on the outcome of government

fiscal policy if they are more difficult to alter than the budget itself (otherwise they would be totally ineffective), and if they have an effect on the final vote and implementation of the budget. For example, one major issue is who holds the power in setting the government's policy agenda and what type of changes can actually be made to this agenda. Generally speaking, theory would suggest that institutional rules which limit universalism (i.e., the property of a budget which includes 'something for everyone') and reciprocity (i.e. an agreement not to oppose another government actor's proposal in exchange for some favour) are conducive to fiscal restraint.[40] Hence, if the decision-making environment in which the budgetary agenda is set is one which promotes universalism and reciprocity, the budget deficit will tend to be larger. This institutional emphasis also ties in with the literature on inefficient fiscal systems (those with higher collection costs) and debt incidence: the more inefficient the fiscal system, the more costly it is to raise taxes and the higher the level of debt incidence.[41]

Fiscal decentralisation

Finally, and in a comparable tone, Tabellini and Alesina stressed the importance of the decentralisation of government fiscal decisions on debt incidence.[42] When the decisions to spend and tax are decentralised among different agents (such as the ministers of a coalition government or between central, regional and local fiscal authorities), there may be an incentive to excessive government spending which is deficit-financed. For example, in a highly decentralised system, it is in the interests of a local fiscal authority to finance increased local expenditure through an increase in the budget deficit. The local fiscal authority realises that the effects of this increase in expenditure on the overall level of the budget deficit are small, given that the authority is representing only a small percentage of the population. Thus, each local fiscal authority has an incentive to increase its expenditure through debt accumulation because, if it does not do this, the benefits to the population of that authority relative to others will decline, given that all of the other local authorities are likely to increase their expenditure through debt accumulation.[43] The more decentralised the fiscal decision-making framework, then, the higher the level of debt incidence.

In models of political instability, then, all the available evidence points to the same conclusion: countries with more fragmented political systems (constitutionally, say, or in terms of decision-making) tend to accumulate more public debt. However, it must be remembered that the time frame of the analysis is also an important factor in these outcomes. Empirical results suggest that fiscal institutions and political factors matter for *short-run deficit dynamics*. States with relatively tight constitutional or statutory rules that make it more difficult to run deficits experience more rapid fiscal adjustment when revenues fall short of expectations or spending exceeds projections than do those states with a more fragmented or unstable constitutional arrangement.[44]

Although, as we have seen, these three approaches (public choice, strategic public debt choice, and government weakness and decentralised government) do not provide the whole picture, they are useful for the insights which they give into the policy-making process. How, though, do frameworks such as these apply when we consider the incidence of debt in the Member States of the European Union and, moreover, what role do they have in regard to the budgetary convergence criterion of the Maastricht Treaty?

EUROPEAN BUDGETARY STABILITY

The Delors Report (echoing the earlier Werner Report) emphasised the relationship between monetary unification and fiscal policy by stressing that 'economic and monetary union form two integral parts of a single whole and would therefore have to be implemented in parallel'.[45] Reinforcing the fiscal implications of the movement towards a greater degree of rigidity in nominal exchange rates, what was needed was:

'an agreed macro-economic framework [which would] ... be subject to binding procedures and rules. This would permit the determination of an overall policy stance for the Community as a whole, avoid unsustainable differences between individual member countries ... public sector borrowing requirements and place binding constraints on the size and financing of budget deficits.'[46]

Indeed, the Report is specific about the constraints to be imposed on national budgetary policy. For example:

'In the budgetary field, binding rules are required that would: firstly, impose effective upper limits on budget deficits of individual member countries of the Community, although in setting these limits the situation of each member country might have to be taken into consideration; secondly, exclude access to direct central bank credit and other forms of monetary financing while, however, permitting open market operations in government securities; thirdly, limit recourse to external borrowing in non-Community currencies.[47]

Note, however, in this last statement, the asymmetric nature of the constraints on the public sector deficit: upper limits but no lower limits. This can only be understood if we assume that without such constraints, there would be a bias towards government deficits that are too large rather than too small.[48] We shall now examine more fully the economic rationale behind such binding policy commitments and consider why it was so necessary that the incidence of debt in the Member States should converge before the final transition to economic and monetary union in Europe. We will do this by first of all examining the link between the budgetary criterion and the rest of the convergence criteria. This will then lead us into our analysis of the role of fiscal policy in a monetary union.

The Economic Rationale

Of all of the convergence criteria, it has been the role of the budgetary criterion which has led to the most heated debate. Very briefly, in economic terms, the requirements laid down in the Maastricht Treaty regarding the fiscal conditions necessary for proceeding towards EMU are linked to the other convergence criteria. For example, with regard to prices, setting a convergence condition upon the level of inflation, whilst at the same time curtailing national central bank financing of budget deficits, prevents the individual Member States from following separate seigniorage policies, and countermands the effect of unanticipated inflation on the debt: GDP ratio. As we saw in the previous chapter, and as Britton and Mayes note more fully:[49]

> 'Fiscal extravagance leads in the end to inflation. It is possible to finance a reasonably large deficit by selling public sector debt to willing holders at home and abroad. Beyond a certain point governments are often forced to resort to bank finance, which adds to the money supply and threatens inflation. Historically, when governments have allowed their stock of debt to rise faster than national income (for example in wartime) there comes a point when the interest on the debt exceeds the taxable capacity of the country. Thereafter the real value of the debt is usually eroded by inflation. To avoid any risk of this happening within EMU the Treaty puts constraints on the behaviour of any persistent debtor countries.'

In terms of fiscal policy and interest rates, one reason why differences in interest rates between countries exist is due to the presence of a national default risk premium for the possible repudiation of debt if the country has an unsustainable fiscal position. Thus, if a country has a high level of debt and a large government budget deficit, the interest rate criterion implies that it is not enough simply to bring inflation down to the level of those states with the best inflation performance. Rather, and in addition, fiscal policy is required to reduce, and eventually eliminate national, default risk premia by providing a binding commitment to maintaining government solvency and allowing entry to the final stage of economic and monetary union (remembering that there will also be budgetary guidelines in operation once EMU has been established). If this did not occur, high budget deficits might lead to an increase in the level of outstanding public debt which, in turn, raises future interest payments, future deficits, and the future levels of outstanding debt.

In terms of the link between the budgetary criterion and the criterion on exchange rates, one of the most obvious consequences of monetary union is that monetary policy is lost as an instrument of national macroeconomic policy. Although, in order to qualify for EMU, monetary policy must be used to defend the exchange rate, once a country is actually in the economic and monetary union the European Central Bank will control monetary policy. According to Kenen, the theory of optimum currency areas, discussed briefly earlier, suggests the following implications for fiscal policy under such circumstances.[50]

First, the theory would suggest that it is beneficial to centralise a significant portion of the member countries, national budgets at the union level. The fact that a country loses its exchange rate instrument when it enters a monetary union means that, if no centralised budget exists to redistribute income automatically, countries have no instrument at hand with which to counter the social costs of a negative shock to a member country or region.[51, 52] Indeed, fiscal policy is the only instrument under such circumstances for dealing with country-specific shocks – those disturbances which a country faces which are different in nature or timing from those affecting other members of the union, as well as those disturbances which are common to all members of the union but which affect them differently. This was a major conclusion of the McDougall Report on the role of public finance in European integration, published in April 1977 (and was a factor also expressed in the Maastricht Treaty).

Second, if such centralisation were not feasible, national fiscal policy should be used flexibly: a country should be allowed, when hit by a negative shock, to increase its budget deficit through automatic budgetary stabilisers (typically by decreasing government revenues or increasing government expenditure). Hence, if a significant portion of the member states' national budgets cannot be centralised at the union level, then substantial autonomy in national fiscal policy-making should be maintained. There are, however various problems with this latter proposition. Most importantly, the idea that national fiscal policy should have a high degree of flexibility reflects a notion that governments can simply increase the level of their budget deficits without regard to whether that deficit is sustainable or not. However, there is a view, in keeping with the previous political perspectives on debt accumulation, that governments have an endemic tendency to overborrow (hence the idea that there would be a bias towards government deficits that are too large rather than too small) – and indeed this can be seen in Europe in the high levels of budget deficits experienced by Italy and by some of the smaller EU countries, such as Greece and the Netherlands.[53] Under such circumstances, governments will be more prone to run up unsustainably high debt levels that will threaten default and financial instability, not just in the short term, but in the long term also. In other words:[54]

'[t]he systematic use of this [fiscal policy] instrument quickly leads to problems of sustainability, which forces countries to run budget surpluses for a number of years.'

Such difficulties were all too obvious to the architects of the Maastricht Treaty. Indeed, there was a significant concern that allowing Member States to continue to exercise their own national fiscal policies in such a way, without regard to the requirements of economic and monetary union, might have serious effects on other EU countries. For example, if a country's public debt becomes unsustainable, other EMU members may be forced to 'bale out' the offending economy. Failure to come to the aid of the stricken economy could lead to financial crisis for the other EMU members because of the high degree of financial interdependence existing within the European economy. In addition, the European Central Bank may then be forced to increase the money supply in such circumstances, thus creating additional inflation throughout the EMU area (and indeed reducing the credibility of the ECB as a mechanism for ensuring price stability). Moreover, even if a country's debt position was not unsustainable, there would still be international interest rate and exchange rate spillovers from national debt financing policies. In these circumstances, it was important that the fiscal policy responses of the individual Member States were consistent with one another and that the collective response of the Member States was consistent with the monetary policy of the central banking system.

These difficulties over the issue of a country being allowed to use its national fiscal policy flexibly resulted in an alternative perspective, seen most clearly in the Delors Report, being put forward as to the part played by national fiscal policies in a monetary union: namely that national fiscal policies, and in particular national government budget deficits, should be subject to binding rules. The Delors Report argued that these were necessary because even though:

'market forces can exert a disciplinary influence . . . experience suggests that market perceptions do not necessarily provide strong and compelling signals and that access to a large capital market may for some time even facilitate the financing of economic imbalances.'

Hence, binding rules were advocated because:

'uncoordinated and divergent national budgetary policies would undermine monetary stability and generate imbalances in the real and financial sectors of the Community.'

This notion, however, was not without criticism. First, the idea that private markets could not provide strong enough discipline to prevent governments from running up unsustainably high debt levels assumes that private capital markets do not work efficiently. If, however, they do work efficiently, and one country is on an unsustainable debt path, then it will be recognised that the debt problem is that country's problem, not a problem for the union as a whole. The market will thus attach a risk premium to the offending country's government debt and the other governments within the union will not suffer any negative effects from the unsustainability of one country's debt position. The difficulty with this, of course, is that lenders might be unable to attach the correct risk premium to the problem country's debt. This may be because, as discussed above, a debt crisis in one country in a monetary union might have serious effects on other EU countries. Under these circumstances, they might thus feel obligated to come to the aid of the offending country, lowering the risk premium on that country's government debt. One solution to this is for the members of the monetary union to issue a solemn declaration that they will not 'bale out' other member countries' governments in such circumstances. Such a 'no bale out' clause was, in fact, introduced in the Maastricht Treaty.

A second problem with the Delors Committee's proposal to impose binding rules on the size of government budget deficits is concerned with the enforceability of these rules once countries are actually inside the economic and monetary union. This stems from the fact that experience with such rules demonstrates the very great difficulty of enforcing them.[55] Such criticism led to a reconsideration of the Delors Committee's Report with regard to its proposal of binding rules for the conduct of fiscal policies in a monetary union; such that by the time the Maastricht Treaty was drafted the proposal had been abandoned, to be replaced by a requirement that the Member States of the European Union avoid 'excessive deficits'. Thus, the Commission has the task of monitoring the budget deficits and the level of the national governments participating in the union in the light of the reference values of 3 per cent (deficit) and 60 per cent (debt).

Despite the modifications made in the Maastricht Treaty, however, over the conduct of fiscal policy in the transition to EMU and after its instigation, there has still been wide-ranging debate about the Maastricht budgetary criterion, with not all analysts convinced of their appropriateness. For example, there has been concern over the arbitrary nature of the numbers chosen for the debt and deficit targets. Buiter, Corsetti and Roubini argue that:[56]

'the wording of the Treaty is sufficiently vague that irrelevant or even harmful political considerations may affect the assessment of whether the fiscal convergence criteria have been met.'

Begg et. al. argued that the figure for the debt-to-gross domestic product ratio of 60 per cent had no economic rationale nor any historical relevance but just happened to be the Community's average in 1991.[57, 58] Other economists argue that the figure of 60 per cent has been derived from a well-known formula which determines the level of budget deficit (conditioned on the future nominal growth rate of GDP) needed to stabilise government debt.[59] This formula demonstrates that, in order to stabilise the government debt at 60 per cent of GDP, the budget deficit must be brought to 3 per cent.[60]

Other concerns over the budgetary criteria centre around the fact that the timing of their implementation was regrettable, in that it coincided with the moment when Europe began to experience one of the worst recessions in the post-World War II period. Thus, the attempt of EU countries to drastically reduce their budgetary deficits by applying strenuous fiscal and monetary restrictions probably intensified the recession. This left serious concerns that the fiscal provisions laid down in the Maastricht Treaty would, in the end, actually prevent a number of states from embarking upon the final stage of economic and monetary union.[61]

In addition, the thorough nature of the budgetary criterion (i.e. including regional and local governments) could have unforeseen results. Coordination may be needed to ensure standardisation of policies among the Member States. For example, 'creative accounting' by Member States (i.e. the shifting of expenditures, revenues, and obligations from one level of government to another) in order to meet the fiscal criteria should be discouraged. In addition to this, central government must supervise the financing policies of local government to ensure that a situation does not arise where a Member State cannot meet the criteria because of the latter's financial imprudence.[62] This was a point noted in the Protocol on the Excessive Deficit Procedure when it states that:

'In order to ensure the effectiveness of the excessive deficit procedure, the governments of the Member States shall be responsible under this procedure for the deficits of general government. . . . [They] shall ensure that national procedures in the budgetary area enable them to meet their obligations in this area.'

Difficulties such as these, then, reiterate the fact that the notion of fiscal convergence, in economic terms, is a problematical one. Moreover, an examination of fiscal convergence, in political terms, does nothing to assuage this conclusion. It is to an analysis of the latter that we now turn.

A Political Framework

The budgetary history of the Member States of the European Union has been varied with regard to the pursuit of budgetary policy. For example (as noted previously) over the last twenty years Italy, Ireland and Belgium have all experienced debt-to-GNP ratios of more than 100 per cent. On the other hand, the United Kingdom, France and

(West) Germany have experienced ratios which are significantly lower than this. Although it may be argued that differences such as these are a result of different policy responses to different types of shock upon the national economies of these countries, the fact that the European countries have economies which are highly interconnected does tend to negate this assumption (it would be expected that the European economies would suffer similar shocks, or that at the very least the shock experienced by one country would be transferred to the rest of the Member States). There must therefore be other reasons for the wide differences which can be seen in European debt-to-GNP ratios. This has two implications. First, an EU country's debt-to-GNP ratio must be explained not only by looking at changes in the European economy as a whole (in terms, say, of whether or not there is a recession), but also by looking at the fiscal policy-making environment of the individual Member States' national governments and fiscal institutions. Second, and following on from this, if indeed it is the case that European debt-to-GNP ratios are significantly effected by differences in the national policy-making environment of Member States, then it may be the case that states will not meet the budgetary convergence criteria unless fundamental changes are made to their national governmental and institutional fiscal frameworks. In this scenario some states may never meet the fiscal criteria because such changes cannot be made. We will now examine both of these implications more fully.

Concerns over the nature of the fiscal policy-making environment of the individual Member States became particularly apparent as the deadline for the creation of a Single European Market drew near. These concerns developed from two broad classes of reasons. The first set of concerns arose from the need for co-ordination of fiscal policies as a result of the increased degree of market integration. For example, the White Paper on the Single European Market noted that it would have 'inescapable implications for the member states as far as indirect taxes [were] concerned' – different rates of value added tax (VAT) would give some countries a preferential competitive position, something which was not in keeping with the spirit of the Single Market Initiative. In addition, the increased mobility of private agents led to concerns over the stabilisation function of national fiscal policy.[63] Specifically, if all Europeans were to be treated alike then (assuming that the benefits go to people who are dependent, unemployed, or poor, and that taxes are raised on the usual principles relating to personal expenditure, income, or wealth) there should generally be transfers from more prosperous to less prosperous regions (for example, from northern European to

Mediterranean regions). This implied a role for a Community-wide fiscal policy (which, undoubtedly, was one of the major motivations behind the increase in the Community's structural funds between 1988 and 1993).

The second set of concerns stemmed more generally from the link between the evolution of private markets and the establishment of new institutions. If we define markets as sets of rules for the exchange of private goods and institutions as organisations for the provision of public goods (or, indeed, the management of public bads), then if private economic decisions are influenced by the provision of public goods (e.g. if the government provides education, individuals will not have to buy it for themselves) then markets and institutions should, ideally, develop together. However, in a Europe-wide context, national boundaries are not necessarily reflective of the location of areas in particular need of public goods provision or of public bads management. For example, 'peripheral regions' within a nation state (which are perhaps considered as having less need for such provision or management – for example, the Highland Region in Scotland) may simply have attained that status because of their national policymakers' definition of national territory. As L. J. Sharpe argues:[64]

> 'peripheral regions are peripheral because the boundary of the state has made them so ... The Midi is peripheral to Paris, but not to Spain's twin economic heartlands, the Basque country and Catalonia; nor is it peripheral to the Italian economic centre – the Turin-Genoa-Milan triangle.'

Under these circumstances, the benefits of local public goods (or the disadvantages of public bads, such as pollution) produced in one country are, in some cases, likely to spill over into another country: for instance, pollution from the Midi spilling into the Basque country and Catalonia. This means that in order to allocate public goods (or deal with public bads) efficiently in a European Union, there should be a degree of co-operation between the Member States over the level of their provision. On the other hand, some public goods will either provide benefits to consumers and producers in an area which is contained entirely within the country or will have a distinctly national character. An important issue, therefore, is to what degree national fiscal autonomy creates problems of efficiency in the provision (or management) of public goods (or bads) and hence what role there is for a Community-wide fiscal policy under such circumstances.[65]

The difficulty with both these sets of concerns, each requiring an increased degree of fiscal co-ordination between the Member States, was that such a degree of co-operation did not seem entirely feasible because of the different fiscal experience of many of these countries. In particular, the evidence suggests that it is differences in the national fiscal policy-making environment of the individual Member States which have contributed to the variations in the pursuit of budgetary policy witnessed in Europe in the post-World War II period.

First, from a public choice perspective, we must consider the use of fiscal policy as a means of manipulation within the context of the desire to achieve certain national and European economic policy goals. While, if we look at the pre-election period in many of the Member States, we are likely to see that the incidence of pre-election promises of low taxation and/or increased government expenditure is significant,[66] what is also interesting from the point of view of this present analysis is the use of fiscal policy as a means for national governments to attain their wider European policy goals. For example, during the early 1980s there was an ideological change in a number of European governments (notably in Belgium, Denmark, Italy, the Netherlands, the then West Germany and the United Kingdom). This change basically represented a shift to the right in European policymaking with a concomitant strengthening of the bargaining position of political and economic groups in favour of anti-inflationary policies. For example, in a speech given in 1984 the then British Chancellor of the Exchequer, Nigel Lawson, stated that the tools of macroeconomic policy – interest rates, public spending and taxation – would no longer be used as a means of regulating demand in the economy, but rather would be used instead to fight inflation. Supply-side policy, which in the past had been used to suppress inflation through price and wage controls, would now be used instead to promote faster growth.[67] Moreover, for those countries in the ERM at that time, this shift to the right in European policy-making represented a strengthening of their commitment to the Mechanism. For example, in France, after the socialist government's fiscal expansion of 1981–83, the contractionary fiscal and monetary policies which were followed after 1983 were sold to the French public as the only ones that would allow France to remain in the ERM and in Europe. The public choice approach thus enables us to explain policy commitments throughout the 1980s in European policymaking. It also helps us partly to understand the way in which the budgetary criteria were designed, because in the public choice view the optimal fiscal policy implies the imposition of rules upon policymakers – hence the Delors Report's recommendations that national fiscal policies, and in particular national government budget deficits, should be subject to binding rules.' What the public choice approach does not really suggest, though, is a full explanation for the large variations in debt to GNP ratios witnessed amongst the EU Member States.

In a similar tone, instances of the strategic public debt choice approach discussed earlier can be seen in many of the Member States' fiscal policy histories. Inherited economic conditions have long been an indicator of how successful a new government's policies are in the short term, and government change has appeared to be more frequent over the last few decades. Thus an incumbent government is less certain of its reappointment and will tend to feel more of a need to use debt strategically. For example, such partisan bias and political polarisation are important roots of the large fiscal deficits in Greece.[68] Again, though, what it does not really suggest is a full explanation of the large variations in debt-to-GNP ratios witnessed amongst the EU Member States. This need for an explanation may be remedied, however, in relation to our third framework for examining the political economy of debt – the government weakness and political instability approach.

If we first of all consider the proposition that high-public-debt countries are almost exclusively parliamentary democracies, often with a highly proportional electoral system, then we can indeed say that this may be an explanation for the debt-to-GNP ratios witnessed in the EU Member States. Every state in Western Europe has, at one time or another during this century, been governed by a coalition government. Even in states with no tradition of coalition government, there have been a number of coalition governments as well as a few minority governments which have needed support in the legislature in order to remain in office.[69] Table 5.1 gives an illustration of just how significant this form of government has been for a selection of the Member States in the post-war period up until 1987.

Thus, for example, the existence of multi-party coalition governments in Italy is important in explaining Italy's fiscal stalemate and inability to curtail its fiscal deficits, as is the existence of multi-party coalition governments in Belgium, two of the states described earlier as having particularly high debt to GNP ratios. Moreover, if we now consider the proposition that it is also a country's budgetary institutional framework which can potentially explain debt incidence in the European Union, we have yet more evidence that the government weakness and political instability approach is a valid one in this instance. Indeed, it was just this framework which von Hagen used when examining

Table 5.1 Frequency of Coalition Cabinet Types, 1945–1987

	Majority situations*	Minority situations**	Total
Belgium	1	21	22
Denmark	0	20	20
Germany	2	10	12
Ireland	4	8	12
Italy	4	31	35
Luxembourg	0	10	10
Netherlands	0	10	10

* A majority situation is where one party controls more than 50 per cent of legislative seats.
** A minority situation is where no party controls more than 50 per cent of legislative seats.

Source: Michael Laver and Norman Schofield, *op. cit.* (1990), p. 71.

the budgetary institutions of the then twelve members of the Community.[70] He tested the hypothesis that the budget procedures of the Member States lead to greater fiscal discipline if they give a large amount of authority to the prime minister or the finance minister; limit universalism, reciprocity and parliamentary amendments; and facilitate a rigorous execution of the budget law.[71] He discovered that budgetary institutions were indeed significant explanatory variables for cross-country differences in the debt to GNP ratios and budget deficits in the 1980s in the European Community. In other words, budgetary institutions influence debt incidence.

Finally, if we consider the notion that decentralisation of fiscal policy decision making may be an incentive towards excessive, deficit-financed government spending we have yet more evidence that the government weakness and political instability approach is a valid one when considering European budgetary conditions. Admittedly, at the moment this evidence is mostly anecdotal.[72] However, it does not take too much of a stretch of the imagination to consider that in a highly decentralised system, as the European Union increasingly is, it is in the interests of local, or regional, fiscal authorities to finance an increase in expenditure through an increase in the budget deficit. Although the 'no bale out' clause of the Maastricht Treaty is designed in such a way that:[73]

'The Community shall not be liable for or assume the commitments of central governments, regional, local or other public authorities, other bodies governed by public law, or public undertakings of any Member State. . . .'

this is an issue which may still become particularly pressing in the future, as the European Union comes increasing to resemble a federal union. Under these circumstances, the European Union is likely to witness higher rather than lower levels of debt incidence, despite the Maastricht fiscal criteria.

To sum up, then, the evidence seems to support the idea that political variables, such as differences in the national policy-making environment, have contributed to the high levels of debt incidence which have been witnessed in Europe in the post-World War II period. Given this, what is important for this present analysis is that some of the Member States may not meet the convergence criteria unless fundamental changes are made to their national governmental and institutional fiscal frameworks. Such changes are not likely to be made either quickly or easily. For example, it could be argued that those countries with a high prevalence of coalition governments should change their electoral systems – but such changes are difficult and time-consuming to make. We are thus faced with a scenario where the way in which budgetary policy in the Member States of the European Union is conducted may also be able to explain the likelihood of the successful achievement and maintenance of the European budgetary convergence criterion, and hence should be of significant concern to the architects of economic and monetary union. Indeed, Table 5.2, which illustrates the forecasts for the budgetary convergence criterion for 1996, does indeed demonstrate that there may be significant difficulties for a number of the Member States in achieving the criteria. Although any interpretation of the fiscal criteria is very much dependent upon how the Commission and the Council choose to apply them, as things stand only Germany, Luxembourg and the UK are forecast to fulfil the deficit criteria. Indeed, in eight of the countries the debt-to-GDP ratio will probably be rising.

Moreover, even if some of the eight states with rising debt to GNP ratios do actually manage, in the end, to meet the budgetary criterion without substantial changes in their policy-making environment, this is still an issue which is unlikely to go away. Even if only one Member State had a debt problem, this could still have wider implications for the policy of economic and monetary union as a whole. For example, a government which desires entry into the EMU but which is heavily in debt may want a future European Central Bank to 'inflate away' its debt by departing from the maintenance of price stability.[74] Given that

Table 5.2   The Budgetary Conditions

	Govt. debt as % of GDP	Govt. Balance as % of GDP	Govt. debt ratio trend
Austria	67.4	−3.9	rising
Belgium	132.3	−3.9	falling
Denmark	75.4	−1.2	stable
Finland	64.6	−1.1	rising
France	52.8	−3.9	rising
Germany	58.1	−2.4	stable
Greece	116.2	10.2	rising
Ireland	80.8	−2.6	falling
Italy	124.4	−8.1	rising
Luxembourg	7.8	1.5	stable
Netherlands	77.1	−2.5	stable
Portugal	70.7	−4.7	rising
Spain	65.2	−4.8	rising
Sweden	85.7	−5.8	rising
United Kingdom	51.5	−2.9	stable

Source: European Commission.

one of the ECB's main roles is to ensure price stability in Europe, this would have far-reaching implications for its credibility as the main financial institution in the future EMU, a fact which would not go unnoticed by speculators in the world's financial markets. Moreover, the amount of government debt outstanding is already an important determinant of interest rates in Europe. After monetary union, would it then be conceivable that a country might default on its debt? This event is generally regarded as impossible. However, given the basic rule of public finance that all debt must be repaid eventually, the obvious difficulty in some countries of reducing their budget deficit figures suggests, again, an eventual threat to the credibility of the anti-inflation commitment in economic and monetary union. The architects of economic and monetary union will surely, then, face many challenges arising from the weaknesses of fiscal policy which have just been described.

CONCLUSION

Establishing sound and sustainable public finances is a central goal of all the Member States' national policies to achieve the convergence criteria: all of them set medium-term targets for deficit reduction, generally aiming to respect the 3 per cent of GDP deficit target and to stabilise the debt ratio and then put it on a declining trend.

This chapter has analysed some of the factors which must be taken into account in considering how achievable these budgetary policy targets actually are. Following a brief introduction on the nature of debt and deficits, we went on to examine the international political economy of the budgetary criterion from a theoretical perspective. In particular, we noted that there are three frameworks within which debt can be analysed: the public choice approach, the strategic debt approach and the government weakness and political instability approach. Although there were difficulties with a widespread application of these models, we could identify valid arguments in all three frameworks. This then brought us to our examination of the economic rationale behind the European budgetary criterion. After a discussion of the links between the fiscal and price criteria, and the fiscal and interest rate criteria, we went on to examine the relationship between fiscal policy and exchange rates. The latter is particularly telling because of the nature of EMU, which entails the loss of the exchange rate instrument. Under such circumstances, fiscal policy takes on a more significant role; hence the need for fiscal criteria to ensure that debt levels in the Member States are of manageable proportions before the accession to EMU takes place. Despite this identification of need, however, there has still been wide-ranging debate over the appropriateness of the fiscal criteria, a debate which takes on an increased significance in the light of a political economy analysis of the criteria and their achievability.

In particular, this analysis found that there was real evidence to suggest that the incidence of debt in the Member States can be explained in terms of the three frameworks of debt incidence described earlier. Most importantly, the applicability of these approaches has particular significance for the actual achievement of the budgetary criteria laid down at Maastricht, as they imply that debt will continue to be a problem so long as some countries have national fiscal policymaking environments which are conducive to an unsustainable budgetary scenario.

NOTES

1. Although, whether or not a budgetary policy which does not put the sustainability of the debt/deficit path at stake can be deemed undisciplined is also a matter of discussion.

2. T. Sargent and N. Wallace, 'Some Unpleasant Monetarist Arithmetic', *Federal Reserve Bank of Minneapolis, Quarterly Review*, 5 (1981), pp. 1–17.
3. J. K. Galbraith, *Money – Whence it came, where it went* (London: Penguin, 1995).
4. Robert J. Barro and Vittorio Grilli, *European Macroeconomics* (New York: McMillan, 1995).
5. *Treaty on European Union*, Office for Official Publications of the European Communities (1992), pp. 27–9.
6. *Ibid.*, pp. 27–9.
7. J. M. Buchanan, 'La Scienza Delle Finanze: The Italian Tradition in Fiscal Theory', *Fiscal Theory and Political Economy* (Chapel Hill, North Carolina: University of North Carolina Press, 1960), pp. 145–73.
8. This section draws on the work of: W. Buiter, G. Corsetti and N. Roubini, 'Excessive deficits: sense and nonsense in the Treaty of Maastricht, *Economic Policy*, 16 (1993) p. 57–99; and A. Alesina and R. Perotti, 'The Political Economy of Budget Deficits', *IMF Staff Papers*, vol. 2, no. 1 (1995), pp. 1–32.
9. Because the literature in this area is so large, it goes beyond the scope of this present analysis to conduct an exhaustive literature survey on the public choice approach. Instead, we focus only on some of the key assumptions. See: Lars Udehn, *The Limits of Public Choice*, (London: Routledge, 1996) for a comprehensive analysis of this approach.
10. J. M. Buchanan and R. E. Wagner, *Democracy in Deficit: The Political Legacy of Lord Keynes* (New York: Academic Press, 1977). They talk of the electorate as being fiscally 'illuded'. This present analysis, on the other hand, prefers to talk of fiscal 'delusion' rather than fiscal 'illusion', as we feel that the former term more comprehensively captures the notion that the government uses the fact that the electorate do not understand the mechanics of the budgetary process, rather than doing something to educate the electorate on the process.
11. J. M. Wagner, C. K. Rowley and R. D. Tollison, *Deficits* (Oxford: Basil Blackwell, 1986).
12. James M. Buchanan and Richard E. Wagner, *Democracy in Deficit* (New York: Academic Press, 1977), pp. 93–94.
13. J. M. Buchanan and R. E. Wagner, *op. cit.* (1977).
14. W. D. Nordhaus, The Political Business Cycle, *Review of Economic Studies*, 42 (1975), pp. 169–90.
15. This is perhaps most famously illustrated by the words of George Bush during his 1988 election campaign, when he asked the American electorate to 'Read my lips – no new taxes.' In June 1990, the White House issued a statement saying 'tax revenue increases' were imminent, thus breaking the Republican promise of 1988.
16. C. D. Macrae, 'A Political Model of the Business Cycle', *Journal of Political Economy*, 85 (1977), pp. 239–63.
17. J. A. Alt and K. A. Chrystal, *Political Economics* (Brighton, Sussex: Wheatsheaf Books, 1983), p. 125.
18. B. T. McCallum, 'The Political Business Cycle: An Empirical Test', *Southern Economic Journal*, 44 (1977), pp. 504–15; T. J. Sargent and N. Wallace, 'Rational Expectations, the Optimal Monetary Instrument and the Optimal

Money Supply Rule', *Journal of Political Economy*, 83 (1975), pp. 241–54; R. E. Lucas Jr, 'Some International Evidence on Output-Inflation Trade-offs', *American Economic Review*, 63 (1973), pp. 326–34; R. E. Lucas Jr, 'An Equilibrium Model of the Business Cycle', *Journal of Political Economy*, 83 (1975), pp. 1113–1144.

19. T. J. Sargent and N. Wallace, 'Rational Expectations, the optimal monetary instrument and the optimal money supply rule', *Journal of Political Economy*, 83 (1975), pp. 241–54.

20. For an excellent overview of the approach, see: C. L. F. Attfield, D. Demery and N. W. Duck, *Rational Expectations in Macroeconomics, An Introduction to Theory and Evidence*, 2nd. ed. (Oxford: Blackwell, 1991).

21. For some recent explanations of the cobweb theorem, see: C. H. Hommes, 'Dynamics of the cobweb model with adaptive expectations and nonlinear supply and demand', *Journal of Economic Behaviour and Organization*, 24, 3 (1994), p. 315 and, J. A. C. Gallas and H. E. Nusse, 'Periodicity versus chaos in the dynamics of cobweb models', *Journal of Economic Behaviour and Organization*, 29, 3 (1996), pp. 447–64.

22. A similar idea is put forward in the literature on how fiscal decisions create links across generations. See: A. Cukierman and A. Meltzer, 'A Political Theory of Government Debt and Deficits in a Neo-Ricardian Framework', *American Economic Review*, 79 (1989), pp. 353–98.

23. The origin of this work is in Alesina's work on partisan effects in monetary policy, but the same methodological approach has been applied to the issue of fiscal policy, and domestic and foreign debt accumulation.

24. See: Douglas Hibbs, 'Political Parties and Macroeconomic Policy', The *American Political Science Review*, 71 (December, 1977), pp. 1467–87; and Thomas Havrilesky, 'A Partisan Theory of Fiscal and Monetary Regimes', *Journal of Money, Credit and Banking*, 19 (August, 1987), pp. 308–25.

25. A. Alesina and G. Tabellini, 'Positive and normative theories of public debt and inflation in historical perspective', *European Economic Review*, 36 (1992), pp. 337–344.

26. A. Alesina and G. Tabellini, 'A Positive Theory of Fiscal Deficit and Government Debt, *Review of Economic Studies*, 57 (1990), pp. 403–414.

27. Such instability could be prevented (or at least mitigated) by a fiscal policy rule, such as a constitutional balanced budget amendment. This would limit the ability of each political party to pursue its electoral aims by manipulating aggregate demand. In addition to this, it would also limit redistribution efforts by the liberal party if the increase in transfer payments needed to implement such a policy required new taxes (depending upon one's views concerning income redistribution).

28. A. Alesina and G. Tabellini, *op. cit.* (1990).

29. T. Persson and L. Svensson, 'Why should a stubborn conservative run a deficit?' *Quarterly Journal of Economics* 104, 2 (1989), p. 325.

30. G. Tabellini and A. Alesina, *op. cit.* (1990).

31. The median voter theorem assumes that there is an electoral system involving two political parties, both of whom care only about winning office. Over time, both parties will tend to approach the centre ground in politics, i.e. the policy position preferred by the 'median voter'.

32. T. Sargent and N. Wallace, 'Some unpleasant monetarist arithmetic', *Federal*

Reserve Bank of Minneapolis Quarterly Review, January (1981), pp. 1–17. See also: A. Alesina and A. Drazen, 'Why are stabilizations delayed?', *American Economic Review*, (1991); and A. Alesina and G. Tabellini, *op. cit.* (1992), pp. 341–42.

33. *Ibid.*, p. 342.
34. The following analysis is not done in any way exhaustively. See: A. Alesina and R. Perotti, 'The Political Economy of Budget Deficits', *IMF Staff Papers*, 42, 1 (1995), pp. 15–24 for a more comprehensive analysis.
35. N. Roubini and J. Sachs, 'Political and Economic Determinants of Budget Deficits in the Industrial Democracies', *European Economic Review*, 335 (1989), pp. 903–38; V. Grilli, D. Masciandaro and G. Tabellini, 'Political and monetary institutions and public financial policies in the industrial countries', *Economic Policy*, 13 (1991).
36. A. Alesina and G. Tabellini, *op. cit.* (1992).
37. A. Alesina and A. Drazen, 'Why are stabilisations delayed?' *American Economic Review*, 81, 5 (1991), p. 1170.
38. N. Roubini and J. Sachs, *op. cit.* (1989).
39. In this study, political instability was proxied by a number of variables such as the type of government (single-party majority, presidential, presidential with divided government, multi-party coalition, minority) or low average duration of the government.
40. K. A. Shepsle, 'Institutional Arrangements and Equilibrium in Multidimensional Voting Models', *American Journal of Political Science*, 23, 1 (1979), pp. 27–59.
41. A. Cukierman, S. Edwards and G. Tabellini, 'Seignorage and political instability', *American Economic Review* 82, 3 (1992), p. 537.
42. G. Tabellini and A. Alesina, 'Voting on the budget deficit', *American Economic Review* (1990), pp. 17–32.
43. B. R. Weingast, K. A. Shepsle and C. Johnsen, 'The Political Economy of Benefits and Costs: A Neoclassical Approach to Distributive Politics', *Journal of Political Economy*, 89 (1981), pp. 642–64.
44. Moreover, Alesina and Tabellini noted that detailed information on fiscal institutions and political matters is readily available only for the industrial countries. In this sense, results of this type of analysis may be biased towards the decision-making environment of the industrialised countries. No more will be said on such a bias as, in this present analysis, only industrialised countries are examined. However, for more information, see: A. Alesina and G. Tabellini, *op. cit.* (1992), p. 343.
45. The 'Delors' Report, *op. cit.* (1989), paragraph 42.
46. *Ibid.*, p. 18.
47. *Ibid.*, p. 222.
48. W. Buiter and K. M. Kletzer, *op. cit.* (1991), pp. 221–22.
49. A. Britton and D. Mayes, *op. cit.* (1992), pp. 51–2.
50. P. Kenen, 'The Theory of Optimum Currency Areas: An Eclectic View' in R. Mundell and A. Swoboda (eds.), *Monetary Problems of the International Economy* (Chicago: University of Chicago Press, 1969).
51. This argument also assumes that there are rigidities in the labour market which preclude workers from relocating within the monetary union. See the earlier arguments in Chapter 1.

52. See: Paul De Grauwe, 'Fiscal Policies in Monetary Unions', Chapter 8 in *op. cit.* (1994).

53. C. Corsetti and N. Roubini, 'Fiscal Deficits, Public Debt and Government Solvency: Evidence from OECD Countries', *Journal of the Japanese and International Economies*, 54 (1991), pp. 354–80.

54. P. De Grauwe, *op. cit.* (1994), p. 199.

55. J. von Hagen, 'A Note on the Empirical Effectiveness of Formal Fiscal Restraints', *Journal of Public Economics*, 44 (1991), pp. 199–210.

56. Willem Buiter, Giancarlo Corsetti and Nouriel Roubini, 'Excessive deficits: sense and nonsense in the Treaty of Maastricht', *Economic Policy*, 16, 1993, p. 61.

57. D. Begg et. al., *op. cit.* (1991), p. 24.

58. Similarly, Begg et. al. note that any rule that deficits can be incurred only to finance capital expenditures necessarily relies upon an accounting distinction between current and capital expenditures which in many instances fails to capture the concepts that are economically relevant. Much current public spending is in fact in the nature of investment. For example, education and research expenditure should be considered as investment in human capital; much modern work on the sources of long-term economic growth identifies human capital as the single most important factor.

59. $d = xb$, where b is the (steady state) level at which the government debt is to be stabilised (in % GDP), x is the growth rate of nominal GDP, and d is the government budget deficit (in % GDP).

60. P. de Grauwe, *op. cit.* (1995), pp. 157–58.

61. *Ibid.*, (1995), p. 159.

62. P. B. Kenen, *Economic and Monetary Union in Europe – Moving Beyond Maastricht*, (Cambridge: Cambridge University Press, p. 107.

63. Willem H. Buiter and Kenneth M. Kletzer (1991), page 240–41.

64. L. J. Sharpe, 'Fragmentation and Territoriality in the European States System', *International Political Science Review*, vol. 10 (1989), p. 236.

65. W. M. Buiter, *op. cit.* (1994), pp. 648–49.

66. See Kenneth A. Schultz, 'The Politics of the Political Business Cycle', *British Journal of Political Science*, 25 (1995), pp. 79–99. He considers the case of a political business cycle in the UK in the period 1961–92 and finds, at times, a sizeable electorally motivated economic cycle.

67. Nigel Lawson, 'The British Experiment', *Fifth Maise Lecture* (H.M. Treasury, 18 June 1984).

68. The argument also works in reverse. The drastic fiscal adjustment in the early 1980s in countries such as Belgium, Ireland and Denmark began in 1982 after the election of new and stable political majorities. Similarly, fiscal improvement in Spain and Portugal has occurred under stable one-party majorities (socialist in Spain, conservative in Portugal). See: W Buiter, G. Corsetti and N. Roubini, *op. cit.* (1993), p. 85.

69. Michael Laver and Norman Schofield, *Multiparty Government, The Politics of Coalition in Europe* (Oxford: Oxford University Press, 1990), p. 1.

70. Cited by Alberto Alesina and Robert Perotti, *op. cit.* (1995), pp. 22–23, but see also: J. von Hagen and Ian J. Harden, 'Budget processes and commitment to fiscal discipline', *European Economic Review*, 39 (1995), pp. 771–779; and J. von Hagen and Ian J. Harden, 'Budgeting procedures

and fiscal performance in the EC', *Economic Papers*, 96 (Brussels: European Commission).

71. Specifically, he constructed various indices summarising budgetary institutions, including one which classified countries as a function of the following variables: the success of the prime minister (or finance minister) in intragovernmental negotiations; the quality of parliamentary amendments; the form and timing of parliamentary votes (item by item, global, etc); the level of transparency of the budget; and the degree of flexibility of the implementation process.

72. See Guido Tabellini, 'Comment on Hughes and Smith', *Economic Policy*, no. 13 (1991), pp. 454–457, for some suggestive evidence.

73. *Treaty on European Union*, Article 104b.

74. K. A. Froot and K. Rogoff, 'The EMS, the EMU, and the Transition to a Common Currency', *NBER Macroeconomics Annual* (Cambridge: MIT Press, 1992). They predict that those governments who are heavily in debt will deliberately raise their inflation rates immediately prior to Stage Three. They will thus engineer 'one final realignment' of the EMS currencies and thus undermine exchange rate stability.

6 Exchange Rates and Interest Rates: An IPE Approach

'When a nation is running to decay and ruine, the merchant and monied man, do what you can, will be sure to starve last.'
John Locke, *Some Considerations of the Consequences of the Lowering of Interests and Raising the Value of Money* (1692).

INTRODUCTION

This chapter departs from the previous two analyses in structure. This is because the analyses of exchange rates and interest rates – particularly within an international political economy framework – are so interlinked that to divide their examination would, in many ways, prove artificial. This chapter, then, will first provide brief introductions to the concepts of exchange rates and interest rates before going on to discuss the approach which will be used for their examination. This will consist, first, of an examination of the concept of interest rate parity, which provides an explanation of the intrinsic relationship between exchange rates and interest rates; and second, of an analysis of the so-called inconsistent quartet of a fixed (or at least pegged) exchange rate, full capital mobility, an independent monetary policy and free trade.[1] This quartet is 'inconsistent' because macroeconomic theory would suggest that a country can have no more than three of these four conditions, for reasons which will be discussed later.[2] This latter analysis, in keeping with earlier chapters, will emphasise that political theories of the behaviour of major economic variables must be concerned not only with the domestic policy-making environment, but also with the international economic conditions which may affect that domestic decision-making environment.

EXCHANGE RATES

At a very general level, the exchange rate is simply the price of foreign currency which clears the market for foreign exchange; the price (or rate) at which one currency is exchanged for another currency, for gold or for special drawing rights (SDRs).[3] These transactions are carried out in the foreign exchange market, and are very much determined by the conditions of supply and demand for the relevant currencies in the market, which are in turn dependent, amongst other things, upon the demand for currencies to meet obligations, expectations about future movements in the exchange rate and the balance-of-payments position of the relevant economies.[4]

The behaviour of exchange rates is of vital importance to any state in the contemporary international political economy. Exchange rates link a country's macro and microeconomies to the rest of the world through the asset market and the goods market. In macroeconomic terms this occurs in two ways.[5] First, in the goods market, the exchange rate establishes a link between prices in the world economy and the given prices in the world market: generally speaking, the higher the exchange rate, the higher the price of foreign goods in home currency. For a given level of domestic costs and prices, a higher exchange rate makes foreign goods less attractive to domestic consumers whilst domestic goods become more attractive to consumers in the rest of the world. Second, in the asset market, the exchange rate is an important variable in the decisions made by domestic wealth holders over how that wealth is to be held. Their choice will depend upon the trade-off between risk and return: the higher the return on foreign assets (in home currency) compared to domestic assets (provided there is no increase in the level of risk) the more chance there is that domestic residents will shift their wealth into foreign assets. For example, for an investment in pounds sterling to be competitive against an investment in dollars, the interest rate on pounds (i.e. the asset return) must be greater than the interest rate on dollars *plus* the expected percentage rate of sterling exchange rate depreciation. If this does not happen, and capital is mobile, then Britain would soon find that it loses reserves selling dollars to domestic residents who prefer them as an investment over the low-yield, domestic currency assets.

In microeconomic terms, the exchange rate links a country to the rest of the world in ways which are of vital importance to the issue of resource allocation. In the goods market, when a change in the exchange rate makes an economy more competitive, resources are drawn into the tradeable goods sector (i.e. the number of tradeable goods increases): more goods become exportable, and fewer goods are imported. On the other hand, when a change in the exchange rate makes an economy less competitive, resources become primarily employed in the domestic market: more goods are imported, and fewer goods are exported. Exchange rate changes therefore effect the allocation of resources in an economy because the distribution of income between different groups or sectors often depends on the level of competitiveness. For example, if the country has a traditional export sector (such as agriculture or mining), then an increase in the exchange rate will make these traditional exports more attractive to consumers in the rest of the world. This sector will then become more profitable. On the other hand, when the exchange rate decreases, firms in the traded goods sector become unprofitable and therefore cut back on investment. The traded goods sector shrinks. In the asset market, the effect of a situation in which the return on domestic assets is lower than the return on foreign assets is that capital flight will take place out of the domestic economy and into the foreign economy. Hence, fewer resources will be available for investment in the home economy which, in turn, will have an affect on the well-being of domestic firms and consumers.

The fact that the exchange rate engenders these links between a domestic economy and the rest of the world means that exchange rate movements are closely monitored by a state's monetary authorities: every country which possesses its own currency must decide upon how that currency is going to be managed and to what extent, if at all, the national authorities will intervene in the foreign exchange markets themselves. For this reason, the value of the exchange rate is a topic which has long exercised the minds of policy makers and academics alike. Indeed, from the 1870s until the 1930s, the exchange rate was one of the economic issues which was most hotly debated in both domestic and international fora. At that time the gold standard (which was at its heyday between 1875 and 1914) was in operation and it was of constant concern to policy makers whether their national currency should be on or off the gold standard and what the value of their national currency should be.[6] For example, the UK came off the gold standard in 1914, partly returned to it in 1925, but was forced to abandon gold finally in 1931, though according to one scholar, 'to go off gold was then thought of as unmitigated disaster, although no one was clear why . . .'.[7]

It is in more recent times, however, especially since the early 1970s, that the significance of the debate over exchange rate policy has increased.

This has been as a result, particularly, of changes in the international economic and political environment. The major turning-point was the collapse of the postwar international monetary order (i.e. Bretton Woods) under which countries had maintained a basically fixed exchange rate arrangement with only occasional adjustments. Its collapse left a vacuum, in that policymakers no longer had to have their currencies pegged to the dollar – they could determine their own values within the new flexible exchange rate system. It was at this point that the real importance of the politics of exchange rates began to be seen.

INTEREST RATES

For borrowers, the rate of interest basically measures the cost of borrowing for investment purposes: the lower that cost of borrowing is, other things being equal, the more borrowers will wish to invest. For lenders, the rate of interest measures the return which will be received when their wealth is invested: the higher the return, the more lenders will wish to invest. If inflation is expected, however, we need to distinguish between the nominal and real rates of interest (where the real interest rate is defined as the nominal rate minus the expected inflation rate) for it is on the real rate of interest that the level of investment will actually depend.

For example, if a firm borrows at a nominal rate of interest of 10 per cent, then at the end of the year it will have to repay £110 for each £100 borrowed. If, over the year, the firm expects the average price level to rise by 10 per cent, then the expected real value of the sum to be repaid – its expected value in terms of goods and services at the end of the year – will be just equal to the value of the £100 the firm borrowed. The real interest rate will be zero. If inflation rates are low and stable, then the nominal interest rate will not be seriously misleading as a measure of the cost of capital because the real and nominal rates will differ only by a small, fairly constant amount. However, when inflation rates are variable and at times very high, and when people come to anticipate inflation, it becomes important to distinguish between the nominal and real interest rate. In this case, it is important to remember that the real interest rate is the relevant borrowing cost for the investment decision.

So far, we have looked at interest rates from the point of view of individual investors. However, from the point of view of national monetary authorities interest rates are at the heart of any strategy which they may select in order to influence business conditions and economic activity. Interest rates affect capital movements as well as the rate of inflation and states, in general, wish to achieve low interest rate targets. In large part this is due to the fact that high interest rates can cause difficulties in the financial system.[8]

First, they may discourage investment plans and therefore long-term growth. Governments might prefer 'less essential' borrowing to be curtailed. Second, they add to the costs of production, to the costs of house purchase and generally to the cost of living. They are thus 'cost inflationary'. Third, and related to the latter point, they are politically unpopular, because the general public do not like paying higher interest rates on overdrafts, credit cards and mortgages. Fourth, high interest rates encourage inflows of money from abroad. This makes it even more difficult to restrain bank lending. The increase in money from abroad increases the amount of bank deposits, and thus the amount of money which banks have at their disposal to lend. Moreover, and fifth, inflows of money from abroad drive up the exchange rate, which can be very damaging for export industries competing with import industries, as described earlier.

Elsewhere, we have noted that the amount of currency trading which now takes place in global financial markets goes far beyond the amount of resources which any individual government has at its disposal for the purpose of defending the national currency should it get into difficulty. In this way, the process of globalisation of financial markets which has taken place to an increasing degree in the post-World War II period subordinates national economies to international markets, and changes the nature of financial policy making. For example, monetary policy management has gone through fundamental changes, one of the most important of which, for this present analysis, has been the desire for the widespread deregulation of financial markets during the 1980s and its consequent effect on interest rates. In the United States, the Depository Institutions Deregulation and Monetary Control Act of 1980 provided for the eventual elimination of ceilings on interest rates payable on deposits held at 'depository institutions'; and in Australia, the profitability of banks, together with their unwillingness or inability to satisfy demands for particular services (due to the fact that banking in Australia was, up until the early 1980s, a heavily regulated industry) at competitive prices, encouraged the growth of non-bank financial institutions. In many instances, the non-banks provided financial products that were close but imperfect substitutes for those provided by the banks. Eventually the growth of the non-banks eroded the profitability and market share of the banks, who reacted by petitioning the

Australian government to deregulate the banking industry, with the result that the ceilings on deposit interest rates were completely abolished.[9]

This desire for deregulation in the 1980s, however, did not always bring with it financial stability. In particular, there are a number of reasons why interest rate deregulation might cause financial market instability, largely due to the fact that with deregulation, interest rate values can change in any given time period. This can happen for a number of reasons. First, interest rate values can change because of changes in time preference. When money is lent, this represents a sacrifice of consumption at the present time. The lender is, in effect, postponing consumption from the present to some time in the future. The stronger the preferences for present as opposed to future consumption, the more they must be paid to induce them to postpone consumption, i.e. the higher must be the rate of interest. Second, interest rate deregulation increases the possibility of a default, because the lender may not be absolutely sure that the borrower will repay the loan, owing to the possibility of a sudden increase in interest rates (the extent of the risk depends on the type of loan being made). Third, and importantly, there is the issue of inflation – the factors just mentioned would make for a positive rate of interest even if the general level of prices was expected to remain constant over the duration of the loan. If inflation is anticipated, however, the lender will wish to take account of a fall in the value of money by raising the interest rate by a much more significant degree. The process of financial globalisation, then, has changed the very nature of the importance of interest rates in contemporary international economic policymaking. As Krugman and Obstfeld note:[10]

> 'If a financier named Rip Van Winkle had gone to sleep in the early 1960s and awakened two decades later, he would have been shocked by changes in both the nature and scale of international financial activity.'

It is with these thoughts in mind that we now turn to the international political economy of exchange rates and interest rates.

AN IPE APPROACH TO EXCHANGE RATES AND INTEREST RATES

Perhaps nowhere can the three issues of importance in the contemporary international political economy (i.e. the link between economics and politics; the relationship between the domestic and international domains; and the role of the state) be more clearly seen than in the behaviour of exchange rates and interest rates. For example, it is now widely recognised that exchange rate behaviour consists of an intimate mix of political and economic factors. As Yann Eichinard powerfully noted:[11]

'. . . . the currency not only has an economic dimension but also a political one – currency is an object of power. When a group recognises exchanges by the medium of currency, this currency becomes a centre of truth, this currency is the expression of a certain economic and social cohesion. . . . [It] cannot be dissociated from the state, the state which is the organised form of a nation – a huge human group in which each member realises his/her preferences and social needs.'

Moreover, common to all (monetised) societies are the political implications of currency *movement*; implications which have no historical or geographical boundary. For example, a monetary crisis in Poland in the seventeenth century, which saw the Polish penny fall to 40 per cent of its traditional value, became, in the eyes of the Polish populace, 'the apocalyptic symbol of the misfortunes of the age, the apparent cause of all their worries and torments in the eyes of contemporaries'.[12] Some of the consequences of this included increased xenophobia, anti-Semitism, and class hatred; all as a result of the search for those responsible for the decline in the Polish currency's economic fortunes. In the words of one historian, 'the situation in Poland was reminiscent of the psychopathic states to which a society falls victim in times of great scourges or epidemics.'[13]

Importantly for this present analysis, one of the major reasons for currency movement is the value of the interest rate, with investors moving their money around in order to secure the best financial return. This has become an issue of extreme importance in our contemporary globalised system and in turn has created a situation in which the role of the state is undermined, with the national economy being seen as being of secondary importance when compared to the mechanism of international markets. In this scenario, capital responds so quickly that national governments are powerless to carry out aggressive domestic macroeconomic policies.

In order to examine these issues more fully we will utilise the so-called 'inconsistent quartet' of a fixed (or at least pegged) exchange rate, full capital mobility, an independent monetary policy and free trade.[14] Before this can be done, however, we will begin with a basic principle in the exchange rate literature, that of interest rate parity, which provides the foundation for basic exchange-rate and balance-of-payments models and which hinges upon the relationship between exchange rates and interest rates. Only once this relationship has been analysed can the full implications of the inconsistent quartet be explained.

Interest Rate Parity

By the late nineteenth century, thanks partly to the experience gained in conducting British monetary policy during the gold standard era, it was common knowledge among policy makers that the behaviour of exchange rates could be influenced through the adjustment of interest rates. By increasing domestic interest rates, the foreign exchange value of the domestic currency unit could be strengthened. Likewise, by reducing domestic interest rates, the authorities could resist an undesired appreciation of the domestic currency. Knowledge of this relationship was reinforced as an awareness of the mechanism of the forward exchange market, particularly in Austrian gulden and Russian roubles, spread through banking circles throughout the second half of the nineteenth century.[15]

This theory of forward exchange basically explains the difference between forward (future) and spot (current) exchange rates in terms of the differential between domestic and foreign interest rates. By the turn of the century, the beginnings of a theory of forward exchange could be seen in the work of the German economist, Walther Lotz, who realised that the forward rate was determined not by one interest rate but by several.[16] However, even during the early part of the twentieth century, hardly any of the theoretical writers on exchange rates demonstrated their awareness of the phenomenon of forward exchange. Thus, it was not until organised trading in forward exchange expanded rapidly in the aftermath of the World War I that any systematic analysis was undertaken, in this case by Keynes in his articles in the *Manchester Guardian Reconstruction Supplement* and in his *Tract on Monetary Reform*.[17]

Keynes focused on the difference over time between forward and spot exchange rates, reasoning that:[18]

'If dollars one month forward are quoted cheaper than spot dollars to a London buyer in terms of sterling, this indicates a preference by the market, on balance, in favour of holding funds in New York in the month in question rather than in London – a preference the degree of which is measured by the discount on forward dollars.'

He then went on to examine the factors which could be seen as determinants of the market's preference for holding funds in one international centre rather than another, listing the interest rate differential as 'the most fundamental cause'.[19]

His argument was based on the following premise. Let us consider two countries (say, Italy and Sweden) and the issue of an investor deciding whether to invest in either the Italian lira or the Swedish krona. In each of these countries there is a prevailing interest rate which may be earned on local currency investments now, and an interest rate which can be earned on local currency investments at some designated date in the future. In addition, there are prevailing spot and forward exchange rates between the Swedish and Italian currencies. Consequently, if the two investment opportunities were regarded as equivalent in all respects other than currency denominations and interest rates, market pressures would tend to generate an equilibrium. This equilibrium is described by the relationship of covered interest parity (CIP) which provides an expression for the premium that, say, Italian merchants or investors would have to pay now in order to 'cover' the exchange risk associated with a contract to receive or deliver Swedish krona at some designated time in the future. The derivation of the covered interest parity condition is therefore based on a comparison of the alternative ways of accumulating Swedish krona at some designated time in the future from one unit of Italian lira valued now.

For example, if the Italian interest rate is greater than the Swedish interest rate, arbitrageurs will be prepared to move funds from Sweden to Italy as long as the exchange rate for Italian lira is not expected to depreciate by as much as, or more than, the interest differential. In a world of certainty the expected change in the exchange rate and the forward premium or discount would be identical.

An alternative way, however, is to hold the initial unit of Italian lira in a lira-denominated investment and convert into Swedish krona at the spot exchange rate that prevails at the designated time in the future. This leads to an accumulation of Swedish krona. Under this alternative, however, the investor remains uncertain about the exchange rate until the date of conversion arrives: the foreign exchange risk is left *uncovered* during the interval between now and the designated delivery date of foreign exchange in the future, and the interest parity condition is now known as uncovered interest parity (UIP). As noted by Keynes:[20]

'the energies and skill of the professional investor and speculator are mainly occupied. . . . . with what the market will value. . . . [the investment] at, under the influence of mass psychology, three months or a year hence.'

In conditions of uncertainty, the Swedish and Italian interest rates would differ by an amount equal to the risk premium required to persuade speculators to fulfil forward contracts. Uncovered interest parity essentially, then, formalises the notion that market forces equilibrate the return that investors expect to earn on the uncovered investment alternative (i.e. the investment which is exposed to Swedish exchange risk) to the return on the riskless option of initially converting into a particular currency.[21] In other words, bonds, identical in all respects apart from their currency denomination, are perfect substitutes and arbitrage continually ensures that the Italian interest rate equals the Swedish rate adjusted for the expected change in the exchange rate (i.e. the risk premium). At its most comprehensive, therefore, uncovered interest parity implies perfect capital mobility.

As with any of the economic methodologies which are so crucial to our understanding of the contemporary international economic system, these interest rate parity hypotheses have been the subject of rigorous testing. When Keynes was undertaking his initial work on interest parities, he argued that the hypothesis of interest parities was, at best, a reasonable approximation, due to the different credit risks associated with holding deposit balances in different countries. In other words:[22]

'If questions of credit did not enter in, the factor of the rate of interest on short loans would be the dominating one. Indeed, as between London and New York, it probably is so under existing conditions. . . . But elsewhere the . . . possibility of financial trouble or political disturbance . . . deter bankers, even when the exchange risk proper is eliminated, from maintaining large floating balances at certain foreign centres. Such risks prevent the business from being based, as it should be, on a mathematical calculation of interest rate . . . [parity].'

However, the changes in international financial markets which have taken place since Keynes was undertaking his analysis make the interest parity hypothesis a much more reasonable one. In particular, the assets available to investors nowadays include many pairs of financial instruments that do indeed differ only with respect to their currencies of denomination and interest rates – such as dollar deposits and sterling deposits located at the same branch of the same bank. Such investment alternatives are subject to identical credit risks, capital controls, and explicit taxes; and for these cases the evidence should suggest that the interest parity hypothesis is almost always valid, with occasional exceptions during periods of exchange market turbulence.

Recent empirical evidence on covered interest parity comes from two main sources: interviews with marketmakers, and studies of recorded data on exchange rates and interest rates. Interview findings on the whole reveal that covered interest parity is actually used as a formula for determining the level of the exchange rate and the interest rate at which trading is conducted.[23] In particular, foreign exchange traders use interest rates on bank deposits denominated in different currencies to determine the forward exchange premiums or discounts that they quote to customers. At the same time, decision makers in other parts of the banks use the range of values between forward and spot exchange rates to set the interest rates they offer on foreign currency deposits relative to those on domestic currency deposits. On the other hand, studies of recorded data on exchange rates and interest rates have not always generated the same impression as has been given with regard to the interview findings. Such studies have tended to rely on interest rate data associated with claims on different country's currencies and have found that deviations from covered interest parity appeared to be quite prevalent. Such deviations have been rationalised in terms of political risk, capital controls, or transactions costs.

Unlike covered interest parity, the uncovered interest parity hypothesis is formulated in terms of expected future exchange rates and is difficult to test convincingly in isolation, due to the limited availability and questionable quality of data on exchange rate expectations.[24] It must be noted, however, that popular theories of exchange rate determination predict a link between real exchange rates and real interest rate differentials. As noted by Baxter, these theories combine the uncovered interest parity relationship with the assumption that the real exchange rate deviates from its long run level only temporarily.[25] Under these assumptions, changes in the real exchange rate – often viewed as being the result of changes in monetary policy – are expected to reverse themselves over time. For example, if the Swedish krona real exchange rate is above its long-run level with regard to the Italian lira, the lira would be expected to depreciate in real terms in the future. In order to equalise *ex ante* real yields between Sweden and Italy, the *ex ante* real yield on Swedish securities must exceed the *ex ante* real yield on Italian securities by the expected real devaluation of the lira over the term of the bonds. Thus there is a predicted link between the level of the real exchange rate and the real interest rate. For the most part, uncovered interest parity has therefore been assessed jointly with the hypothesis that exchange rate expectations are formed rationally. This joint hypothesis – often called the 'efficient market' hypothesis – implies that interest rate differentials should be unbiased predictors of changes in exchange rates, a hypothesis which can be tested empirically. Why, though, does it matter whether or not the uncovered interest parity hypothesis, in particular, can be tested?

The validity, or otherwise, of the uncovered interest parity hypothesis is important, in terms of this present analysis, due to the effect that validity has on debates over the efficacy of official intervention in exchange markets – those actions taken by national monetary authorities to influence exchange rates.[26] Indeed, during the 1970s it was thought that the case for exchange market intervention was dependent upon whether or not the uncovered interest parity hypothesis could be rejected.[27] If the uncovered interest parity relationship was to be believed, intervention by the national monetary authority would not be able to change the prevailing spot exchange rate relative to the expected future exchange rate unless interest rates were allowed to change. Exchange market intervention would not then be an effective policy instrument for the national monetary authorities to pursue.

In many ways, these arguments fit in with the reasoning of classical economic thought, which maintained that economic activity was subject to its own inbuilt controls and these, by implication, also neutralised political power.[28] If the economy worked efficiently, there would be no need for intrusion by a national monetary authority because the rate of interest would be set competitively to reflect the supply of savings. The more savings available, the lower would be the rate of interest. Investment opportunities previously seen as unprofitable would become attractive and the market would reach a new equilibrium. If the rate of interest was too high, funds available for investment would fail to find employment, and interest rates would come down. Thus, in this classical argument, the relationship between the level of domestic investment, and the level of domestic savings was pivotal.

However, in the contemporary international economic system the national monetary authorities may actually be powerless to undertake such exchange market intervention anyway. The increased incidence of flexible investment arrangements means that a country with an adequate profit rate and a high desired rate of investment, yet with a low rate of saving, can borrow from abroad, while a country with a high savings rate and a low domestic rate of profit can invest abroad. Thus, over the long term there would tend to be only a weak correlation between national saving and national investment across countries: nations would have no ability to set interest rates or profit rates differently from those abroad (although they would have the ability to borrow and lend as much as they would like at the market determined rate of return).[29, 30]

Arguments such as these are of immediate relevance to our analysis of an IPE approach to exchange rates and interest rates for two reasons. The first is that the very strong relationship between interest rates and exchange rates which we have just defined is pivotal. One of the major ways in which interest rates have been used is as a tool of domestic monetary policy designed to influence the behaviour of exchange rates. Indeed, if the uncovered interest parity relationship is to be believed, national monetary authorities would not be able to change the current exchange rate unless interest rates were used to do so.

Second, and following directly on from this, is the issue of the role that interest rates have as a determinant of the market's preferences for holding funds in one international centre rather than another. High interest rates attract foreign funds. On the other hand, high interest rates are commensurate with an exchange rate appreciation, which impairs domestic competitiveness. They are also particularly damaging to sectors of the domestic economy which rely heavily upon their products being bought on credit, such as car manufacturing. Thus policy makers must think carefully in order to achieve the policy mix which will provide the most appropriate interest rate values for their domestic goals, if indeed they can achieve that desired policy mix autonomously in what is an increasingly interdependent policy-making environment. Moreover, as we shall see, it is the relationship between exchange rates and interest rates which is at the heart of the inconsistent quartet. It is to an analysis of the latter that we now turn.

THE INCONSISTENT QUARTET

As was mentioned previously the economist Tommaso Padoa-Schioppa termed the phrase 'inconsistent quartet' to define the relationship between fixed (or at least pegged) exchange rates, full capital mobility, an independent monetary policy, and free trade. In what is perhaps one of the clearest introductions to the political dilemmas of international monetary affairs, Padoa-Schioppa stated three of the basic propositions which must be borne in mind in any analysis.[31]

The first of these is that the boundaries of the economy and the boundaries of the nation state do not correspond. Markets can be larger or smaller than nation states. Because nation states have both political and economic authority, markets, and economic activity in general, tend to suffer both from an excess and from a lack of government rule, something which is true also in monetary affairs as a whole.

The second proposition is that economic life needs some form of government in order to develop. Even if the trend towards non-intervention were pushed to the boundaries, a strong legal foundation would still be necessary for the maintenance of orderly economic affairs. Moreover, whatever happens, these boundaries of non-intervention will not be reached because there will always have to be some form of government intervention in economic life. Certain public goods, for example, will always be provided by the state.

The third proposition presents the inconsistent quartet. Padoa-Schioppa argued that both economic theory and historical experience have repeatedly shown that these four elements cannot coexist, and therefore that at least one of them has to give way:[32] A group of independent countries cannot simultaneously have fixed exchange rates, full capital mobility, an independent monetary policy and free trade. Highly integrated capital markets make it impossible to pursue autonomous economic policies without causing serious trade frictions or major misalignments in real exchange rates. Hence, Padoa-Schioppa argued, the inconsistent quartet was the main reason for disappointment with the floating rate regime, just as it was the main cause for the breakdown of the previous fixed parity system. In other words:[33]

'The international, multi-country economy is permanently confronted with the problems stemming from the . . . "inconsistent quartet".'

Before we go on to analyse the problems which this inconsistent quartet causes in more detail, let us first examine its elements: a fixed (or at least pegged) exchange rate, full capital mobility, an independent monetary policy and free trade.

Fixed Exchange Rates

Every state which has control over its own currency must resolve the issue of what type of exchange rate arrangement to maintain. In this regard, there are two issues of particular relevance to the IPE analyst.

The first is that national policy makers need to decide whether indeed to have an independent monetary policy, allowing a flexible exchange rate, or to abandon an independent monetary policy in the interests of having a fixed, and thus predictable, exchange rate. The second issue is that, assuming that the national monetary authority takes steps to influence the value of the exchange rate (for example, through appropriate monetary and/or fiscal policy and Central Bank intervention),[34] governments have to decide on an appropriate value which is consistent with the prevailing domestic political and economic environment. For example, Frieden concludes that in:[35]

> 'an open economy, clear differences arise among economic agents over both the desired level of the exchange rate and the desired degree to which it will be fixed. All else equal, domestically oriented producers prefer a flexible exchange rate, internationally oriented ones a fixed exchange rate, tradeables producers prefer a weak (depreciated) currency, non-tradeable producers and overseas investors a strong (appreciated) one.'

Thus, a government might decide upon a fixed exchange rate regime because of, say, pressure exerted upon it by domestic firms which are highly oriented towards international trade.

Over the years, much discussion has taken place over the relative merits of flexible versus fixed exchange rates. Indeed, the dichotomy between fixed and flexible exchange rate systems goes as far back in economic analysis as David Ricardo, and has generated an enormous literature on the reasons for the choice of different exchange rate regimes.[36] When a national monetary authority determines to fix the exchange rate of its country's currency against that of another country (or against a combination of other country's currencies) it has an obligation to intervene, using foreign exchange reserves, in the foreign exchange market itself, undertaking to buy or sell its country's currency, when conditions dictate, in order to keep the value of its exchange rate at that predetermined level. By comparison, when the authorities refuse to intervene in the foreign exchange market, they are allowing their exchange rate to float freely. Early supporters of this latter arrangement argued that, compared to the Bretton Woods system, a regime of flexible exchange rates would actually be one in which currency values would be more stable. This view over the efficacy of a flexible exchange rate regime was based on six major arguments.[37]

The first of these was the proposition that a country's price level was sticky (i.e. difficult to move) in a downward direction.[38] Say, for example, that from a position of balance of payments equilibrium, a country's price level rose, therefore making that country's goods less competitive in the world market. With a fixed exchange rate the authorities, in order to maintain balance of payments equilibrium, would have to direct macroeconomic policy towards reducing the price level (with the probable use of foreign exchange reserves). If prices are sticky downwards, this would give a painful economic adjustment, resulting in unemployed resources. Better instead to let the exchange rate rise to compensate for the price increase, so maintaining the country's competitive position and in this way obviating the need for a long-drawn out adjustment process. This is the concept of purchasing power parity (PPP) discussed in Chapter 4.

The second argument was the notion that a flexible exchange rate regime would be relatively stable, in contrast to the supposed inherent instability of the Bretton Woods system. In short, the Bretton Woods system was viewed as one of periodic crises, with sharp, discrete changes in exchange rate values and one-way speculative frenzies as a result of exchange rate misalignment. In contrast, under a more flexible system such serious exchange rate misalignments would hardly ever take place. This issue of whether speculators would behave in a stabilising or destabilising manner in a regime of flexible rates became a key area of disagreement and led to a series of examples and counter-examples as to why speculators might indeed behave in an unstable manner. For example, Milton Friedman argued that if speculators were to destabilise exchange rates they would eventually lose money and go out of business, hence leaving the stable speculators to determine the exchange rate.[39] This idea of only stable speculators remaining in the market thus led to the picture of a floating rate regime being a tranquil one compared to the Bretton Woods system where one-way speculation was regarded as the norm.

The third supposed advantage that a flexible exchange rate system would bring was in insulating a country from shocks emanating from other countries. For example, with fixed exchange rates, a fall in demand for a country's exports due to a recession abroad would eventually lead to a domestic recession. With exchange rate flexibility, however, the exchange rate value would rise, thus reducing the price of exported goods and maintaining balance of payments equilibrium. This, of course, means that a flexible exchange rate regime allows a country to pursue an independent monetary policy, which was the fourth argument put forward for flexible exchange rates.

The fifth argument was that such a system suggested that the world economy could function without requiring a system of tariffs and trade barriers. Thus, if the exchange rate is free continually to equilibrate the balance of payments, a country's policy-makers should not have recourse to protectionist devices for balance of payments reasons: the freeing of exchange rates should usher in a period of more liberal trade relative to the Bretton Woods system.

Finally, in a system of flexible exchange rates, central banks would not need to hold foreign exchange reserves, because there would be no official intervention. This is because the exchange rate would adjust itself until the supply and demand for currencies were brought into balance (although the central bank would still hold reserves to pay for official commercial transactions). Because reserves earn a zero or low return compared to a longer-term investment, this would result in some, perhaps small, savings for the national economy.

Despite these arguments, however, as time went on it was recognised that there were difficulties inherent in a flexible exchange rate system, particularly with regard to exchange rate instability. For example, McKinnon, writing in 1976, noted that in the then prevailing flexible exchange rate system:[40]

'Current movements of spot [nominal] exchange rates of 20 per cent quarter-to-quarter, 5 per cent week-to-week or, even 1 per cent on an hour-to-hour basis are now not unusual by historical standards;. . . . .'

Moreover, evidence of this instability can be seen further by measuring the variation of nominal exchange rates and prices for six major countries in the period January 1973 to December 1987 inclusive.[41]

From the figures in Table 6.1, it can be seen that exchange rates are on average much more volatile than the corresponding prices over the time period analysed. For example, the Canadian exchange rate has a variation value of −8.65 over the sample period, compared to 0.60 for Canadian prices, whilst Germany has an exchange rate variation value of 11.13, compared to 1.02 for German prices.[42] Fluctuations in the exchange rate such as these may be inopportune for trading and are a source of increased instability for a domestic economy. Moreover, because of the pressure of short-term capital movements or speculation, the exchange rate could move in a direction separate from that which may be required by the domestic economy as reflected in its basic balance of payments position.

In addition, historical evidence does seem to bear out the fact that there may be difficulties inherent in a flexible exchange rate regime. For example, after the breakdown of the gold standard, the world economy

Table 6.1   Exchange Rate and Price Variation Values
January 1973–December 1987

Country	exchange rate	price
Canada	99.28	0.54
France	−8.65	0.60
Germany	6.20	1.90
Italy	−20.37	1.82
Japan	11.13	1.02
UK	−12.92	0.59

Source: Watson (1995).

went through a period of freely floating exchange rates. On the basis of that experience, the Norwegian economist Ragnar Nurkse argued that freely floating exchange rates have three major disadvantages.[43] First, they create an element of risk which tends to depress international trade.[44] Second, as a way to adjust the balance of payments, changes in exchange rates involve a constant shift of labour and other resources between import and export production. Such shifts may be costly as they tend to generate frictional unemployment.[45] Third, experience has demonstrated that floating exchange rates cannot always be relied upon to encourage economic adjustment. A major change in the exchange rate may generate expectations of further movement in the same direction, resulting in a large amount of foreign exchange trading taking place. If economic agents act upon these expectations then if, for example, a depreciation in pounds sterling is expected, they will sell pounds in favour of buying another currency (e.g. dollars). Pounds sterling will be bought back at a later date in order that a profit can be made. The act, however, of selling pounds sterling increases the amount of that currency in circulation which, in turn, leads to a depreciation. Hence the initial expectations of a sterling depreciation have generated a self-fulfilling prophecy. From these arguments, it would seem obvious that there are definite advantages for a country in participating in a fixed exchange rate regime. However, it can be argued that fixed exchange rates cannot be maintained for a sufficiently long period of time and conflicts over the stance of monetary policy in the system may continue to undermine the credibility of the fixed exchange rate arrangement, a point to which we will return later in this analysis.[46]

Capital Mobility

Corden argues that the increasing integration of the world capital market has been 'the single most important development' in the world economy in the last two decades.[47] From the 1960s onwards, private international financial activity has grown at a phenomenal rate, far more rapidly than the rate of growth of international goods trade. Indeed, by the late 1980s, the volume of foreign exchange trading (e.g. of the type mentioned in the previous section) exceeded that of foreign goods trade by almost forty times, totalling $650 billion per day.[48]

This tremendous growth can be explained by the process of financial liberalisation which has taken place in all the major industrial countries (as well as some others) over the last few decades. Moreover, as private firms started to benefit from a less restrictive transnational financial system, they increased their pressure upon governments to further ease restrictions on business activity, particularly financial institutions, and to deregulate domestic markets; the result of which has been an even greater movement toward the global integration of capital markets and an ever-increasing amount of mobile capital.

Before this movement, there were several different kinds of capital control in operation.[49] One type consisted of measures which placed *direct* quantitative constraints upon the external asset and liability capacities of domestic residents, sometimes distinguishing financial institutions (particularly banks) from other residents. Alternatively, capital flows could be hindered in a more *indirect* manner, either by preserving separate exchange rates for commercial and financial transactions (i.e. a so-called dual or multiple exchange rate system) or by levying taxes upon international capital transactions or on income from foreign capital holdings.

The effectiveness of these capital control measures – whether direct or indirect – clearly relied upon the authorities' ability to prevent the flow of capital transactions through channels that either evaded detection or legitimately avoided the protection of the controls. However, the increasing integration of capital markets significantly hindered the ability of the authorities to do this, particularly given the creation of new financial products and services;[50] the increased ability of financial markets and intermediaries to migrate between different regulatory jurisdictions throughout the world;[51] changes in information processing communication technologies which lowered the costs of switching between domestic and foreign assets; and a whole range of other improvements, all of which worked to make markets more liquid and international in character.[52]

The overall result of this tremendous liberalisation of capital flows has been the complete transformation of the post-war international political economy. Owners of capital can now 'shop' among a variety of economies for the investment climate which suits their needs most – lower inflation, better interest rates, less restrictive labour policies, etc. In this sense, the increase in capital mobility over the last few decades has meant that investors (particularly large investors) are no longer restricted to searching for investment opportunities in their domestic economy. Thus, domestic economic policy must increasingly accommodate the needs of the international marketplace.[53] In particular, the threat of capital flight wields immense influence over state behaviour and state policies, largely due to its distributional consequences (i.e. when residents of a country attempt to acquire foreign assets, hence shifting their wealth from domestic to foreign investments, meaning that fewer resources will be available for investment in the home economy. In this way, in the contemporary globalised economic environment, if investors want to move their capital, either in order to sidestep regulation, or because they fear financial or political instability (such as high inflation levels or domestic political and economic disturbances), they can do so – a fact which provides a significant hindrance to the ability of national monetary authorities to conduct independent monetary policies.[54]

An Independent Monetary Policy

The higher the level of interdependence existing within the international political economy, the larger the number of actors who have to be taken into account in the decision-making process, and hence the larger the number of potential policy problems confronting the national authorities. For example, if we consider a financially open economy where the level of financial and commercial integration is high, the use of monetary policy (interest rates and money growth) will have a major influence on the exchange rate. For this reason, in such an economy, one of the consequences of such intervention is in its role in the maintenance of balance of payments equilibrium, in that it changes the relative prices of tradeable and non-tradeable goods and services. A monetary stimulus, for example, leads to a fall in the value of the domestic currency, thus making domestically produced goods cheaper and stimulating their demand. Those goods which traditionally make up a large portion of the export market will become more attractive to consumers in the rest of the world. In this scenario the exchange rate then becomes more distributionally divisive as firms that produce these goods will become more profitable. Those who are employed to manufacture these goods will thus be able to command higher wages than workers manufacturing non-traded goods. Under these circumstances macroeconomic policy then becomes more politicised.[55]

An issue of further importance is whether foreign exchange intervention by a national monetary authority affects the exchange rate if it does not also change domestic monetary conditions. During the 1980s, the majority of international economists were sceptical of the power of such managed intervention. However, recent studies suggest that intervention is effective when it is publicly announced or otherwise communicated to currency traders, and the latter believe that the intervention is credible and consistent with existing monetary policy.[56] This is particularly the case in respect of a state's external monetary policy, i.e. those actions which a state takes in order to affect the external value of a currency, including the international use of the national currency and the state's stance towards the prevailing international monetary regime.[57]

It can be argued that the more national monetary authorities pursue increased competitiveness and stable monetary policies, the more they will intervene in the foreign exchange markets, i.e. the more proactive will be their stance.[58] In addition, although under certain circumstances governments can drive wedges between domestic and external monetary policy successfully, with the high degree of capital mobility existing in the contemporary international political economy external monetary policy must be broadly consistent with domestic monetary policy. Often this is achieved by adjusting exchange rate targets in order to conform to domestic monetary objectives; but, sometimes, domestic monetary policy is adjusted in order to conform to exchange rate objectives. Hence, domestic monetary policy as an exchange rate instrument may lie at the heart of the policymaking process.

Free Trade

The political origins of free trade can be traced back to the nineteenth century when the French emperor Napoleon imposed an economic embargo upon Great Britain, the effect of which was to encourage the British economy to pursue trade overseas as opposed to merely in the Continent, a trend which continued after the French defeat and the ending of the embargo. Thus, Britain's military and political dominance at this time allowed her to adopt and encourage a liberal economic trading system.[59]

A century later it was the dominance, politically and militarily, of the United States which allowed the adoption and encouragement of the post-World War II Western liberal economic trading system. The benefits of free trade are well known and often quoted.[60] First, trade leads to specialisation in production, which improves the allocation of resources and leads to a lower cost structure. This in turn means that prices for the domestic consumer are at their lowest level possible. Second, trade can increase output through export-led growth. However, trade can have a negative impact too. For example, an increased dependence on trade can make countries more vulnerable in general to external shocks – shocks, that is to say, which may be initiated by national or international factors but whose impact is transmitted through trade (e.g. as was the case with the oil price shocks of the 1970s). More specifically, the distributional impact of exchange rate movement increases as economies become more open, with any given exchange rate movement causing a greater redistribution of income within the domestic economy (i.e., if a change in the exchange rate makes an economy more competitive, there will be an increase in international trade which, in turn, may lead to a redistribution of income within the domestic economy from non-traded goods producers to traded goods producers). In addition, changes in trade performance under these conditions may lead to persistent divergences in growth, with international trading success becoming cumulative as the increasing demand for exports – usually of goods which are highly sensitive to changes in income, such as high-technology goods – from strong trading countries allowing them to exploit economies of scale, improving their competitiveness and leading to further improvements in their trade performance. Japan, for example, is one country which has exploited trading success in such a way.

On the other hand, weaker trading nations exporting goods which are less sensitive to changes in consumer incomes may find that their export volumes are falling and may thus fail to maintain balance of payments equilibrium at a high level of economic activity, and may then pursue deflationary policies in an attempt to maintain external balance. Hence, the combined impact of poor trade performance and domestic policies geared towards deflation is likely to lead, in aggregate, to a deterioration in relative economic growth as these countries fail to exploit the increasing returns associated with a high level of economic activity.[61] What would therefore be required would be a system with mechanisms that maintain the balanced development of the world economy, while at the same time allowing those countries in difficulty some means of adjustment.

To bring some of these issues more clearly into focus, particularly within an international political economy framework, let us now examine the so-called 'inconsistent quartet' and consider the difficulties caused by the fact that no country in the contemporary international political economy no country can expect the above four elements to coexist.[62]

An IPE Analysis

The twin phenomena of free trade and a high degree of capital mobility are an undisputed part of the contemporary international political economy. If there is perfect capital mobility, then interest rates should not vary across countries.[63] We saw this in our earlier analysis when we noted that, at its most comprehensive, uncovered interest parity implies perfect capital mobility. This is because if there were higher interest rates in any one country, there would be a capital inflow into that country by those investors who wish a higher return on their assets. Under these circumstances, if the interest parity condition holds, then monetary policy will operate primarily via the exchange rate: a rate of money growth faster than the rest of the world leads to an exchange rate depreciation, which (in general) results in economic expansion.[64, 65]

The most important implication of this is that a high degree of capital mobility leads to a trade-off between exchange rate stability and monetary independence in an economy, because a government can only ensure currency stability by giving up its autonomy in monetary policymaking. This trade-off therefore constrains monetary policy in purely economic terms – the scenario of the inconsistent quartet can clearly be seen. Importantly, however, for the present analysis, this also has a political impact because of the effect that it has on the activity of different socioeconomic groups.

For example, in an economy with a low level of capital mobility, a monetary stimulus leads to an increase in nominal income, a reduction in real interest rates (resulting in a decrease in borrowing costs) and the stimulation of both investment and credit-financed consumer spending. In such an economy monetary policy therefore affects the economy-wide price level which, in turn, has widespread effects on that economy's growth and upon the fortunes of debtors and creditors. In particular, political divisions may be expected to arise between a country's borrowers and savers. This is due to the fact that some industries, such as housing construction and car manufacture, are more sensitive to changes in interest rates because their products are typically bought on credit. Workers and management involved in such sectors typically support lower interest rates. On the other hand, some industries, such as financial services, typically favour higher interest rates because this increases the return which they receive on the money lent to borrowers. Hence, it can be assumed that there will be a degree of political conflict over monetary policy in a closed economy – but it will be modest, because those who are chiefly affected will be either relatively small groups (e.g. those employed in interest rate-sensitive industries) or the broad masses of borrowers and savers, workers and consumers who are affected by macroeconomic trends in general, such as an overall change in the interest rate.

On the other hand, in an economy with a high level of capital mobility monetary policy has a large impact upon the exchange rate and operates by altering the relative prices of tradeable and non-tradeable goods and services. As we have already seen, a monetary expansion drives the value of the currency down, making domestically produced goods cheaper and thus stimulating demand for them. A change in the exchange rate therefore has an immediate impact on those exposed to international competition. Eventually this has an effect on economic conditions for producers of non-tradeable goods and services because of the overall changes wrought in the domestic economy through the increase in international trade.

Therefore, in an open economy the use of monetary policy, through its impact on the exchange rate, has effects which are immediate and significant for specific interests. Political pressures from interested groups of the electorate can be expected. It is for this reason that political leaders and parties may find that their destinies are intimately linked with the fate of their currencies – all because currency movements have a more immediate effect on relative prices than do overall movements in the nominal price level. In particular, factors in the international political economy may oppose both devaluation and revaluation. One important issue here is that voters, it is believed, interpret devaluation as an admission of financial failure, with negative consequences for the government in power. In addition to this, in the case of a political agreement regarding the exchange rate value, voters hold their political leaders, in particular, responsible for devaluations (although it is by no means clear why devaluation should be more of an embarrassment (and thus a more effective constraint) to an incumbent government than inflation, unemployment, worsening trade deficits, or the failure to meet an exchange rate commitment assumed unilaterally.[66]

Monetary politics are affected in a similar way by the phenomenon of free trade. While increasing levels of capital mobility alter the effect of monetary policy, in a similar way free trade increases the degree to which monetary policy affects different groups of economic actors. Even non-tradeable goods producers care more about exchange rates as the economy is opened to trade, because the import component of their inputs rises (i.e. they are likely to import more of their production inputs), as does the effect on them of the expenditure-switching caused by exchange rate movements (i.e. as more and more substitute goods are traded).[67] Increased trade intensifies the interest of producers in policies that move exchange rates in their favour. How, then, should exchange rate policy be conducted in such an open economy?

Depending on their specific concerns, economic agents will have different views as to what is important in the macroeconomy: exchange rate stability or the ability of policymakers to pursue an independent monetary policy. Uncertainty regarding the future value of exchange rates introduces uncertainty about the future revenues of firms. It is generally accepted that this leads to a loss of welfare in a world populated by risk-averse individuals. These will, generally speaking, prefer a future return that is more certain than one that is less so, at least if the expected value of these returns is the same. Having a fixed exchange rate means that eliminating the exchange risk reduces a source of uncertainty and should therefore increase welfare. Firms that trade solely in the domestic market – those for whom foreign trade and payments are insignificant – will prefer that national policy makers maintain their autonomy over national monetary policy making. Their prosperity is dependent upon domestic business conditions. The government's ability to affect national monetary conditions in their favour therefore necessitates a flexible exchange rate.

On the other hand, for firms that are heavily involved in international trade and investment, having exchange rate predictability is vitally important, as this has a major impact on their economic performance. Indeed, inasmuch as they can move production or sales easily from home to foreign markets, they care less about domestic conditions than about the predictability of currency values – indeed, if flexible exchange rates prove to be excessively volatile, those heavily involved in international trade and investment may prefer a fixed exchange rate regime.

However, neither of these views on the preferences of domestic and international businesses is unqualified. Preferences over the level of the exchange rate may vary in intensity and over time. Where policy towards the level of the exchange rate and its variability are linked and actors' interests cut in different directions, they must decide what matters more to them. Exporters weigh the relative importance of the increased competitiveness given by a devaluation against the uncertainty that devaluations introduce. For some – particularly those with long-term contracts where hedging is difficult – variable exchange rates may lead to a substantial loss of business. For others, the added competitive edge is the most important factor. To take another example, international investors may care less about the level of the exchange rate than about its variability. Firms with globally diversified production may be insensitive to particular levels of the exchange rate. However, their ability to formulate investment plans may be very sensitive to exchange rate instability.

CONCLUSION

This chapter has analysed the international political economy of exchange rates and interest rates. After a brief introduction of the nature of exchange rates and interest rates, we went on to examine the relationship between the two, in particular in the form of the interest parity relationship. This was important from the point of view of this analysis because of the way in which interest rates have been used as a tool of domestic monetary policy designed to influence the behaviour of exchange rates, and also because of the importance of interest rates in the decisions made by wealth-holders over where to locate their wealth. These nuances are important to the detailed evaluation of political debates over monetary and exchange rate policy making, but they are also of particular importance to the analysis of the 'inconsistent quartet', because the fact that free trade and a high degree of capital mobility are inherent in the contemporary international economic system means that countries continually have to trade off the benefits of exchange rate stability against the costs of giving up autonomy in monetary policy making, of which the interest rate is a part. With this analytical framework in place, let us now turn to an analysis of interest and exchange rate policy making in Europe, in order to examine how the problems stemming from the 'inconsistent quartet' apply to the future economic and monetary union.

NOTES

1. A variation of this well-known model is used by Jeffry Frieden in his excellent article on exchange rate politics. See: Jeffry A. Frieden, 'Exchange rate politics: contemporary lessons from American history', *Review of International Political Economy*, Vol. 1 (1994), pp. 81–103.
2. See, for example: Richard T. Froyen, *Macroeconomics – Theories and Policies* (London: Macmillan, 1990).
3. The exchange rate is defined here as the home currency price of a unit of foreign exchange.
4. See any basic economics textbook for a fuller explanation.
5. Rudiger Dornbusch and Luis Tellez Kuenzler, *op. cit.* (1993), pp. 91–95.
6. In the gold standard each country defined its currency in terms of gold. Hence, £1 was worth $5 because £1 was defined as containing five times as much gold as $1. Any private individual, business or bank in any country who owned dollars, francs, marks, roubles or sterling could freely exchange them for each other or for gold at the defined exchange rates.
7. Jonathan Kirshner, *Currency and Coercion, The Political Economy of International Monetary Power* (Princeton: Princeton University Press, 1995), p. 12.
8. See: Sérgio Pereira Leite and V. Sundararajan, 'Issues in Interest Rate Management and Liberalization', *IMF Staff Papers*, Vol. 37, No. 4, December (1990).
9. J. Eichberger and I. R. Harper, 'On Deposit Interest Rate Regulation and Deregulation', *The Journal of Industrial Economics*, vol. XXXVIII, no. 1 (1989), p. 20.
10. Paul R. Krugman and Maurice Obstfeld, *International Economics: Theory and Policy* (Glenview, Il: Scott, Foresman and Co., 1988), p. 622.
11. Yann Eichinard, *op. cit.* (1987), p. 124.
12. Maria Bogucka, 'The Monetary Crisis of the XViith Century and its Social and Psychological Consequences in Poland', *Journal of European Economic History*, 4, no. 1 (1975), p. 149, as quoted in J. Kirshner, *op. cit.*
13. *Ibid.*, pp. 150 (first quote), 152 (second quote).
14. See: Jeffry A. Frieden, *op. cit.* (1994) for a variation of this.
15. P. Einzig, *op. cit.* (1962), p. 214.
16. Walther Lotz, 'Die Wahrungsfrage in Osterreich-Ungarn', *Schmollers Jahrbuch*, vol. 13 (1889), pp. 34–5.
17. P. Einzig, *op. cit.* (1962), p. 275.
18. J. M. Keynes, *A Tract on Monetary Reform* (London: Macmillan, 1923), p. 123.
19. *Ibid.*, p. 124.
20. J. M. Keynes, *The General Theory of Employment, Interest and Money* (London: Macmillan, 1936), chapter 12.
21. The conceptual framework from which this hypothesis emerges as a special case is generally referred to as the international asset pricing model. For a further explanation of this, see Richard A. Meese, 'Empirical Assessment of Foreign Currency Risk Premiums', in Courtenay C. Stone (ed.), *Financial Risk: Theory, Evidence and Implications* (Boston: Kluwer Academic Publishers, 1989), pp. 157–80; and, Robert J. Hodrick, *The*

Empirical Evidence on the Efficiency of Forward and Futures Exchange Markets, (Chur, Switzerland: Harwood Academic Publishers, 1987).

22. J. M. Keynes, *op. cit.* (1923), pp. 126–27.
23. Richard J. Herring and Richard C. Marston, 'The Forward Market and Interest Rates in Eurocurrency and National Money Markets', in Carl H. Stem, John H. Makin and Dennis E. Logue (eds) (Washington: American Enterprise Institute, 1976), pp. 139–63; Richard C. Marston, 'Interest Arbitrage in the Eurocurrency Markets', *European Economic Review*, 7 (1976), pp. 1–13; Richard M. Levich, 'Empirical Studies of Exchange Rates: Price Behaviour, Rate Determination and Market Efficiency', in Ronald Jones and Peter B. Kenen (eds), *Handbook of International Economics*, Vol. 2 (Amsterdam: North Holland, 1985), pp. 979–1140.
24. Although recent work would tend to suggest that earlier studies of the standard UIP model may be flawed in that they formulate the hypothesis for testing incorrectly. See: Antoine Frachot, 'A re-examination of the uncovered interest rate parity hypothesis', *Journal of International Money and Finance*, vol. 15, no. 3 (1996), pp. 419–37.
25. Marianne Baxter, 'Real exchange rates and real interest rate differentials – Have we missed the business cycle relationship?', *Journal of Monetary Economics*, 33 (1994), pp. 5–37. See also the discussion in Chapter 2 of: Alison M. S. Watson, *Aspects of European Monetary Integration*, Ph.D. Thesis, University of Dundee (1995).
26. Or the efficacy of monetary policy.
27. However, more recently it has been recognised that, even if UIP was valid, intervention could be useful if it signalled new information about the intentions of policymakers to adjust interest rates or other policy instruments in order to achieve their exchange rate objectives.
28. John Kenneth Galbraith, *Money, Whence it came, where it went* (London: Penguin, 1995).
29. This ability is of course subject to an intertemporal budget constraint that says they cannot borrow more than they are able to repay. Note that the asset balance model imposes a different constraint: they cannot borrow more than they are willing to pay.
30. However, although governments may actually seem powerless, governments may still have to be seen to be doing something in response to a perceived problem, whether it be in the area of social policy or of social affairs. See: Richard Jeffrey, 'More than a gesture?', *Accountancy* (International Edition), February 1996, pp. 56–7.
31. Tomasso Padoa-Schioppa, 'Squaring the Circle, or the Conundrum of International Monetary Reform', *Catalyst, a Journal of Policy Debate*, 1, 1 (1985), pp. 64–5.
32. *Ibid.*, and see: T. Padoa-Schioppa, 'The European Monetary System: A Long-term View', in F. Giavazzi, S. Micossi and M. Miller (eds), *op. cit.* (1988), pp. 372–75.
33. Tomasso Padoa-Schioppa, *op. cit.* (1985), p. 64.
34. See: C. A. E. Goodhart, 'The Conduct of Monetary Policy', *The Economic Journal*, 99 (1989), pp. 293–346.
35. Jeffry A. Frieden, *op. cit.* (1994), p. 87.
36. See, for example: Terence C. Mills and Geoffrey E. Woods, 'Does the

Exchange Rate Regime Affect the Economy?', *Review of the Federal Reserve Bank of St Louis*, vol. 75, no. 4 (1993), p. 3; Marianne Baxter and Alan C. Stockman, 'Business Cycles and the Exchange Rate Regime: some international evidence', *Journal of Monetary Economics*, vol. 23, no. 3 (1989) p. 377; A. Velasco and A. Tornell, 'Fiscal discipline and the choice of exchange rate regime', *European Economic Review*, vol. 39, no. 3 (1995), p. 759.

37. R. MacDonald, *op. cit.* (1988), pp. 1–4.

38. See M. Friedman, 'The case for flexible exchange rates', in *Essays in Positive Economics* (Chicago: University of Chicago Press, 1953), pp. 157–203.

39. *Ibid.*

40. R. I. McKinnon, 'Floating exchange rates 1973–74: the emperor's new clothes', *Carnegie Rochester Supplement to the Journal of Monetary Economics*, vol. 3 (1976), pp. 79–114.

41. This is done by measuring the coefficient of variation for exchange rates and prices, where the coefficient of variation is a measure of the dispersion of a set of data and is defined here as: the standard deviation/the mean of the series.

42. Note, however, that the variation in the exchange rate for the three ERM countries in the above sample is much lower than the corresponding non-ERM countries in the above sample.

43. Quoted in Peter Kenen, 'Macroeconomic Theory and Policy: How the Closed Economy Was Opened', in Ronald Jones and Peter Kenen, eds, *Handbook of International Economics*, Volume II (North Holland: Amsterdam, 1985).

44. Where a forward exchange market exists, this risk may be covered by 'hedging' operations but this type of insurance, if obtainable, carries with it a price.

45. Frictional unemployment arises from the lags in time associated with labour redeployment. Even if the amount of vacancies for each type of labour were exactly equal to the number seeking employment, in practice it still takes time for the unemployed to find vacancies, be interviewed, etc. Thus there will always be a small pool of unemployed due to the fact that the labour market does not adjust instantaneously.

46. P. de Grauwe, *op. cit.* (1994), p. 159.

47. W. Max Corden, *op. cit.* (1994), p. 3.

48. Philip Turner, *Capital Flows in the 1980s: A Survey of the Major Trends* (Basle: Bank for International Settlements, 1991), pp. 9–10.

49. See: C. Randall Henning, *op. cit.* (1994) for a fuller analysis.

50. The process of financial innovation has been closely associated with the extensive liberalisation and deregulation of domestic financial markets since the beginning of the 1980s. By the early 1990s, competitive forces had substantially reduced the traditional roles of banks in the provision of financial services, with corporate borrowers in major industrial countries increasingly able to satisfy their liquidity, risk-management, and financing needs directly in markets for liquid securities.

51. An important example of this phenomenon was the development of the Eurodollar market – specifically, the market in US dollars held on deposit in banks or bank branches located outside the United States – which was

stimulated, inter alia, by the desires of the Soviet Union and other communist countries during the 1950s to build up holdings of dollars outside the United States; by the US interest equalisation tax of 1964, which was designed to discourage foreign borrowers from issuing debt obligations in the US market; and by the rise in Eurodollar interest rates above the ceiling rates that banks in the United States were permitted to pay (under Regulation Q) on certificates of deposit during the tight money years of 1968–69.

52. The International Monetary Fund's Articles of Agreement specifically declare that member countries 'may exercise such controls as are necessary to regulate international capital movements,' provided that these do not impede current account transactions or unnecessarily hinder the resolution of international contracts. At the end of 1993, around three-quarters of the members of the IMF still supported the maintenance of restrictions, of one form or another, on international capital flows (although in many cases the remaining controls were comparatively unimportant). Such restrictions may be of several different kinds.

53. R. Stubbs and G. R. D. Underhill, 'Global Issues in Historical Perspective', in Richard Stubbs and Geoffrey R. D. Underhill (eds), *op. cit.* (1994), p. 153.

54. J. A. Frieden, *op. cit.* (1994), p. 83.

55. *Ibid.*, p. 57.

56. Kathryn Dominguez and Jeffrey A. Frankel, *Does Foreign Exchange Intervention Work?* (Washington Institute for International Economics, 1993).

57. C. Randall Henning, *op. cit.* (1994).

58. Note that a policy oriented toward 'competitiveness', in the sense that the term is used here, seeks an exchange rate consistent with expanding or maintaining market share in tradeable goods. The term does not mean 'competitive devaluation' and is consistent with either a depreciating or stable currency.

59. See: P. J. Cain, *Economic Foundations of British Overseas Expansion 1815–1914* (London: Macmillan, 1980); and, C. P. Kindleberger, 'The rise of free trade in Western Europe 1820–1875', *Journal of Economic History*, 35 (1975), pp. 20–55.

60. For a fuller discussion, see any elementary economics textbook, e.g. Richard G. Lipsey, *An Introduction to Positive Economics* (London: Weidenfeld and Nicholson, 1989).

61. M. Kitson and J. Michie, 'Trade and Growth: A Historical Perspective', in J. Michie and J. G. Smith (eds), *Managing the Global Economy* (Oxford: Oxford University Press, 1995), p. 5.

62. Jeffry A. Frieden, *op. cit.* (1994), p. 83.

63. This refers to covered real interest rates; currency, country, and inflation risk all affect interest rates.

64. Robert Mundell, 'The appropriate use of monetary and fiscal policy under fixed exchange rates', *IMF Staff Papers*, 9 (1962), pp. 70–9; Robert Mundell, 'Capital mobility and stabilisation policy under fixed and flexible exchange rates', *Canadian Journal of Economics and Political Science*, 29 (1963), pp. 475–85.

65. Keith Cuthbertson and Mark P. Taylor, *Macroeconomic Systems* (Basil Blackwell: London, 1987), pp. 203–204.

66. Witness, for example, the sacking of the British Chancellor of the Exchequer, Norman Lamont, in the aftermath of the British 'Black Wednesday' ERM crisis. See also: J. Melitz, *op. cit.* (1988), p. 58; and J. T. Woolley, *op. cit.* (1992), p. 163.
67. Obviously, in an increasingly interdependent world economy there are few goods that are completely non-traded between countries – but, nevertheless, it can be said that there are some goods which are more heavily traded in the international marketplace than others.

7 The Convergence Criteria: Exchange Rates and Interest Rates – A European Perspective

'We are worried about the exchange rate developments in the Community. There is at present no effective Community framework for the coordination of policies in this area among all members, while recent developments have surely indicated the urgent need for common action.'

Wilhelm Duisenberg (1976)[1]

It is filthy gaines, and a worke of darknesse, it is a monster in nature: the overthrow of mighty kingdoms, the destruction of flourishing States, the decay of wealthy cities, the plagues of the world, and the misery of the people ... This is Usury.

Bishop Jewell[2]

INTRODUCTION

Our previous chapter outlined the way in which exchange rates and interest rates could be viewed from an IPE perspective. Specifically, we used the methodology of the inconsistent quartet to outline the way in which interest rate and exchange rate movements impact upon the international political economy. This chapter will take this analysis one stage further by applying the previously discussed methodology to the issue of the convergence of exchange rates and interest rates, as set out in the Maastricht Treaty. After brief outlines of European exchange rate and interest rate policies (bearing in mind the Maastricht requirements and including an overview of their economic rationale), we go on to examine the dilemmas which the inconsistent quartet poses for a future economic and monetary union.

EUROPEAN EXCHANGE RATE STABILITY

If there was one economic issue, more than any other, which gave
added impetus to the process of European monetary integration, it was
that of creating a stable exchange rate regime in Europe.[3] The achievement
of exchange rate stability has been a continuing goal in the drive towards
European monetary integration: the Treaty of Rome set the fixity of
currency parities as a fundamental objective and Article 107 stated
that the exchange rate policy of each Member State was a 'matter of
common interest'.[4] Thus, just as the efficacy of fixed versus flexible
exchange rate regimes has been long-debated, as we saw in our previous chapter, the issue of the fixity of currency parities first brought up
in the Treaty of Rome has led to long history of argument over just
how fixed or flexible a European exchange rate regime should be.[5] For
example, a system of fixed *but adjustable* exchange rates, as in the
Exchange Rate Mechanism, may, under certain circumstances, be seen
as superior to the type of regime proposed in economic and monetary
union. For example in a truly unified market, such as the United States,
the overall economy would be more likely to adjust to regional-specific
shocks and regional disparities in productivity and growth through factor
movements (i.e. labour and capital movement) and fiscal transfers (that
is, increased federal expenditures in affected regions). However, in the
EU, because of the vast differences which still exist in levels of economic
development (for example, as between Germany and Portugal), significant
differences in productivity and growth are very likely to persist. Moreover,
structural differences between national economies mean that country-
specific shocks are likely to occur.[6] Since factor mobility across countries
(especially for labour) and EC fiscal transfers (namely, the regional
funds) remain limited, that avenue of adjustment in the face of such
shocks is blocked. In this case, exchange rate changes remain a viable
means of adjusting to cross-national differences without imposing
unacceptable costs on any one economy.[7]

Yet despite the latter arguments, for the Member States of the European Union, the objective of greater economic and political integration
has nevertheless led many officials to reject both flexible exchange
rates and frequent variations in fixed exchange rates as instruments for
adjusting to asymmetric shocks. This is in large part due to the desire
of policy makers to eliminate the high levels of risk which emanate
from the uncertain nature of future exchange rate movements, i.e. speculation. National monetary authorities can avert the difficulties caused
by speculators in the international capital markets by forming a monetary union, thus fixing their mutual exchange rates for good. The

establishment of such a union will not only eliminate capital movements among its member countries, but thereafter unfavourable consequences will have to be handled by means of policy instruments analogous to those available to national governments for offsetting the undesired effects of monetary movements between the constituent regions of their countries (for example, by altering the money supply).[8]

It is fair to say, then, that one of the advantages of a monetary union most frequently claimed by policy makers is its effect upon the reduction of exchange rate volatility. However, the value of any reduction in exchange rate volatility depends, in the main, on whether movements in exchange rates primarily reflect underlying economic fundamentals (e.g. relative price levels, balance of payments positions, national monetary policy stances) or whether autonomous movements in market sentiment play a significant role. If exchange rate volatility only reflects fundamentals, then it simply reflects the proper functioning of the market mechanism. On the other hand, if changes in market sentiment lead to a sustained exchange rate misalignment, a misallocation of resources may result due to speculation (as we saw in Chapter 6).

It is true, of course, that currencies which have been subject to considerable volatility against one another are not likely to participate easily together in a monetary union. For example, a fixed exchange rate regime *with narrow bands* can be extremely destabilising in the absence of the convergence of economic fundamentals and credibility.[9] In such a regime, a movement towards the end of a band provides speculators with a potential 'one-way bet' (this was seen in the previous chapter in regard to the Bretton Woods regime's potential for 'one-way speculative frenzies'). As market participants (hedgers as well as speculators) position themselves for a possible realignment, they push a currency to the bottom of its band, at which point the authorities concerned are compelled to take defensive action. This involves intervention in the exchange market and possibly an increase in interest rates. As has become evident in the recent past, such defensive actions are not always effective in stabilising the market. If higher interest rates are perceived to create an unsustainable conflict between domestic and external objectives, they can add to, rather than alleviate, speculative pressures.[10] However, although (for some of the reasons outlined above) it may be argued that exchange rates should be irrevocably fixed within a monetary union, many economists have questioned the point of the exchange rate criterion in the Maastricht Treaty.

To recapitulate, the Maastricht Treaty requires that a Member State respects the normal exchange rate fluctuation margins (which at the time of the treaty were 2.25%), without undue pressure, for at least the last two years before the Member States' performances are examined prior to their possible accession to economic and monetary union; and, in particular, that the Member State will not have devalued its currency against that of another Member State's (on its own initiative) for that same period. Nevertheless, some have argued that this need for an exchange rate criterion to be met before economic and monetary union can take place is not a strong one.[11] In particular, politicians in the Member States have queried the notion that a country is being asked to maintain stable exchange rates as a precondition for entering an economic and monetary union in which it will have no exchange rate of its own. The exchange rate criterion may be defended, however, if we consider that it is meant to facilitate the reduction of realignments during the transition stage of EMU in order that credibility is bestowed upon the process of exchange rate fixing at the start of Stage Three.[12] In this way the infant monetary union would be protected from exchange rate crisis before it had moved to using the Euro as its single currency.[13] However, if this was indeed the reason for the inclusion of the exchange rate criterion, the authors of the Treaty did not consider the issue of how currency conversions should take place after exchange rates have been locked and before the shift to the Euro.[14]

Other analysts, notably Begg, Giavazzi, Spaventa and Wyplosz, have nevertheless argued that the exchange rate criterion is the only one of the convergence criteria to which attention should be paid.[15] The reasoning for this is that the success of the EU countries in avoiding realignments during the run-up to Stage III would then be an adequate test of their ability to bear the costs of reducing inflation in Stage III itself.[16] However, a speculative attack which forces a devaluation, thereby preventing a Member State from satisfying this requirement, might, by eliminating the lure of membership in the monetary union, induce its government to abandon its current policy regime. This is because the country, once driven out of the ERM, might no longer qualify for EMU membership and would thus have no incentive to continue pursuing the policies necessary to gain entry. Under these circumstances, and if the exiting country has devalued, a speculative attack could prove self-fulfilling.[17]

These, then, are some of the difficulties with the economic rationale behind the exchange rate criteria. Before going on to discuss this further within an IPE framework, let us first examine the issue of European interest rate policy.

INTEREST RATE POLICY AND MAASTRICHT

The Maastricht Treaty emphasises the importance of the role of the convergence of long-term interest rates to the future economic and monetary union of Europe. In particular, it requires that Member States' average nominal long-term interest rates do not exceed by more than two percentage points that of, at most, the three best performing Member States in terms of price stability for the period of a year before the Member State's examination for suitability for EMU accession. In the end, there were a variety of reasons for this emphasis. First, it was a result of the Member States' experiences in the previous decade when interest rates in all of the industrialised countries had stayed persistently high. This was particularly the case in the United States, where financial instability was much more pronounced in that period than in the other major countries, a fact which had obvious implications for European interest rate policy. MacDonald, for example, noted that:[18]

'In 1981 and 1982 the USA was pursuing a tight monetary policy and had correspondingly high interest rates. Although the European countries did not desire or require such a tight monetary policy they were forced to pursue one nevertheless, since to have had interest rates below the US ones would have meant large capital outflows from Europe to the USA, sharp exchange rate depreciations and the consequent deleterious effect this would have had on inflation and the value of real assets. . . . So the European countries in this period were forced to adopt interest rate policies which were more in tandem with US policy than the needs of their domestic economies.'

By the beginning of the 1990s, therefore, the Member States felt the need to take control of European interest rate policy in the face of external pressures.

The second reason for the emphasis on interest rates in the Maastricht Treaty is that the interest rate is at the heart of the interface between fiscal and monetary policy in an economic and monetary union. As has been noted elsewhere, analysts and policymakers have long mapped the links between monetary and fiscal policy in EMU. In particular, an incorrect fiscal policy can sabotage an otherwise effective monetary policy. Excessive fiscal deficits can lead either to debt monetisation or to the need for bale-outs by other Union members, and bring about the twin dangers of inflation through excess money creation or stagnation through high long-term interest rates on public debt. However, fiscal policy in EMU as a whole has a wider significance (as we saw in Chapter 5), and that is in its contribution to economic stabilisation. The sum of fiscal decisions by individual governments cannot guarantee a collective fiscal stance that is optimal from the point of view of the monetary union as a whole. The danger is that loose fiscal policy does not merely offset but also undermines tight monetary policy, and thus becomes counterproductive by raising long-term as well as short-term interest rates – depressing rather than stimulating economic activity.[19] Achieving the correct interest rate in an economic and monetary union is thus a matter of particular concern to the Member States.

The final reason for the emphasis on long-term interest rate policy was that, in economic terms, the interest rate convergence criterion is different from the other criteria in that it is forward-looking. This means that unlike the other convergence criteria, it contains information about expectations. Thus a large long-term interest rate relative to that of other countries could indicate a future currency devaluation.[20] For example, when a Member State's long-term interest rate is larger than that of other countries, this may be due to the market's expectations regarding a large future increase in that Member State's short-term interest rate. On the other hand, it could be an indicator of the future possibility of a large increase in its inflation rate. In these terms, the interest rate criterion can basically be thought of as an indicator of the credibility of a government's commitment to low inflation. In other words, as noted by Artis:[21]

'This criterion can be thought of as relying on the forward-lookingness of financial markets to provide an assurance that inflation convergence, if observed, is not simply a 'flash in the pan'. If it were, then the country would be likely to fail the interest rate criterion, because the expected future inflation would be built into a high-interest differential against the good performers.'

Thus, just as volatile exchange rates are a threat to government credibility and European economy competitiveness, so unpredictable changes in interest rates wreak similar difficulties. Indeed, one of the advantages of economic and monetary union, stemming from the relationship between exchange rates and interest rates covered in our previous chapter, is in the reduction in the risk of exchange rate realignment and devaluation: EMU should result in a reduction in the risk premia currently included in the interest rates of most EC countries, relative to German rates,[22] the existence of which is clear.[23] The significance of this can be seen more fully if we consider what happens if two countries, say France and Italy, set their interest rates independently and simultaneously. At equilibrium, by definition, neither country wishes to cut its rate unilaterally, because such a cut would raise demand and output but would give a double stimulus to inflation – directly because of demand and indirectly because of import prices. On its own the output increase would be desirable but the overall inflation cost would just offset the gain (at the margin). It follows at once that a co-ordinated cut would benefit both countries, because the import price component of the extra inflation would not arise.

There is yet another issue, however, with regard to the relationship between exchange rates and interest rates in the Maastricht Treaty. Every system of fixed exchange rates faces the problem of how to set the system-wide level of the money stock and the interest rate. This issue essentially arises from the so-called *n-1* problem. In a system of *n* countries, there are only *n-1* exchange rates. Therefore *n-1* monetary authorities will be forced to adjust their monetary policy instrument so as to maintain a fixed exchange rate. There will be one monetary authority which is free to set its monetary policy independently. This leads to the issue of which Member State's central bank will use this degree of freedom and whether or not there are alternatives to the asymmetric solution where one central bank does what it likes and others follow. If we assume that there is perfect capital mobility, and thus that un-covered interest parity holds, this leads to the following scenario: if economic agents expect a depreciation of currency A, the interest rate of country A will have to exceed the interest rate of country B in order to compensate holders of assets of country A for the expected loss. Now suppose countries A and B decide to fix their exchange rate (as in EMU). Let us also assume that economic agents do not expect that the exchange rate will be adjusted in the future (again, as in EMU). This means that the interest rates in the two countries will be identi-cal. However, there is still a problem: the so-called '*n-1* problem', to which there are two solutions: either allow one country within the monetary union to take on a leadership role (the symmetric (hegemonic) solution), or else have the member states decide jointly the level of their money stocks and interest rates (the symmetric or co-operative solution). In the quasi-monetary union represented by the EMS, the former was the solution taken. In the economic and monetary union of the future, it is the latter approach with which the Member States are concerned.[24]

EUROPEAN POLICY MAKING AND THE INCONSISTENT QUARTET

In the previous chapter we noted that the economist Tommaso Padoa-Schioppa had termed the phrase 'inconsistent quartet' to describe the source of some of the difficulties with which the 'international multi-country economy' is permanently confronted. Padoa-Schioppa actually used this phrase in an analysis of the future of the EMS and, in particular, of the effect that the removal of capital controls and remaining non-tariff barriers (as a result of the Single European Act) would have on the stability of the System. In particular, he noted that:[25]

'Unless new items are added to the agenda, the Community will be seeking to achieve the impossible task of reconciling (1) free trade, (2) full capital mobility, (3) fixed (or at any rate managed) exchange rates and (4) national autonomy in the conduct of monetary policy.'

With these issues in mind, and for our present purposes of building an IPE approach to European exchange rate and interest rate policy making, we must therefore examine what problems an economic and monetary union might face as a result of the 'inconsistent quartet'. Only then will we get a full account of how Member States' domestic politics and European political expediency co-exist.

The Inconsistency Dilemma

A currency and its exchange rate are symbolic of a nation's sovereignty in conducting its own monetary affairs. As Kindleberger notes:[26]

'A country's exchange rate is more than a number. It is an emblem of its importance to the world, a sort of international status symbol.'

Giving up this symbol could thus be taken to be a powerful indicator of the depth of trust which the majority of the Member States of the European Union have in the process of economic and monetary union in Europe. However, as was argued previously, in the contemporary global economic framework, the ability of national monetary authorities to conduct a national monetary policy is, in any event, limited. Thus, giving up a national currency for a single currency in EMU is less a matter of trust in the process and more a case of necessity in the face of prevailing economic conditions. If, as we have already argued, the countries in the international economy are permanently confronted with the difficulties which stem from the 'inconsistent quartet', then the issue in this analysis is what this means for European interest rate and exchange rate policy making. In this regard, there are a number of issues which are of particular concern.

Of most notable concern is the level of commercial and financial integration, stimulated by the Single European Act, which exists within the European Union. In the long run, the goal of free trade in goods and services cannot be sustained unless capital is also free of restrictions and is allowed to go where the most efficient economic use can be made of it – hence the provisions of the SEA covering both free trade and capital mobility. Thus, under these twin provisions, interest rates should not vary between the Member States and monetary policy will operate via the exchange rate: a rate of money growth in one of the Member States relative to the others will lead to an exchange rate depreciation. As was mentioned in the previous chapter, under conditions of capital mobility, there is a strong link between interest rates within a country and abroad and the expected rate of depreciation. If interest rate differentials fall short of expected depreciation, capital flight is certain. Policies to depress real interest rates will quickly run into trouble in the exchange market.[27] The most important implication of this is that the high degree of capital mobility in Europe, engendered by the Single European Market, leads to a trade-off between exchange rate stability and monetary independence among the Member States: a country's currency stability can only be assured by relinquishing autonomy in monetary policymaking – the dilemma of the inconsistent quartet. Thus the level of commercial and financial integration generated by the Single European Act made the resolution of the conflict between national monetary autonomy and exchange rate stability pressing.[28] In economic terms, European governments could only ensure exchange rate stability by giving up their autonomy in monetary policy making. If this were not done, then the pursuit of independent monetary objectives would be almost certain, sooner or later, to result in a significant balance of payments disequilibrium, and hence provoke potentially destabilising flows of speculative capital. Under such circumstances, and to preserve exchange rate stability, governments would then be compelled to limit either the movement of capital (via some form of capital control or differential tax rates, both of which go against the spirit of the Single European Act) or their own policy autonomy (via some form of multilateral surveillance or joint decision making). Unwillingness to sacrifice either one would eventually compromise the objective of exchange rate stability. The governments thus chose to relinquish their autonomy in monetary decision-making by embarking upon the process of economic and monetary union in Europe.[29] One issue of concern, however, for those same governments was that such a move also had a political impact because of its effect on the activity of different socioeconomic groups, in this case at both a domestic and at a European intergovernmental level.

Domestic Politics and the Results of the Inconsistent Quartet

At the domestic level, the socioeconomic groups upon whom the dilemmas of the inconsistent quartet particularly impact fall into two categories: first, domestic firms; and second, the electorate.

With regard to the interests of domestic firms, as trade and capital flows within the EU grew, ever larger segments of EU business communities developed more important markets and investments in other EU nations. The amount of goods being traded in European (as opposed to simply domestic) markets grew. This growth of intra-EU trade and investment therefore increased the real or potential support base for economic policies that would facilitate and defend such economic activities. Stabilising exchange rates within the EU was a prominent example of a policy that benefited the growing ranks of domestic economic actors with cross-border intra-EU economic interests, whether these were export markets or investment sites.[30] By the same token, however, import-competing tradeables producers – especially those in traditionally high inflation countries – faced the prospect that fixing their exchange rate would lead to a real appreciation of the currency that would harm them in important ways, particularly in terms of their competitiveness. There is in fact substantial anecdotal evidence that much of the private sector's support for monetary integration came from internationally oriented firms in the EU. Perhaps more striking, however, is the evidence that shows that the principal opposition to fixing exchange rates came from import-competing producers in relatively high-inflation countries who anticipated that fixed exchange rates meant real appreciations. This can be seen by looking at some of the most prominent cases of domestic political divisions over European monetary relations – in particular, in France and Italy in the mid-1980s. Along with Ireland, these countries had inflation rates which had been higher than those of West Germany for a significant period of time, and in the first half of the 1980s their domestic political situation was dominated by debate over whether or not to undertake the sacrifices necessary to keep their currencies fixed to the Deutschmark, sacrifices which would harm their competitiveness in the short term.

With regard to the concerns of the electorate, we noted previously that voters may interpret a currency devaluation as an admission of financial failure by the incumbent government and that, in particular, voters hold their political leaders responsible for devaluations in the case of a political agreement regarding the exchange rate value.[31] Once more, we need only look back to the Black Wednesday of the ERM crisis of 1992 in the United Kingdom to see that this is the case. Echoing this, in the contemporary international political economy, arguments about the decline of the state's role are often implicitly based on the model of mobile asset-holders 'voting with their feet' in order to 'prevent politicians from eroding national wealth by adopting policies favouring special interest groups at the expense of the country as a whole.'[32, 33] This may be particularly the case with regard to the value of the exchange rate. As De Grauwe concedes:[34]

> 'The argument that exchange rate changes are dangerous instruments in the hands of politicians is important. The experience of many countries illustrates that when devaluations are used systematically, they will lead to more inflation without gains in output and employment. In addition, they easily lead to macroeconomic instability as economic agents continuously tend to expect future devaluations. Contrary to the old view, devaluations are not instruments that policy-makers can use flexibly and costlessly.'

In other words, a devaluation is not, as it was in the analysis of Mundell, a flexible instrument that can be used frequently. Policy-makers will have to evaluate the advantages obtained today against the possible costs which may be incurred in the long run, i.e. that it will be more difficult to use this instrument effectively in the future.[35] For this reason, we can see that there is a sound political rationale for relinquishing the use of the exchange rate as an instrument of monetary policy by irrevocably fixing its value within an economic and monetary union. However, as a counter-argument, there were many cases observed in Europe during the 1980s in which devaluations were used very successfully. The ingredients of this success have typically been that the devaluation was coupled with other drastic policy changes (sometimes a change in government, e.g. Belgium in 1982 and Denmark in the same year). As a result, the devaluation was perceived as a unique and an extraordinary change in policies that could not easily be repeated in the future. Under those conditions, the negative reputation effects (i.e. of manipulating the exchange rate value for electoral advantage) could be kept under control. Some countries, for example Denmark in 1982, even seem to have improved their reputation quickly after such a devaluation.[36]

Intergovernmental Politics and the Results of the Inconsistent Quartet

These issues of the costs to a particular nation of the loss of the exchange rate instrument bring us to the matter of the resolution, in particular, of the conflict between national monetary autonomy and exchange rate stability at the intergovernmental level. To examine this further, we must first of all look to those factors in European politics which led to an increased impetus for a European internal market. This will help to explain the depth of feeling, at an intergovernmental level, regarding the need for free trade and increased capital mobility in Europe.

One of the most important political developments within the Community in the early 1980s was a series of changes, as mentioned elsewhere of varying magnitude, in the partisan composition of the national governments. For some Member States this involved dramatic changes in the ideological centre of gravity of government as one party replaced another in office. In other cases, one party in a coalition government was replaced by another. There was even one important ideological and programmatic switch in a government that remained in office. Despite these differences, however, these changes shared one feature in common: they all represented a shift toward a more conservative position.[37]

The most marked change occurred in Britain, in 1979. With the election of a Conservative majority and with Margaret Thatcher as Prime Minister, the British government embarked on a radical programme of tax reduction, disinflation, privatisation and deregulation, which, in sanctifying the principle of the market, sought to reduce or eliminate various government-imposed barriers to commercial activity. Thus, throughout the 1980s, the Thatcher government was a strong proponent of pro-market positions within the Community, including the elimination of barriers to trade and commerce.

Moreover, in 1981 and 1982 three of the Member States experienced changes in the nature of their coalition governments. Although less dramatic than the change in Britain, all three resulted in a rightward ideological shift. The first of these occurred in Belgium, after the parliamentary election of November 1981, when Wilfred Martens formed a centre-right government composed of the two Christian Social parties (the CVP in the Flemish-speaking region and the PSC in the French-speaking region of the country) and the two liberal parties (the PVV (Flemish) and the PRL (French)). This government was subsequently renewed after the 1985 elections.

In the Netherlands the experience was similar, with a realignment of the government in May 1982. In this case, a centre-left coalition of the Christian Democrats, the Labour Party and a smaller centre-left party was succeeded by a centre-right government, headed by Ruud Lubbers and formed by the Christian Democrats and the right-wing People's Party for Freedom and Democracy. As with the centre-right government in Belgium, this government was renewed in office in the subsequent election in the mid-1980s. In the case of Denmark, when the Social Democratic minority government resigned in 1982, it was succeeded by a four-party non-Socialist government, formed by the Conservative Party, the Liberal Party (a conservative party despite its name), the Centre Democrats, and the Christian People's party. Although a minority government, this coalition, headed by Poul Schluter, remained in office throughout the 1980s.

In addition, and at about the same time as these three changes were taking place, the coalition of Social Democrats (SPD) and Free Democrats (FDP) which had been in power in West Germany since 1969 began to break up. In part because of disagreements over economic strategy, public expenditure, and the size of the budget deficit, the FDP decided in June 1982 to ally itself with the opposition Christian Democrats (CDU) in the state of Hesse. In September the FDP ministers in the Federal government, headed in 1974 by Helmut Schmidt, resigned and their party began negotiations with the CDU and its Bavarian sister party, the CSU, to form a new government. In October 1982, after a vote of no confidence in the Schmidt government, a three-party coalition, formed by the CDU, the CSU, and the FDP and headed by Helmut Kohl, took office.

In each of these five cases, a Labour, Socialist, or Social Democratic party was replaced with one or more non-Socialist parties. France, however, shifted toward the right not because one party replaced another in government but because the Socialist government elected in 1981 changed its programme. The story of that shift, which occurred in 1982 and 1983, has been told in great detail elsewhere and need not be repeated here.[38] Suffice it to say that in the wake of three devaluations of the franc between October 1981 and March 1983 the Socialist-controlled government shifted from its initial policy of reflation to one of fiscal and monetary restraint. In 1983–84 restraint had evolved into full-fledged austerity in spending, consumption, and incomes, and active support for profit-making, investment, and corporate restructuring and reorganisation.

As different as these six changes in government were, all represented, in varying degrees, a rightward shift in the ideological centre of gravity. Taken together, they may have greatly facilitated the development of an initiative that, above all, sought to create a market free of the intrusions and obstacles erected by interventionist governments. Free trade and increased capital mobility in Europe were the order of the day.

More than this, however, as was noted earlier and particularly since the 1980s, exchange rate problems have become a central policy issue resulting in many prominent political debates: the issue of exchange rate stability was thus a pressing one. In this sense, there are two factors which are of particular concern. First, and as we already noted, the Member States of the European Union have economies which are already largely open to foreign trade, and thus they depend to a large extent on international markets for the sale of their products, and on international producers for the products which they themselves consume.[39] Moreover, as we have already seen, in addition to being dependent on international trade in general, the Member States are also highly dependent on trade with other members of the Community. This means that exchange rate fluctuations, particularly those of European currencies, have a strong impact not only on the trade balance of the Member States but also on their gross domestic products.[40]

Second, in addition to this intra-Community trade dependence, there is a large degree of competition between the economies of the European Union. Member States no longer have any significant means to protect themselves from competition from the other Member States. Exchange rate instability, particularly if engineered by a Member State's independent monetary policy, might give one country, or one group of countries, the type of competitive advantage which the Single Market has worked to rule out.[41]

Under such circumstances, then, the free trade and capital mobility being pressed for by domestic actors and by Member States at the intergovernmental level, coupled with the pressing need for exchange rate stability which those same actors had, meant that – given the methodology of the inconsistent quartet – an independent monetary policy had to be relinquished for those goals to be achieved. It is for

Table 7.1   The Maastricht Interest Rate Criterion
(long bond interest rate)

Austria	7.5	Belgium	8.0
Denmark	8.7	Finland	8.7
France	7.5	Germany	7.3
Greece	17.5	Ireland	8.5
Italy	11.7	Luxembourg	7.5
Netherlands	7.3	Portugal	8.5
Spain	8.8	Sweden	10.8
UK	8.1	Three best	7.8

Source: European Commission 1995 Annual Report.

these reasons that the convergence criteria of the Maastricht Treaty contain both a requirement for exchange rate stability before EMU proceeds and a requirement that long-term interest rates remain at a low and stable level. The issue is still, however, whether such requirements will actually be achieved.

The Achievement of Convergence

How the interest rate criterion is currently being met by the EU Member States is set out in Table 7.1. Optimistically, only three of the fifteen Member States (Greece, Italy and Sweden) are at present forecast to fail the convergence criterion on interest rates. The problem still remains, however, that to the extent that these interest rates are being consulted as an index of sustainable inflation performance, the countries with the best inflation performance are not necessarily the countries with the lowest interest rates. This is a problem in so far that – if the interest rates are being consulted as an index of sustainable inflation performance – it might seem more appropriate to base the convergence limit on the countries' best interest rate performance.

Moreover, with regard to the exchange rate criterion (that a currency will have remained for at least two years within the 'normal fluctuation margins') the issues are even more problematical. In particular, the exchange rate criterion was drafted on the assumption that the ERM would continue to observe its original margins of 2.25 per cent, i.e. before the currency crises of 1992 and 1993. Thus, when the decision is taken on which Member States have achieved the convergence criteria necessary for accession to EMU, the European Council could interpret the Treaty criterion as meaning that a currency must be within a 'reasonably stable' relationship with its peers for two years before a decision is made about Stage III (although it is far from certain that Germany, for one, would accept less rigour than was originally envisaged).

CONCLUSION

This chapter has analysed the interest rate and exchange rate convergence criteria from the standpoint of the 'inconsistent quartet'. In particular, given the fact that free trade and increased capital mobility are a fundamental part of the ethic of European integration, we argued that there would then necessarily be a trade-off between a Member State being able to pursue an independent monetary policy (of which the interest rate is a part) and the level of exchange rate stability. Having a fixed exchange rate, as in economic and monetary union, means that a state will, in the end, have to give up its ability to conduct an independent monetary policy. This has an impact in two main ways. First, with regard to domestic politics, both domestic firms and individual consumers (i.e. the electorate) require that exchange rates are as stable and predictable as possible. It is therefore in their interests that, in particular, exchange rate convergence takes place. However, actions required to keep exchange rates stable can sometimes involve very high costs. Foreign exchange rates are always difficult to forecast and central banks are traditionally very cautious in this area. In addition, in terms of intergovernmental interests and the inconsistent quartet, contemporary economic thought generally recognises the vital part played by interest rate policy in the achievement of both internal and external balance in an economy, as well as its importance in ensuring the efficient allocation of financial resources. It is therefore important that interest rates in Europe converge, particularly because of the effect that such convergence has on the credibility of EMU's low inflation stance. Despite the progress made towards fulfilling the interest rate and exchange rate convergence criteria, however, the issue still remains of whether or not that stability will be enough to fulfil the criterion laid down at Maastricht. If it does not, the result would threaten the entire process of European integration.

NOTES

1. D. Gros and N. Thygesen, *op. cit.* (1992), p. 39.
2. Cited by John Ruskin, Introduction to *'Usury and the English Bishops'*, 1885.
3. J. A. Frieden, *op. cit.* (1994), p. 81.
4. Susan M. Nelson, *op. cit.* (1993), p. 20. The Article goes on to state that:

   '[i]f a Member State makes an alteration in its rate of exchange which is inconsistent with the objectives set out in Article 104 [i.e. that a Member State shall pursue balance of payments equilibrium, and maintain confidence in its currency] . . ., the Commission may, after consulting the Monetary Committee, authorise other Member States to take for a strictly limited period the necessary measures, . . ., in order to counter the consequences of such alteration.'

   This was the first sign that a mechanism for punishing Member States for financial imprudence was a possibility.
5. See: Charles Engel and Craig S. Hakkio, 'Exchange Rate Regimes and Volatility', *Economic Review*, vol. 78, no. 3 (1993), pp. 43–58, for an analysis with particular reference to Germany.
6. For an example of an analysis of these types of issues, see: Mark D. Partridge and Dan S. Rickman, 'Differences in State Unemployment Rates: The Role of Labour and Product Markets in Structural Shifts', *Southern Economic Journal*, vol. 6, no. 1 (1995), p. 89.
7. Wayne Sandholtz, 'Choosing Union: Monetary Politics and Maastricht', *World Politics*, 47, 1 (1993), pp. 106–107. See also the literature on optimal currency areas outlined in Chapter 1.
8. See the previous chapter for an outline of the difficulties caused by speculative currency movements in the contemporary world economy. Because the single currency of the monetary union can be expected to become one of the world's major currencies, periodic pressures on the single currency are likely as a result of capital movements between the union and outside countries (a possibility acknowledged in the text of the Maastricht Treaty, which provides for safeguard measures in the event that such capital movements are a source of serious difficulties for the operation of the union). See: Yilmaz Akyuz and Andrew Cornford, 'International Capital Movements: Some Proposals for Reform', in J. Michie and J. G. Smith, *op. cit.* (1995), p. 184.
9. For a fuller discussion of the relationship between exchange rates and fundamentals see, amongst others: S. P. Peterson, 'Forecasting dynamics and convergence to market fundamentals', *Journal of Economic Behaviour and Organization*, vol. 22, no. 3 (1993), p. 269; Alun H. Thomas, 'Expected Devaluation and Economic Fundamentals', *International Monetary Fund Staff Papers*, vol. 41, no. 2 (1994), p. 262; Shady Kholdy and Ahmed Sohrabian, 'Testing for the Relationship between Nominal Exchange Rates and Economic Fundamentals', *Global Finance Journal*, vol. 6, no. 2 (1995), p. 121; and, Hohn T. Harvey, 'Long-term Exchange Rate Movements: The Role of Fundamentals in Neoclassical Models of Exchange Rates', *Journal of Economic Issues*, vol. 30, no. 2 (1996), p. 509.

10. As, it could be said, occurred during the British crisis over the Exchange Rate Mechanism – 'Black Wednesday'. See: Andrew Crockett, (1994), *op. cit.* p. 180.

11. For a fuller analysis of this issue, see Peter B. Kenen, *op. cit.* (1995), pp. 129–30.

12. See Chapter 1 for an outline of the Three Stages of the economic and monetary union process.

13. E. Langfeldt, 'European Monetary Union: Design and Implementation', in R. Barrell (ed.), *Economic Convergence and Monetary Union in Europe*, (London: Sage for the Association for the Monetary Union of Europe and the National Institute of Economic and Social Research).

14. Conversions can and should take place through the European Central Bank and the national central banks, without recourse to the foreign exchange market. In this case, the ECB would not have to defend the locked exchange rates by intervention, and there would be little reason to worry about exchange rate crises in Stage III.

15. D. Begg, F. Giavazzi, L. Spaventa and C. Wyplosz, 'European Monetary Union – The Macro Issues', in *Monitoring European Integration: The Making of Monetary Union* (London: Centre for Economic Policy Research, 1991).

16. D. Begg et al., *op. cit.* (1991).

17. For a fuller economic discussion, see: Peter B. Kenen, *op. cit.* (1995); and Paul De Grauwe, *op. cit.* (1994).

18. Ronald MacDonald, *op. cit.* (1988), pp. 14–15.

19. Christopher Johnson, 'Fiscal and Monetary Policy in Economic and Monetary Union', *op. cit.* (1994), p. 74.

20. The vast majority of exchange rate theory suggests that an increase in a country's interest rate relative to a comparable foreign interest rate should lead to a capital inflow and an appreciation in the exchange rate (and conversely to a fall in the domestic rate – strictly speaking in real terms).

21. M. Artis, *op. cit.* (1994), p. 360.

22. C. A. E. Goodhart, *op. cit.* (1995), p. 166.

23. Compare, for example, French, Danish, or Spanish real interest rates in the winter of 1992–93 with those of Germany.

24. Nowhere is this more clearly explained than in Paul De Grauwe, *op. cit.* (1994), pp. 105–116.

25. T. Padoa-Schioppa, *op. cit.* (1988), p. 373.

26. Charles P. Kindleberger, *Power and Money* (New York: Basic Books, 1970), p. 198.

27. Rudiger Dornbusch, *op. cit.* (1993), p. 13.

28. This was not a new phenomenon, however, as this issue had been on the European agenda since the 1960s. One of its primary motors in the early years of the European Community was the Common Agricultural Policy and the threat that exchange rate instability posed to that intricate political bargain. At an international level, this linkage became especially prominent as a result of the rise in protectionism in the United States in the early 1980s (during a time of exchange rate overvaluation). As the US stance became more unilateral, so the stance of the EC Member States towards tighter monetary control became more multilateral. Moreover, the

threat of US trade protectionism and monetary unilateralism in the face of economic mismanagement stimulated both the launch of the Uruguay Round of GATT trade talks and the reinvigoration of macroeconomic policy coordination (beginning with the Plaza accord). See: Miles Kahler, *International Institutions and the Political Economy of Integration* (The Brookings Institution: Washington D.C., 1995), p. 124.

29. Benjamin Cohen, *op. cit.* (1992), p. 261.

30. There is in fact substantial anecdotal evidence that much of the private sector's support for monetary integration came precisely from such firms within the European Community.

31. J. Melitz, *op. cit.* (1988), p. 58.

32. John Cuddington, *op. cit.* (1987), p. 11.

33. This idea of 'voting with the feet' first came to prevalence through the writings of Charles Tiebout, and once again is indicative of the public choice approach to issues of international political economy. In his model, voters delineate their preferences through the device of allowing people to sort themselves out into groups of like tastes. Strategising is eliminated, and the voluntary exchange principle implicit in much of public choice is operationalised through the assumption of mobility between communities.

The Tiebout model rests on a number of extreme assumptions, however, and there are difficulties in that each additional public good on offer raises the number of polities required to a higher exponent. If the number of public goods is very large, one reaches a solution in which the number of communities equals the size of the population. Each community-individual becomes a polity with a basket of public-private goods tailored to his own tastes. This was a possible consequence of the model that Tiebout himself observed.

34. Paul De Grauwe, *op. cit.* (1994), p. 59.

35. *Ibid.*, p. 54.

36. *Ibid.*, pp. 54–5. Indeed, recently, some analysts have argued that France and Germany, as the 'core' states in the EU, should be relaunched on a growth path before EMU takes place – and one way of doing this would be to devalue their currencies. This would have the effect of actually creating credibility in the eyes of market opinions, because it would be a 'first-class [exercise] in credible joint-decision making before EMU'. See: Henri Bourguinat and Alfred Steinherr, 'The weak heart of Europe needs stimulus, not surgery', *The European*, 3–9 October, (1996), p. 20.

37. David Cameron, *op. cit.* (1992), pp. 56–59.

38. See, for example, John B. Goodman, 'Monetary Policy and Financial Deregulation in France', *French Politics and Society*, vol. 10, no. 4 (1992), pp. 31–40.

39. For a discussion of trade openness, see: D. A. Cameron, 'The Expansion of the Public Economy: A Comparative Analysis', *American Political Science Review*, 72 (1978), pp. 1243–61.

40. A. Icard, 'Exchange Rate Stability and the European Construction', in C. Border, E. Girardin and J. Melitz (eds), *European Currency Crises and After* (Manchester: Manchester University Press, 1994), pp. 244–45.

41. *Ibid.*, p. 245.

8 An Elysian Harmony

The money changers have fled from their high seats in the temple of our civilization. We may now restore that temple to the ancient truths. The measure of the restoration lies in the extent to which we apply social values more noble than mere monetary profit.

F. D. Roosevelt, 4 March 1933.

INTRODUCTION

The convergence criteria are at the heart of economic and monetary union in Europe. In the absence of reform of the Maastricht Treaty, they provide the clearest set of economic targets which countries must meet on their road to EMU. Yet, the process of economic and monetary union is, as we have seen during the course of this analysis, not only an economic process but also a political one. Thus, for a full explanation of the motives for such targets to take place, what is required is an examination of the convergence criteria both in terms of economic rationale and political expediency.

This analysis has used, largely, the methodologies of economics and of international political economy to examine the reasoning behind the nature of the Maastricht convergence criteria. With the latter in mind we have attempted, in each chapter, to examine a particular criterion, not only in terms of the economic rationale, but also in terms of the three basic but related issues which are of particular importance in any examination of contemporary international economic relations: the relationship between economics and politics; the relationship between domestic and international factors, and the role of the state. From these analyses emerged a number of particularly pertinent issues.

ECONOMICS AND POLITICS

In terms of the relationship between economics and politics, the convergence criteria represent the result of both considered economic judgement and political bargaining between the Member States. At the Intergovernmental Conference in 1991, the result of which was the Maastricht Treaty, one of the first issues of concern was the nature of the convergence conditions necessary to allow a state to proceed to

Stage III of EMU. From the outset, the concern was with resolving differences in the Member States' positions.

First, with regard to the technicalities and legalities of the convergence criteria, one significant consideration was whether or not they should be given treaty status (i.e. whether they should be specified in the Treaty or in a protocol annexed to the Treaty) in which case they could be changed only by a unanimous vote; or whether they could be ensconced in secondary Community legislation, in which case they could be changed by qualified majority.[1] Those for whom the achievement of the convergence criteria might prove difficult were very much in favour of the latter proposal, whereas those states with far stronger economies were much more in favour of the convergence criteria being enshrined within the Treaty. The solution adopted was very much in keeping with the views of those states with a more significant bargaining position, that is that the convergence criteria may be changed only by a unanimous decision of the Council.[2]

Second, with regard to solving the issue of how assessment should actually be examined, we have seen throughout the course of the analysis that the economic reasoning behind the actual variables which are used for such measurement was at times tenuous. The actual discussion was conducted at the IGC and, for the more technical aspects, in the Monetary Committee. Membership of the two bodies was largely the same. However, the technical nature of the matters being discussed and the fact that those ministers and national officials who were keen on seeing the process of European integration continue to move forward were preoccupied with the parallel IGC on political union, led the consensus over the precise nature of the convergence criteria to drift compared to the level of agreement amongst interested parties regarding the provisions put forward earlier by the Delors Committee.[3] In the end, the result was a set of convergence criteria which were sufficient to pass the Maastricht Treaty ratification process, but which did not necessarily reflect the sound principles of economic logic (see, in particular the discussions over the nature of the criteria in Chapters 4 and 5). Nevertheless, with the convergence criteria in place, the issue then became who would actually meet those requirements. In this regard, one point which has been emphasised throughout this analysis is that the relationship between domestic and international factors is crucial.

DOMESTIC AND INTERNATIONAL FACTORS

In Chapter 4, we examined European price convergence from an international political economy perspective, and discovered that certain characteristics inherent within the domestic society would strongly influence to the achievement or non-achievement of the inflation requirement. These included structural factors, such as the nature of organised labour unions, as well as issues such as the aspirations of the incumbent national government. These domestic factors were important in considering whether or not a Member State could be said to favour a low-inflation stance. Moreover, the issue of the creation of supranational institutions for the achievement and maintenance of price stability led to a discussion of the nature of credibility and reputation in these institutions and how this could be achieved. Domestic and international factors go hand in hand in this, because the European institutions which have been designed to achieve price stability will only achieve such stability if the Member States relinquish their national authority in this area to a supranational institution and, perhaps more importantly, if speculators in international markets actually believe that this has taken place. Only when the latter has occurred will the supranational authority be said to have credibility in the decision-making process.

In Chapter 5, we considered this issue of the domestic policy-making environment further by examining the budgetary convergence criterion. In particular, we took a public choice perspective to consider why some states may be expected to have larger budget deficits than others. Issues such as the type of government (coalition, majority, etc.), and its duration have long been cited in the literature as being instrumental in determining the size of a state's budget deficit. More importantly for this analysis, however, we can see quite clearly that the same is true in regard to the ability of the Member States to achieve the budgetary convergence criteria. Changes in the ideological composition of the governments of the Member States, coupled with the proportionality of the electoral process in countries such as Italy and Belgium, lead directly to the conclusion that the current national fiscal policy-making environments of many of the Member States are conducive not to sustainability of the budgetary position but to unsustainability. Moreover, the impact that this has is not only relevant with regard to the domestic policy-making environment: difficulties in achieving the budgetary criteria will eventually impact upon the international decision-making environment. The reason for this is that failure to achieve the budgetary criteria will present an eventual threat to the anti-inflation commitment of EMU in Europe, a factor which has obvious repercussions on the attitudes of speculators in international financial and goods markets to the monetary integration project.

What was gauged from these chapters on the price and budgetary criteria, then, was the significance of the relationship between domestic and international factors to their analysis. In particular, the domestic policy-making environment was the significant factor in deciding the likelihood of whether these criteria were met, and this in turn impacted upon how the process of EMU was viewed in the international arena. For the analysis of the interest rate and exchange rate criteria, however, the causality was reversed in that the important factor was, instead, how the international policy-making environment constrained policymakers in the domestic arena. In particular, the methodology of the inconsistent quartet demonstrated that a group of independent countries cannot simultaneously have free trade, capital mobility, fixed exchange rates and autonomy in monetary policy making. The increasing integration of capital markets makes it impossible to pursue an independent monetary policy without the threat of either major trade conflicts or significant exchange rate volatility. With regard to economic and monetary union in Europe, this means that the policy of relinquishing national monetary policies in order to ensure exchange rate stability is a sound one. The issue is that actions taken to keep exchange rates stable can sometimes involve very high costs. Thus, in the long run, the achievement of exchange rate convergence, as well as the necessity of interest rate convergence in order to ensure external and internal balance in an economy, may prove problematical. In these circumstances the issue then becomes who will achieve the convergence criteria and, perhaps more importantly, what will happen if, as seems increasingly likely, economic and monetary union leads to a European financial framework where some states are part of an EMU and other states are not – what is referred to as a 'two-speed' Europe. In this case, the role of the individual Member States in the policy process becomes paramount.

EMU AND THE ROLE OF THE STATE: FRUITION OR REFORM?

Although the European Commission forecasts, optimistically, that a significant number of EU Member States will be capable of meeting the convergence criteria by the time the European Council takes its decision, given the current economic position of many of the Member States vis-à-vis the targets laid down in the Maastricht Treaty (as reported in earlier chapters) as well as some of the political attitudes towards them, it seems increasingly likely that a number of Member States will be unsuccessful in their bid to join EMU at the earliest opportunity and that the path towards a 'two-speed Europe' is an inevitable one.[4]

In this regard, there are a number of issues which are particularly worthy of examination. First, in terms of the type of institutional framework which would deal with such an arrangement, as was noted elsewhere, the Maastricht Treaty provisions on EMU embrace two basic principles. The first is that the transition to monetary union should be gradual: a long transition period is felt necessary in order that states have sufficient time to attempt to meet the convergence criteria. The second is that not all EU Member States are required to join the monetary union at the same time: their accession to the union is made dependent on satisfying the convergence criteria. If they do not do this they are not allowed into EMU. It has always, then, been considered that an EMU without all of the Member States was a possibility, particularly given the British and Danish attitudes to the possibility of such an arrangement as laid down in the Treaty. The debate at Maastricht, then, was how the question of such a 'two-speed' scenario was going to be resolved institutionally. This was particularly pressing in the light of the care which had been taken over designing institutions which would lend the future economic and monetary union a high degree of credibility, as we have seen in previous chapters.[5]

The debate over an appropriate institutional framework in the event of a two-speed Europe has focused around two issues in particular. Those governments of Member States who it seemed would be unlikely to proceed to EMU after the initial European Council reports were concerned lest they be left out of future EMU decision making. Under these circumstances, they wanted (if indeed a two-speed EMU took place and they were to proceed at a slower speed) their national central bank governors to continue to take part in the discussions of the Governing Council of the European Central Bank, even if they could not vote on policy.[6] On the other hand, those governments of Member States who expected to proceed at a faster pace wanted the slower states to be excluded from any formal role in the EMU decision-making process.

In the end, the Maastricht Treaty reflected a compromise between these two positions. Article 109l asserts that if a 'two-speed' Europe does occur, a 'General Council' will be established as a third decision-making body of the European Central Bank. Its membership would consist of the president and vice-president of the ECB and the governors of all the Member States' national central banks; and its role would be to take over the responsibilities of the European Monetary Institute for those member States who have not yet achieved the convergence criteria. The General Council would thus be entrusted with the job of continuing to help with regard to the transition process of the non-EMU states, for example in strengthening the coordination of monetary policies with a view to ensuring price stability, and in monitoring exchange rate stability. At the same time, however, the functions of the General Council will be restricted in that it will not have the authority to make any policy recommendations to individual Member States or indeed to be consulted in advance about the nature of the future development of monetary policies within the economic and monetary union.

The actual significance of this institutional framework to the future European policy landscape is, not unnaturally, highly dependent upon how many non-EMU participant Member States there turn out to be and how important these particular Member States are to the present EU decision-making apparatus. If there are very few and they are minor actors in European policy making (i.e. some of the smaller states, or some of the more recent members) then there will still be the need for consultation over monetary and exchange rate policies – but, in general, they will have to adapt their policies to those of the ECB and peg their currencies to the Euro if they wish to qualify for eventual EMU participation. If, however, there are a significant number of non-EMU Member States and some of these are major actors (as is a more likely scenario, particularly given the fact that the UK, for one, is highly unlikely to be among the 'fast-speed' EMU participants) then the issue of policy co-ordination will be a far more significant one, not only to the non-EMU participants but to the EMU participants as well.[7] Under such conditions, the ECB and the non-EMU Member States' national central banks, would have to closely consult. Despite these institutional mechanisms, however, doubts still remain as to the way in which exchange rates should be managed in what is the increasingly likely situation that there will be a two-speed Europe.

Exchange Rate Management

As was noted earlier, the achievement of exchange rate stability has been a continuing goal in the drive towards European monetary integration. It is surprising, however, given the extent of the concern which has historically been expressed over exchange rate management in Europe, that the question of such management in a two-speed Europe should be dealt with so ambiguously. In fact, even though institutionally the General Council is charged with contributing to the arrangements for irrevocably fixing the exchange rates of the non-EMU states against the participant EMU states, the Maastricht Treaty is actually unclear about how exactly this should be done. For example, Article 109k of the Maastricht Treaty does state that unsuccessful EMU states cannot enter Stage III until they meet the conditions which call for 'the observance of the normal fluctuation margins provided for by the exchange-rate mechanism of the European Monetary System'.[8] Nowhere does the Treaty impose any corresponding responsibility on the European Central Bank to manage exchange rates between the Euro and non-EMU currencies.

There are, however, basically two ways of managing such rates. The first is to have the non-EMU Member States unilaterally peg their currencies to the Euro and then charge them with maintaining their exchange rates within predetermined bands. To do this, they would have to intervene using their own currency reserves and would set their interest rates at levels which would maintain exchange rate stability. Assuming such responsibilities, however, might also lead them to insist upon the right to alter their exchange rates as and when necessary and, moreover, without the permission of the European Central Bank, something which would be contrary to the spirit of ever increasing monetary integration in Europe.

On the other hand, exchange rates could be managed such that the decision-making would be shared between the ECB and the non-EMU national central banks – the so-called 'residual EMS' framework. Central rates would then be chosen on a collective basis and the ECB would intervene whenever the Euro reached its margins (and would be expected to adjust interest rates in order to maintain exchange rate stability).

Although both policy makers and academics have expressed support for this 'residual EMS' framework in the face of a two-speed Europe (most notably in a recent speech by the president of the EMI, Alexandre Lamfalussy)[9] there is always the likelihood that such an arrangement might interfere with the ECB's goal of achieving price stability.[10] In addition, there is also the issue of whether or not a 'residual EMS' would place undue strain upon those economies yet to proceed to EMU. For example, it is unlikely that if a country fails to satisfy the exchange rate criterion for entering Stage III at the earliest opportunity (whilst being in the Exchange Rate Mechanism with the rest of the Member States) that it would find it any easier to satisfy the criterion after some of the other states have already embarked upon the third stage. Moreover, the EMS crises examined in Chapter 3 have only complicated the scenario further. In particular, and given the British and Italian withdrawals from the Exchange Rate Mechanism, the 1992–93 crises made it more likely that there will be several countries unable to achieve EMU at the faster speed. This would have an impact not only upon the non-EMU participants, but also on the EMU participants. Again, the significance of this depends very much on the number of non-EMU participants and on their significance to the EU decision-making process. If they are all small countries, the monetary policy apparatus of the ECB will not be greatly effected. If, on the other hand, some of the non-EMU countries are large and significant players in the EU (again, as is more likely), the European Central Bank may find its position in monetary policy decision making compromised. With such difficulties in mind, it becomes even more important to consider the issue of whether a one-speed monetary union could, or would, actually take place.

A One-Speed European Monetary Union

The process of economic and monetary union in Europe is still at a stage when many difficulties have yet to be overcome. Moreover once, as is likely, a two-speed Europe is embarked upon, those difficulties are set not to decrease but to increase in magnitude as concerns mount over the need to draw the non-EMU Member States into the EMU participation. In this regard, there are two, possibly hazardous, scenarios. The first is that a non-EMU country might have an incentive never to participate in EMU. The second is that the EMU countries might never admit those countries that stayed outside.

The question of the incentive for non-EMU states to eventually participate in EMU stems from the notion that those countries who traditionally take a low-inflation policy stance (such as Germany) may not invite the high-inflation non-EMU states to participate until the latter have sufficiently diminished their inflation bias.[11] If the EMU participants wait too long, however, before admitting additional members (i.e. until after the previously high-inflation Member States have been enjoying the benefits of low and stable inflation for a considerable period of time) then the non-EMU participants will be gaining from their new, low and stable, inflation stance, without the policy limitations of being a member of the economic and monetary union., i.e. the non-EMU state will be free-riding. Alessandra Casella, in an examination of the dynamics of small countries in a currency union, similarly comes to the conclusion that it might be in a non-EMU Member State's best interests to remain outside a one-speed EMU.[12] In particular, he argues that unless such a country can exercise a significant influence upon the decision-making process in a monetary union, it might be better to remain outside. Doing this may actually lead a small non-participant EMU state to have more of an influence on policymaking than its size warrants.

With regard to the second possible scenario, that EMU participant countries might never actually want to admit those countries that have initially stayed outside, the first issue of importance is to consider why a country with a low and credible inflation stance (e.g., Germany) would agree to help other countries, without such economic attributes, to achieve them. The answer is that Member States with a low and stable inflation stance have a significant amount of bargaining power because of this superior economic position. If, however, they are to maintain this power, they must ensure that when economic and monetary union takes place they are at the heart of the institutional process and, in particular, they must hold a dominant position within the mechanisms of the European Central Bank.[13]

For example, if, following Alesina and Grilli, we assume that in 1999 only three Member States make the transition to EMU in Europe, we can see that those three Member States must subsequently resolve the issue, by majority, of whether or not to allow additional members to join EMU. Given such a situation, it is possible that those first three countries will never choose to admit subsequent members (for example, because of their fear over the future monetary policy stance of the enlarged EMU) and a one-speed EMU will never take place. Under such circumstances, embarking upon a two-speed EMU would appear to threaten the entire integration process. What would be important is whether or not the EMU-participants can be compensated for their concerns over future EMU monetary policy stance in return for allowing additional members to be admitted, thus safeguarding the integration project. As an example, it is often stated that Germany has nothing to gain economically from EMU, the reason being that Germany already has the dominant economic position in Europe (see Chapter 4). On the other hand, Germany could be argued to have something to gain politically, in that monetary union is a necessary step towards the future political integration of Europe which Germany desires. In this way, the increased political role which Germany has sought in the post-World War II period would be able to be achieved.[14]

This section has outlined the possible difficulties which a two-speed EMU might face. In particular, these difficulties are magnified depending upon whether the non-EMU participants are large or small in number and/or important or unimportant in terms of political leverage. The fact that the UK and Denmark are likely to be two of the nonparticipant EMU states tends to suggest that the difficulties which a twospeed EMU would bring with it would be significant. Moreover, one additional consideration is that the EC may admit more members. Indeed, an EU enlargement would be likely to present much greater problems with regard to the appropriate institutional arrangements and entry times for new EMU members. For example, the prospective accession of Poland, Hungary, the Czech Republic and other eastern European states – poorer, more agricultural, and threatening the voting weight of smaller existing members – may make a complex multi-speed design even more likely. Whether we are considering non-EMU states from the existing membership of fifteen, or future non-EMU members from an enlarged Europe, relations between EMU participants, EMU-institutions and the non-participant countries are likely to require close attention for many years to come.

CONCLUSION

'By the end of the century, Europe will have a single currency. It will be strong and stable. This is the wish of the leaders and peoples in signing and then ratifying the Treaty on European Union.'

These opening lines of the Green Paper on the Practical Arrangements for the Introduction of the Single Currency demonstrate the confidence which the European Commission has regarding the viability of the EMU project.[15] The achievement of the convergence criteria is seen as being of primary importance in achieving this long-term goal, yet, in many ways, the Maastricht convergence criteria can actually be seen as being obstacles to the process of monetary union in Europe because of the possible difficulties in their achievement rather than advantages. Although the Treaty allows considerable discretion for the Council of Ministers in deciding whether countries are fit to join the union, the convergence criteria still create the opportunity for political conflict.[16] For example, although, as we have seen in this chapter, the possibility that a two-speed Europe would result from the EMU project has always been present, the political realities of such a scenario are just beginning to be savoured by the possible non-participant EMU states. For example, the tensions amongst the Member States increased on October 1 of this year when French President Jacques Chirac said that the monetary union start date would come too quickly for some countries, notably the Italians.[17] The Italians quickly retaliated by summoning the French ambassador in Rome and threatening to cancel an imminent summit meeting to be held between President Chirac and Prime Minister Romano Perodi.

Whatever happens, however, the criteria must be adhered to. Anything less than this would ensure that the task of creating credibility for the European single currency would prove fruitless. The reason for this is that non-achievement of the convergence criteria would lead to the need for a complete review of the EMU process, and how it could be attained. Thus, just how strong the belief in these criteria is can be seen in the introduction to the Green Paper, with the words: 'the need to raise awareness of the technical issues involved does not in any way weaken the primary importance of economic convergence. This is at the heart of the Treaty and the indispensable condition for a strong and stable single currency, at least as strong as the strongest national currency.'

Despite this, however, the hope that all fifteen Member States will go through as a one-speed Europe is a vain one. Not only does this cause practical difficulties for the realisation of the EMU project, but it should also be borne in mind that failure to achieve the Maastricht objectives entails serious dangers for the Single European Market and for the Union itself. Economic and monetary union was by far the most ambitious objective of Maastricht. All EU governments, except Britain and Denmark, have bound themselves by Treaty to the aim of EMU. If the objective now were to be abandoned or postponed indefinitely, contrary to the Treaty's terms, it would be the most serious failure since the founding of the Community. A return to devaluation of EU currencies would weaken the Single Market more than if the goal of EMU had never been declared. This is because a return to a regime of flexible European exchange rates would allow the Member States to use the exchange rate as a way of improving national competitiveness (see the arguments in Chapter 6). In the light of such circumstances, states could no longer be said to be holding to the tenets of the Single Market, because of the impact of such 'competitive devaluations' on the free movement of goods and services. The result would be a return to national protectionism as Member States attempt to safeguard their domestic economies in the face of European competition. The goals of the Single European Market would have been overturned. For reasons such as these, it is important that the goal of economic and monetary union in Europe be successfully achieved – at least to what can be seen to be a credible extent. However, one issue must continually be borne in mind in regard to the practicality of such EMU arrangements: that in the light of our present analysis whatever happens, the concerns of the domestic and international arenas must be reconciled. In order to attempt to achieve EMU, Member States must pursue domestic policies which are not always in the interests of the electorate. Such policies, however, have to be followed in order that the EMU process attains credibility in the international marketplace. Only when this is done, can we truly say that we are anywhere on the road to a United States of Europe.

NOTES

1. Lorenzo Bini-Smaghi, Tommaso Padoa-Schioppa and Francesco Papadia, *op. cit.* (1994), p. 23.
2. See Appendix A: Treaty, Article 104c, No. 14, and Protocol on the Convergence Criteria, Article 6.
3. Lorenzo Bini-Smaghi, Tommaso Padoa-Schioppa, and Francesco Papadia, *op. cit.* (1994), p. 24.
4. The European Commission, 'Preparing for EMU stage 3', *The Week in Europe*, 13 June (1996).
5. For an excellent discussion of this issue, see: John T. Woolley, 'Policy Credibility and European Monetary Institutions', in Alberta M. Sbragia, *Europolitics* (Washington D.C.: The Brookings Institution, 1992), pp. 157–90.
6. The responsibilities of the Governing Council are defined in Article 12 of the Statute of the ESCB, in that it:

> 'shall adopt the guidelines and take the decisions necessary to ensure the performance of the tasks entrusted to the ESCB under this Treaty and this Statute. The Governing Council shall formulate the monetary policy of the Community including, as appropriate, decisions relating to intermediate monetary objectives, key interest rates and the supply of reserves in the ESCB, and shall establish the necessary guidelines for their implementation.'

7. Peter B. Kenen, *op. cit.* (1995), p. 147.
8. From this it can be argued that non-EMU states will still be expected to assume an exchange rate obligation of some form.
9. Mark Milner, 'ERM mark 2 second-best plan, says Lamfalussy', *The Times*, 20 June (1996), p. 19.
10. A factor which was given much attention at the Maastricht summit. See Article 109 of the Treaty on European Union.
11. Phillippe Martin, 'Free-riding, convergence and two-speed monetary unification in Europe', *European Economic Review*, 39, 7 (1995), pp. 1345–1364.
12. Alessandra Casella, 'Participation in a Currency Union', *American Economic Review*, 82, 4 (1992), pp. 847–63.
13. Alberto Alesina and Vittorio Grilli, 'On the Feasibility of a One-Speed or Multispeed European Monetary Union, *Economics and Politics*, 5, 2, (1993).
14. An additional issue is whether or not it might be in the interests of the non-EMU to form their own union, a question which goes to the heart of the differentiated integration debate. See, for example: B. Langeheine and U. Weinstock, 'Graduated integration: a modest path towards progress', *Journal of Common Market Studies*, 23 (1985), pp. 185–97; H. Wallace with A. Ridley, *Europe: The Challenge of Diversity*, Chatham House Paper, No. 29 (1985), London; and, Alexander C-G Stubb, 'A Categorisation of Differentiated Integration', *Journal of Common Market Studies*, 34 (1996).
15. *Green Paper on the Practical Arrangements for the Introduction of the Single Currency*, Office for Official Publications of the European Communities (1995).
16. Paul de Grauwe, *op. cit.* (1994), pp. 161–162.
17. Victor Smart, 'Tensions rise as monetary union rolls on', *The European*, 3–9 October (1996), p. 1.

Selected Bibliography

F. Abraham and P. Van Rompuy, 'Regional Convergence in the European Monetary Union', *Papers in Regional Science: The Journal of the RSAI*, 74 (1995), pp. 125–142.

N. Abuaf and P. Jorion, 'Purchasing power parity in the long run', *Journal of Finance*, 45 (1990), pp. 157–174.

M. Adler and B. Lehmann , 'Deviations from purchasing power parity in the long-run', *Journal of Finance*, 38 (1983), pp. 1471–87.

R. K. Akhtar and R. S. Hilton , 'Effects of Exchange Rate Uncertainty on German and U.S. Trade', *Federal Reserve Bank of New York Quarterly Review*, 9 (1984), pp. 7–16.

Yilmaz Akyuz and Andrew Cornford, 'International Capital Movements: Some Proposals for Reform', in J. Michie and J. G. Smith (eds), *Managing the Global Economy* (Oxford: Oxford University Press, 1995), pp. 172–196.

Alberto Alesina, 'Macroeconomics and Politics', *NBER Macroeconomics Annual* (1988), pp. 13–61.

A. Alesina and A. Drazen, 'Why are stabilisations delayed?', *American Economic Review*, 81, 5 (1991).

A. Alesina and V. Grilli, 'On the Feasibility of a One-Speed or Multispeed European Monetary Union', *Economics and Politics*, 5, 2 (1993).

A. Alesina and R. Perotti, 'The Political Economy of Budget Deficits', *IMF Staff Papers*, vol. 2, no. 1 (1995), pp. 1–32.

A. Alesina and G. Tabellini, 'Positive and normative theories of public debt and inflation in historical perspective', *European Economic Review*, 36 (1992), pp. 337–344.

A. Alesina and G. Tabellini, 'A Positive Theory of Fiscal Deficit and Government Debt', *Review of Economic Studies*, 57 (1990), pp. 403–414.

C. Allsopp, 'Inflation', in A. Boltho (ed.), *The European Economy, Growth and Crisis* (Oxford, Oxford University Press, 1982).

J. A. Alt and K. A. Chrystal, *Political Economics* (Brighton, Sussex: Wheatsheaf Books, 1983).

A. Amin, B.Gills, R. Palan and P. Taylor, 'Editorial: Forum for Heterodox International Political Economy', *Review of International Political Economy*, 1 (1994), pp. 1–12.

J. W. Angell, 'International trade under interconvertible paper', *Quarterly Journal of Economics*, 36 (1922), pp. 309–324.

C. Archer, *Organising Western Europe*, (London: Edward Arnold 1990).

M. J. Artis, 'The European Monetary System: A Review of the Research Record', in Graham R. Bird and R. MacDonald (eds), *The International Financial Regime* (Surrey: Surrey University Press, 1990), pp. 145–196.

M. J. Artis, 'European Monetary Union', in M. J. Artis and N. Lee (eds), *The Economics of European Union* (Oxford: Oxford University Press, 1994), pp. 346–367.

M. J. Artis, and M. P. Taylor, 'Exchange Rates, Interest Rates, Capital Controls and the European Monetary System: Assessing the Track Record', in

F. Giavazzi, S. Micossi and M. Miller (eds), *The European Monetary System* (Cambridge: Cambridge University Press, 1988), pp. 185–206.

M. J. Artis, and M. P. Taylor, 'The Achievements of the European Monetary System', *The Economic and Social Review*, 20 (1989), pp. 121–145.

C. L. F. Attfield, D. Demery and N. W. Duck, Rational Expectations in Macroeconomics, *An Introduction to Theory and Evidence*, 2nd ed. (Oxford: Basil Blackwell, 1991).

G. D. Baer and T. Padoa-Schioppa, 'The Werner Report revisited', in *Report on Economic and Monetary Union in the Community* ('Delors Report'), Office for Official Publications of the European Community (1989).

M. J. Bailey, G. S. Tavlas and M. Ulan, 'The Impact of Exchange Rate Volatility on Export Growth: Some Theoretical Considerations and Empirical Results', *Journal of Policy Modelling*, 9 (1987), pp. 225–43.

B. Balassa, 'The Purchasing Power Parity Doctrine: A Reappraisal', *Journal of Political Economy*, 72 (1964), pp. 584–596.

Lionel Barber, 'Europe's Political Co-operation: An American Perspective on European Union', *Europe*, December, no. 301 (1990).

R. J. Barro and D. B. Gordon , 'Rules, discretion and reputation in a model of monetary policy', *Journal of Monetary Economics*, 12 (1983), pp. 101–121.

Robert J. Barro and Vittorio Grilli, *European Macroeconomics* (New York: McMillan, 1995).

R. J. Bartel, 'International Monetary Unions: the 19th Century Experience', *Journal of European Economic History*, 3 (1974), pp. 689–704.

Michael J. Baun, 'The Maastricht Treaty as High Politics', *Political Science Quarterly*, 110, 4 (1995–96), pp. 605–24.

Marianne Baxter, 'Real exchange rates and real interest rate differentials – have we missed the business cycle relationship?', *Journal of Monetary Economics*, vol. 33 (1994), pp. 5–37.

Marianne Baxter and Alan C. Stockman, 'Business Cycles and the Exchange Rate Regime: some international evidence', *Journal of Monetary Economics*, vol. 23, no. 3 (1989).

D. Begg, 'Discussion – Economic Growth and Exchange Rates in the European Monetary System: Their Trade Effects in a Changing External Environment', in F. Giavazzi, S. Micossi and M. Miller (eds), *The European Monetary System* (Cambridge: Cambridge University Press, 1988), pp. 178–182.

D. Begg, F. Giavazzi, L. Spaventa and C. Wyplosz, 'European Monetary Union – The Macro Issues', in *Monitoring European Integration: The Making of Monetary Union* (London: Centre for Economic Policy Research, 1991).

J. Bendor and D. Mukherjee, 'Institutional Structure and the Logic of Ongoing Collective Action', *American Political Science Review*, 81 (1987), pp. 129–54.

W. T. Bianco and R. H. Bates, 'Co-operation by Design: Leadership, Structure and Collective Dilemmas', *American Political Science Review*, 84 (1990), pp. 133–47.

Lorenzo Bini-Smaghi, Tommaso Padoa-Schioppa and Francesco Papadia, 'The Transition to EMU in the Maastricht Treaty', *Princeton University Essays in International Finance*, No. 194, November (1994).

G. R. Bird, and R. MacDonald (eds), *The International Financial Regime* (Surrey: Surrey University Press, 1990).

O. J. Blanchard and P. A. Muet, 'Competitiveness through disinflation: an assessment of the French macroeceonomic strategy', *Economic Policy*, 16 (1993), pp. 11–56.

A. Blundell-Wignall and F. Browne, 'Increasing Financial Market Integration: Real Exchange Rates and Macroeconomic Adjustment' (1991), OECD Working Paper.

Maria Bogucka, 'The Monetary Crisis of the XVIIth Century and its Social and Psychological Consequences in Poland', *Journal of European Economic History*, vol. 4, no. 1 (1975).

A. Boltho (ed.), *The European Economy: Growth and Crisis* (Oxford: Oxford University Press, 1982).

K.-D. Borchardt, *European Integration, The origins and growth of the European Union*, 4th ed. (Luxembourg: Office for Official Publications of the European Communities (1995).

J. C. Brada and J. A. Mendez, 'Exchange Rate Risk, Exchange Rate Regimes and the Volume of International Trade', *Kyklos*, 41 (1988), pp. 263–280.

W. H. Branson, 'Comment on Frenkel', *European Economic Review*, 16 (1981), pp. 167–171.

W. H. Branson, 'Discussion – The Role of the Exchange Rate Regime in a Disinflation: Empirical Evidence on the European Monetary System', in F. Giavazzi, S. Micossi and M. Miller (eds), *The European Monetary System* (Cambridge: Cambridge University Press, 1988), pp. 108–111.

A. Britton and D. Mayes, *Achieving Monetary Union in Europe* (London: SAGE, 1992).

K. Brunner and A. H. Meltzer (eds), *The Phillips Curve and Labour Markets,* Carnegie-Rochester Conference Series on Public Policy, 1 (Amsterdam: North Holland, 1985).

K. Brunner and A. H. Meltzer (eds), *Understanding Monetary Regimes*, Carnegie-Rochester Conference Series on Public Policy, 22 (Amsterdam: North Holland, 1985).

M. Bruno and J. Sachs, *Economics of Worldwide Inflation* (Oxford: Basil Blackwell, 1985).

J. M. Buchanan, 'La Scienza Delle Finanze: The Italian Tradition in Fiscal Theory', in *Fiscal Theory and Political Economy* (Chapel Hill, North Carolina: University of North Carolina Press, 1960), pp. 145–73.

J. M. Buchanan and R. E. Wagner, *Democracy in Deficit: The Political Legacy of Lord Keynes* (New York: Academic Press, 1977).

W. Buiter, G. Corsetti and N. Roubini, 'Excessive deficits: sense and nonsense in the Treaty of Maastricht', *Economic Policy*, 16 (1993), pp. 57–100.

R. C. K. Burdekin, C. Wihlborg and T. D. Willett, 'A Monetary Constitution Case for an Independent European Central Bank', *The World Economy*, March (1992).

P. J. Cain, *Economic Foundations of British Overseas Expansion, 1815–1914* (London: Macmillan, 1980).

L. Calmfors and J. Driffill, 'Bargaining Structure, Corporatism and Macroeconomic Performance', *Economic Policy*, 6, pp. 13–61.

D. Cameron, 'The Expansion of the Public Economy: A Comparative Analysis', *American Political Science Review*, 72 (1978), pp. 1243–61.

D. R. Cameron, 'The 1992 Initiative: Causes and Consequences' in A. Sbragia (ed.), *Euro-politics* (Washington: The Brookings Institution, 1992), pp. 23–74.

J. Y. Campbell, and R. H. Clarida 'The Dollar and Real Interest Rates', in A. Meltzer and K. Brunner (eds), *Carnegie-Rochester Conference Series on Public Policy*, 24 (North Holland: Amsterdam 1987).

G. Cassel, 'The Present Situation of the Foreign Exchanges I', *Economic Journal*, 26 (1916), pp. 62–65.

G. Cassel, 'The Present Situation of the Foreign Exchanges II', *Economic Journal*, 26 (1916), pp. 319–323.

G. Cassel, 'Comment', *Economic Journal*, 30 (1920), pp. 44–45.

G. Cassel, *The World's Monetary Problems* (London: Constable, 1921).

G. Cassel, *Post-war Monetary Stabilisation* (New York: Columbia University Press, 1928).

G. Cassel, *Money and Foreign Exchange after 1919* (London: Macmillan, 1930).

Alessandra Casella, 'Participation in a Currency Union', *American Economic Review*, 82, 4, (1992), pp. 847–63.

A. Chrissanthaki and D. M. Nachane , 'Purchasing power parity in the short and long run: a reappraisal of the post-1973 evidence', *Applied Economics*, 23 (1991), pp. 1257–1268.

E.-M. Claasen and E. Peree, 'Discussion – Exchange Rates, Interest Rates, Capital Controls and the European Monetary System: Assessing the Track Record', in F. Giavazzi, S. Micossi and M. Miller (eds), *The European Monetary System* (Cambridge: Cambridge University Press, 1988), pp. 206–210.

Inis Claude, *Swords into Ploughshares*, (New York: Random House, 1956).

D. P. Cobham, 'Strategies for Monetary Integration Revisited', *Journal of Common Market Studies*, 27 (1989), pp. 203–218.

D. P. Cobham, 'European Monetary Integration: A Survey of Recent Literature', *Journal of Common Market Studies*, 29 (1991), pp. 362–383.

P. Coffey, and J. R. Presley, *European Monetary Integration* (London: Macmillan, 1971).

N. Colchester and D. Buchan, *Europe Relaunched: Truths and Illusions on the Way to 1992* (London: The Economist Books/ Hutchinson, 1990).

S. M. Collins, 'Inflation and the European Monetary System', in F. Giavazzi, S. Micossi and M. Miller (eds) (Cambridge: Cambridge University Press, 1988), pp. 112–136.

Committee for the Study of Economic and Monetary Union, *Report on Economic and Monetary Union in the European Community (The Delor's Report)* (Luxembourg: Office for Official Publications of the European Community, 1989).

W. M. Corden, *Economic Policy, Exchange Rates and the International Currency System* (Oxford: Oxford University Press, 1994).

C. Corsetti and N. Roubini, 'Fiscal Deficits, Public Debt and Government Solvency: Evidence from OECD Countries', *Journal of the Japanese and International Economies*, 5, 4 (1991), pp. 354–80.

C. C. Coughlin and K. Koedijk , 'What Do We Know About the Long-Run Real Exchange Rate?', *St Louis Federal Reserve Bank Review*, 72 (1990), pp. 36–48.

Council-Commission of the EC Report to the Council and the Commission on the Realization by Stages of Economic and Monetary Union in the Community – 'Werner Report', Supplement to the *Bulletin*, 11 (1970).

Robert Cox and Harold Jacobson, *The Anatomy of Influence: Decisionmaking in International Organisations* (New Haven, Conn.: Yale University Press, 1983).

A. Cukierman and A. Meltzer, 'A Political Theory of Government Debt in a Neo-Ricardian Framework', *American Economic Review*, 79 (1989), pp. 353–98.

A. Cukierman, S. Edwards and G. Tabellini, 'Seigniorage and political instability', *American Economic Review*, 82, 3 (1992).

D. O. Cushman, 'The Effects of Real Exchange Rate Risk on International Trade', *Journal of International Economics*, 24 (1983), pp. 45–63.

Keith Cuthbertson and Mark P. Taylor, *Macroeconomic Systems*, (London: Basil Blackwell, 1987).

P. Dankert, 'The European Community – Past, Present and Future', *Journal of Common Market Studies*, 21 (1983), pp. 3–18.

M. Darby, 'Does purchasing power parity work?', *NBER Working Paper*, (No. 607, 1980).

M. Davies, 'Interest Rates in the ERM', *The Business Economist*, 23 (1992), pp. 44–58.

P. De Grauwe, 'Exchange Rate Variability and the Slowdown in Growth in International Trade', *IMF Staff Papers*, 35 (1988), pp. 63–84.

P. De Grauwe, *The Economics of Monetary Integration*, 2nd ed. (Oxford: Oxford University Press, 1994).

P. De Grauwe, 'Towards European Monetary Union without the EMS', *Economic Policy*, 18 (1994), pp. 147–185.

P. De Grauwe and L. Papademos , *The European Monetary System in the 1990's* (Longman, 1990).

G. de Malynes, 'A Treatise of the Canker of England's Commonwealth', in R. H. Tawney and E. Power (eds), *Tudor Economic Documents* (New York: Barnes and Noble, 1963).

Renaud Dehousse, 'European Political Cooperation', *European Journal of International Law*, vol. 1, no. 1/2 (1990).

G. R. Denton, (ed.), *Economic Integration* (Wiedenfield and Nicholson, 1969).

P. Dollinger, *The German Hansa*, (1964), translated by D. S. Ault and S. H. Steinberg (London: George Allen and Unwin, 1984).

Kathryn Dominguez and Jeffrey A. Frankel, *Does Foreign Exchange Intervention Work?* (Washington: Washington Institute for International Economics, 1993).

R. Dornbusch, 'Expectations and Exchange Rate Dynamics', *Journal of Political Economy*, 84 (1976), pp. 1161–76.

R. Dornbusch and D. Jaffee, 'Purchasing power parity and exchange rate problems: Introduction', *Journal of International Economics*, 8 (1978), pp. 157–62.

R. Dornbusch, 'The European Monetary System, the dollar and the yen', in F. Giavazzi, S. Micossi and M. Miller (eds), *The European Monetary System*, (Cambridge: Cambridge University Press, 1988), pp. 23–41.

R. Dornbusch, 'Two-Track EMU, Now!', in *Britain and EMU* (London: Centre for Economic Performance, 1990).

R. Dornbusch and L. T. Kuenzler, 'Exchange Rate Policy and Issues', in R. Dornbusch (ed.), *Policymaking in the Open Economy* (Oxford: Oxford University Press, 1993).

J. Driffill, 'The Stability and Sustainability of the European Monetary System with Perfect Capital Markets', in F. Giavazzi, S. Micossi and M. Miller (eds) (Cambridge: Cambridge University Press, 1988), pp. 211–228.

D. Dyker, *The European Economy* (London: Longman 1992).

K. Dyson, *Elusive Union: The Process of Economic and Monetary Union in Europe* (London: Longman, 1994).

H. J. Edison, 'Purchasing Power Parity: A Quantitative Reassessment of the 1920's experience', *Journal of International Money and Finance*, 4 (1985), pp. 361–372.

H. J. Edison, 'Purchasing Power Parity in the Long Run: A Test of the Dollar/Pound Exchange Rate (1890–1978), *Journal of Money Credit and Banking*, 19 (1987), pp. 376–87.

H. J. Edison and E. O. N. Fisher, 'A long-run view of the European Monetary System', *Journal of International Money and Finance*, 10 (1991), pp. 53–70.

H. J. Edison and B. D. Pauls, 'Reassessment of the Relationship Between Real Exchange Rates and Real Interest Rates: 1974–90', *International Financial Discussion Papers* (No. 408, 1991).

J. Eichberger and I. R. Harper, 'On Deposit Interest Rate Regulation and Deregulations', *The Journal of Industrial Economics*, vol. XXXVIII, no. 1 (1989).

B. Eichengreen, 'Is Europe an Optimal Currency Area?' *CEPR Discussion Paper*, No. 414 (1990).

B. Eichengreen, 'European Monetary Unification', *Journal of Economic Literature*, vol. 31 (1993).

B. Eichengreen and J. A. Frieden, 'The Political Economy of European Monetary Unification: An Analytical Introduction', in J. A. Frieden and D. A. Lake (eds), 3rd ed., *International Political Economy, Perspectives on Global Power and Wealth* (London: Routledge, 1995).

B. Eichengreen and C. Wyplosz, 'The Unstable EMS', *CEPR Discussion Paper*, No. 817 (1993).

Charles Engel and Craig S. Hakkio, 'Exchange Rate Regimes and Volatility', *Economic Review*, vol. 78, No. 3 (1993), pp. 43–58.

E. C. Commission, 'One Market, One Money', *European Economy*, (Brussels: Directorate-General for Economic and Financial Affairs, 44 1990).

M. Feldstein, 'Does One Market Require One Money?', in P. King (ed.), (1995).

S. Fischer, 'Towards an understanding of the costs of inflation: II', *Carnegie Rochester Series on Public Policy*, (1981), 15, pp. 5–42.

J. M. Fleming, 'Domestic financial policies under fixed and under floating exchange rates', *IMF Staff Papers*, 3 (1962), pp. 369–80.

Antoine Frachot, 'A re-examination of the uncovered interest parity hypothesis', *Journal of International Money and Finance*, vol. 15, no. 3 (1996), pp. 409–37.

J. A. Frankel, 'On the Mark: A Theory of Floating Exchange Rates Based on Real Interest Differentials', *American Economic Review*, 69 (1979), pp. 610–622.

P. Fraser, and C. D. Rogers, 'Some Evidence on the Potential Role of Commodity prices in the Formulation of Monetary Policy', *University of Dundee Discussion Papers in Economics* (No. 13, 1990).

P. Fraser, C. V. Hellier and D. M. Power, 'European Capital Market Convergence: A Disaggregated Perspective', *University of Dundee Discussion Papers in Financial Markets* (No. 3, 1992).

P. Fraser, M. P. Taylor and A. Webster, 'An Empirical Analysis of Long-Run Purchasing Power Parity as a Theory of International Commodity Arbitrage', *University of Dundee Discussion Papers in Economics*, (No. 3, 1990).

M. Fratianni and J. von Hagen, 'German Dominance in the EMS: The Empirical Evidence', *Open Economies Review*, 1 (1990).

J. A. Frenkel, 'Purchasing Power Parity: Doctrinal perspective and evidence from the 1920's', *Journal of International Economics*, 8 (1978), pp. 169–91.

J. A. Frenkel, 'Flexible exchange rates, prices and the role of 'news': lessons from the 1970's', *Journal of Political Economy*, 89 (1981), pp. 665–705.

J. A. Frenkel, and K. W. Clements, 'Exchange rates, money and relative prices: the dollar-pound in the 1920's', *Journal of International Economics*, 10 (1980), pp. 249–62.

B. S. Frey, 'Politico-Economic Models and Cycles', *Journal of Public Economics*, April, 9 (1978), pp. 203–220.

B. S. Frey, 'The Public Choice View of International Political Economy', *International Organization*, 38, 1, Winter (1994).

B. S. Frey and F. Schneider, 'On the Modelling of Politico-Economic Interdependence', *European Journal of Political Research*, Dec. (1975), pp. 339–360.

J. A. Frieden, 'Exchange rate politics: contemporary lessons from American history', *Review of International Political Economy*, 1 (1994), pp. 81–103.

M. Friedman, 'The case for flexible exchange rates', in *Essays in Positive Economics* (Chicago: University of Chicago Press, 1953), pp. 157–203.

K. A. Froot and K. Rogoff, 'The EMS, the EMU, and the Transition to a Common Currency', *NBER Economics Annual* (Cambridge: MIT Press, 1992).

Richard T. Froyen, *Macroeconomics – Theories and Policies* (London: Macmillan, 1990).

J. K. Galbraith, *Money – Whence it came, where it went* (London: Penguin, 1995).

J. A. C. Gallas and H. E. Nusse, 'Periodicity versus chaos in the dynamics of cobweb models', *Journal of Economic Behaviour and Organization*, 29, 3 (1996), pp. 447–464.

G. Gallorotti, 'The Limits of International Organization: Systemic Failure in the Management of International Organizations', *International Organization*, 45 (1991), pp. 183–220.

H. Genberg, 'Purchasing Power Parity Under Fixed and Flexible Exchange Rates', *Journal of International Economics*, 8 (1978), pp. 247–76.

F. Giavazzi, S. Micossi and M. Miller (eds), *The European Monetary System* (Cambridge: Cambridge University Press, 1988).

F. Giavazzi and A. Giavannini, 'The Role of the Exchange-Rate Regime in a Disinflation: Empirical Evidence on the European Monetary System', in F. Giavazzi, S. Micossi and M. Miller (eds) (Cambridge: Cambridge University Press, 1988), pp. 85–107.

F. Giavazzi and A. Giavannini, *Limiting Exchange Rate Flexibility: The European Monetary System* (Cambridge, Mass: MIT Press, 1989).

F. Giavazzi and M. Pagano, 'The Advantage of Tying One's Hands: EMS Discipline and Central Bank Credibility', *European Economic Review*, 32 (1988), pp. 1055–82.

R. Gilpin, *The Political Economy of International Relations* (Princeton University Press, 1987).

A. Giovannini, 'The Transition to European Monetary Union', *Essays in International Finance* (No. 178, 1990 Princeton University).

D. Glasner, *Free Banking and Monetary Reform* (Cambridge: Cambridge University Press, 1989).

C. A. E. Goodhart, 'The Conduct of Monetary Policy', *The Economic Journal*, 99 (1989), pp. 293–346.

P. Gotur, 'Effects of Exchange Rate Volatility on Trade', *IMF Staff Papers*, 32 (1985), pp. 475–512.

C. A. E. Goodhart, 'Economists' Perspectives on the EMS: A review essay', *Journal of Monetary Economics*, 26 (1990), pp. 471–87.

C. A. E. Goodhart, 'The Political Economy of Monetary Union', in C. A. E. Goodhart, *The Central Bank and the Financial System* (London: Macmillan, 1995), pp. 156–202.

C. A. E. Goodhart, 'A European Central Bank', in C. A. E. Goodhart, *The Central Bank and the Financial System* (London: Macmillan, 1995), pp. 303–332.

John B. Goodman, 'Monetary Policy and Financial Deregulation in France', *French Politics and Society*, vol. 10, no. 4 (1992), pp. 31–40.

F. Graham, *Exchange prices and production in hyperinflation Germany 1920–23* (Princeton: Princeton University Press, 1930).

V. Grilli, D. Masciandaro and G. Tabellini, 'Political and monetary institutions and public financial policies in the industrial countries', *Economic Policy*, 13 (1991).

D. Gros, 'Discussion – The Stability and Sustainability of the European Monetary System with Perfect Capital Markets', in F. Giavazzi *et. al.* (eds) (Cambridge: Cambridge University Press, 1988), pp. 229–231.

D. Gros, 'Paradigms for the Monetary Union of Europe', *Journal of Common Market Studies*, 27 (1989), pp. 219–230.

D. Gros and N. Thygesen, *European Monetary Integration: From the European Monetary System to Economic and Monetary Union* (London: Longman, 1992).

D. Gros and G. Vandille, 'Seigniorage and EMU: The Fiscal Implications of Price Stability and Financial Integration', *Journal of Common Market Studies*, 33 (1995).

E. Haas, *The Uniting of Europe: political, social and economic forces, 1950–57* (Stanford: Stanford University Press, 1958).

G. Haberler, *The Theory of International Trade* (London: William Hodge, 1936).

S. Haggard, 'Inflation and Stabilisation, in J. A. Frieden and D. A. Lake, *International Political Economy: Perspectives on Global Power and Wealth*, 3rd ed. (London: Routledge, 1995).

C. S. Hakkio, 'A Re-examination of purchasing power parity: A multi-country and multi-period study', *Journal of International Economics*, 17 (1984), pp. 265–277.

A. G. Haldane and M. Pradhan, 'Real Interest Parity, Dynamic Convergence and the European Monetary System', *Bank of England Discussion Paper* (1992).

S. G. Hall, D. Robertson and M. Wickens, 'Measuring Convergence of the

EC Economies', *London Business School Centre for Economic Forecasting* (Discussion Paper No. 01.92, 1992).

P. Hallwood, and R. MacDonald, *International Money: Theory, evidence and Institutions* (Blackwell, 1986).

L. Harris, 'International Financial Markets and National Transmission Mechanisms', in J. Michie and J. G. Smith (eds), *Managing the Global Economy* (Oxford: Oxford University Press, 1995).

D. M. Harrison, *The Organisation of Europe – Developing a Continental Market Order*, (London: Routledge, 1995).

John T. Harvey, 'Long-term Exchange Rate Movements: The Role of Fundamentals in Neoclassical Models of Exchange Rates', *Journal of Economic Issues*, vol. 30, no. 2 (1996).

Thomas Havrilesky, 'A Partisan Theory of Fiscal and Monetary Regimes', *Journal of Money, Credit and Banking*, 19 (1987), pp. 308–25.

R. G. Hawtrey, *Currency and Credit* (Longmans, Green: London 1950)(1st edition, 1919).

E. Helleiner, 'Explaining the globalisation of financial markets: Bringing states back in', *Review of International Political Economy*, 2 (1995), pp. 315–41.

C. Randall Henning, *Currencies and Politics in the United States, Germany and Japan* (Washington: Institute for International Affairs, 1994).

B. Hettne (ed.), *International Political Economy – Understanding Global Disorder* (London: Zed Books, 1995).

Douglas Hibbs, 'Political Parties and macroeconomic Policy', *The American Political Science Review*, 71 (1977), p. 1467–87.

A. O. Hirschman, *Exit, Voice and Loyalty: Responses to Decline in Firms, Organisations and States* (Cambridge: Harvard University Press, 1970).

T. Hitiris and A. Zervoyianni, 'Monetary integration in the European Community' in J. Lodge (ed.), *Institutions and Policies of the European Union* (London: Frances Pinter, 1983), pp. 130–141.

Robert J. Hodrick, *The Empirical Evidence on the Efficiency of Forward and Futures Exchange Markets* (Chur, Switzerland: Harwood Academic Publishers, 1987).

P. Hooper and S. W. Kohlhagen, 'The Effect of Exchange Rate Uncertainty on the Prices and Volumes of International Trade', *Journal of International Economics*, 8 (1978), pp. 483–511.

K.-L. Holtfrerich, 'The Monetary Unification Process in 19th-century Germany: Relevance and Lessons for Europe Today', in M. de Cecco and A. Giovannini (eds), *A European Central Bank* (Cambridge: Cambridge University Press, 1989).

C. H. Hommes, 'Dynamics of the cobweb model with adaptive expectations and nonlinear supply and demand', *Journal of Economic Behaviour and Organization*, 24, 3 (1994).

A. J. Hughes-Hallett, P. Minford and A. Rastogi, 'The European Monetary System: Achievements and Survival', *CEPR Discussion Paper* (No. 502, 1991).

A. J. Hughes Hallett and D. Vines, 'On the Possible Costs of European Monetary Union', *Manchester School Journal*, 61 (1993), pp. 35–64.

A. Icard, 'Exchange Rate Stability and the European Construction', in C. Border, E. Girardin and J. Melitz (eds), *European Currency Crises and After* (Manchester: Manchester University Press, 1994).

Harold K. Jacobsen, William Reisinger and Todd Mathers, 'National

Entanglements in International Governmental Organizations', *American Political Science Review*, 80 (1986), pp. 141–59.

P. Jacquet, 'The Politics of EMU: A Selective Overview', in *The Monetary Future of Europe* (London: Centre for Economic Policy Research, 1993).

R. R. James (ed.), *Winston S. Churchill: His Complete Speeches, 1897–1963*, Vol. VII, 1943–49.

Miles Kahler, *International Institutions and the Political Economy of Integration* (Washington D. C.: The Brookings Institution, 1995).

G. J. Kalamotousakis, 'Exchange rates and prices: the historical evidence', *Journal of International Economics*, 8 (1978), pp. 163–168.

G. Kaminsky, 'The Real Exchange Rate Since Floating: Market fundamentals or bubbles?', Mimeo, University of California, San Diego (August 1988).

Peter B. Kenen, 'The Theory of Optimum Currency Areas: An Eclectic View', in R. Mundell and A. Swoboda (eds), *Monetary Problems of the International Economy* (Chicago: University of Chicago Press, 1969).

Peter B. Kenen, 'Macroeconomic Theory and Policy: How the Closed Economy was Opened', in Ronald Jones and Peter Kenen, (eds), *Handbook of International Economics*, Volume II (North Holland: Amsterdam, 1985).

Peter B. Kenen, *Economic and Monetary Union in Europe – Moving beyond Maastricht* (Cambridge: Cambridge University Press, 1995).

P. B. Kenen and D. Rodrik, 'Measuring and Analysing Effects of Short-term Volatility in Real Exchange Rates', *Review of Economics and Statistics*, 68 (1986), pp. 311–19.

E. Kennedy, *The Bundesbank Germany's Central Bank in the International Monetary System* (London: Pinter, 1991).

R. O. Keohane and J. S. Nye, *Power and Interdependence: World Politics in Transition* (New York: Little, Brown, 1977).

J. M. Keynes, *The General Theory of Employment, Interest and Money* (Macmillan 1936, Reprinted 1967).

Shady Kholdy and Ahmed Sohrabian, 'Testing for the Relationship between Nominal Exchange Rates and Economic Fundamentals', *Global Finance Journal*, vol. 6, no. 2 (1995).

C. P. Kindleberger, 'The rise of free trade in Western Europe 1820–1875', *Journal of Economic History*, 35 (1975), pp. 20–55.

C. P. Kindleberger, *A Financial History of Western Europe* (London: George, Allen and Unwin, 1984).

G. Kirchgassner, 'Ökonometrische Untersuchungen des Einflusses der Wirtschaftlage auf die Popularität der Parteien', *Schweizerische Zeitschrift für Volkswirtschaft und Statistik*, 110 (1974), pp. 409–45.

Jonathan Kirshner, *Currency and Coercion, The Political Economy of International Monetary Power* (Princeton: Princeton University Press, 1995).

M. Kitson and J. Michie, 'Trade and Growth; A Historical Perspective', in J. Michie and J. G. Smith, (eds), *Managing the Global Economy* (Oxford: Oxford University Press, 1995).

U. W. Kitzinger, *The Politics and Economics of European Integration: Britain, Europe and the United States* (Greenwood Press, 1976).

F. Kratochwil and John C. Ruggie, 'International Organization: A State of Art or an Art of the State', *International Organization*, 40, (1986).

I. B. Kravis and R. E. Lipsey, 'Price behaviour in the light of Balance

Payments Theories', *Journal of International Economics*, 8 (1978), pp. 193–246.

P. B. Krugman, 'Purchasing Power Parity and exchange rates: another look at the evidence', *Journal of International Economics*, 8 (1978), pp. 193–246.

Paul Krugman and Maurice Obstfeld, *International Economics: Theory and Policy* (Glenview, Il: Scott, Foresman and Co., 1988).

P. B. Krugman, *Rethinking International Trade* (London: M.I.T. Press, 1990).

D. C. Kruse, *Monetary Integration in Western Europe: EMU, EMS and Beyond* (London: Butterworths, 1980).

F. E. Kydland, 'On the econometrics of world business cycles', *European Economic Review*, 36 (1992), pp. 476–482.

F. Kydland and E. Prescott, 'Rules Rather than Discretion: The Inconsistency of Optimal Plans', *Journal of Political Economy*, 85 (1977).

B. Laffan, *Integration and Co-operation in Europe* (Routledge, 1992).

M. W. J. Lak, 'Interaction between European Political Co-operation and the European Community: existing rules and challenges', Common Market Law Review, vol. 26, no. 2 (1989).

L. Lambertini, M. Miller and A. Sutherland, 'Inflation Convergence with Realignments in a Two-Speed Europe', *CEPR Discussion Paper* (1991).

B. Langeheine and U. Weinstock, 'Graduated integration: a modest path towards progress', *Journal of Common Market Studies*, 23 (1985), pp. 185–97.

E. Langfeldt, 'European Monetary Union: Design and Implementation', in R. Barrell (ed.), *Economic Convergence and Monetary Union in Europe* (London: Sage, for the Association for the Monetary Union of Europe and the National Institute of Economic and Social Research).

Michael Laver and Norman Schofield, *Multiparty Government, The Politics of Coalition in Europe* (Oxford: Oxford University Press, 1990).

Sérgio Pereira Leite and V. Sundararajan, 'Issues in Interest Rate Management and Liberalization', IMF Staff papers, vol. 37, no. 4, December (1990).

E. Leigh, *An Essay upon Credit* (London, 1715).

R. Levacic and A. Rebmann, *Macroeconomics – An Introduction to Keynesian Neoclassical Controversies* (London: Macmillan, 1982).

Richard M. Levich, 'Empirical Studies of Exchange Rates: Price Behaviour, Rate Determination and Market Efficiency', in Ronald Jones and Peter B. Kenen, (eds), *Handbook of International Economics*, vol. 2 (Amsterdam: North Holland, 1985), pp. 979–1140.

J. Lodge, (ed.), *Institutions and Policies of the European Community* (London: Frances Pinter, 1983).

Walther Lotz, 'Die Währungsfrage in Österreich-Ungarn', *Schmollers Jahrbuch*, vol. 13 (1889).

R. E. Lucas, Jr., 'Some International Evidence on Output-Inflation Trade-offs', *American Economic Review*, 63 (1973), pp. 326–34.

R. E. Lucas, Jr., 'An Equilibrium Model of the Business Cycle', *Journal of Political Economy*, 83 (1975), pp. 241–54.

P. Ludlow, *The Making of the European Monetary System* (London: Butterworths, 1982).

R. MacDonald, 'Some tests of the rational expectations hypothesis in the foreign exchange market', *Scottish Journal of Political Economy*, 30 (1983), pp. 235–250.

R. MacDonald, *Floating Exchange Rates: Theories and Evidence* (London: Unwin Hyman, 1988).

R. MacDonald, 'Exchange Rate Economics: An Empirical Perspective', Ch. 4 in G. R. Bird and R. MacDonald (eds), *The International Financial Regime* (Surrey: Surrey University Press, 1990).

R. MacDonald, 'Long-Run Purchasing Power Parity: Is It For Real?' Mimeo., (I. M. F. Research Department, 1991).

R. MacDonald, and M. P. Taylor, 'The Monetary Approach to the Exchange Rate: Long-Run Relationships and Coefficient Restrictions', Mimeo. (I. M. F. Research Department, 1991).

P. Macmillan and A. M. S. Watson, 'Economic and Monetary Union' in P. Barbour (ed.), *The European Union Handbook* (London: Fitzroy Dearborn, 1996).

C. D. Macrae, 'A Political Model of the Business Cycle', *Journal of Political Economy*, 85 (1977), pp. 239–63.

Richard C. Marston, 'Interest Arbitrage in the Eurocurrency Markets', *European Economic Review*, 7 (1976), pp. 1–13.

Phillippe Martin, 'Free-riding, convergence and two-speed monetary unification in Europe', *European Economic Review*, 39, 7 (1995), pp. 1345–1364.

P. Masson and J. Melitz, 'Fiscal Policy Independence in a European Monetary Union', *CEPR Discussion Paper*, No. 414 (1990).

C. Mastropasqua, S. Micossi and R. Rinaldi, 'Interventions, Sterilisation and Monetary Policy in European Monetary System Countries, 1979–87', in F. Giavazzi, S. Micossi and M. Miller (eds), *The European Monetary System* (Cambridge: Cambridge University Press, 1988), pp. 252–287.

T. Mazowiecki, 'Returning to Europe', *European Affairs*, vol. 46, no. 4 (1990), pp. 41–43.

B. T. McCallum, 'The Political Business Cycle: An Empirical Test', *Southern Economic Journal*, 44 (1977), pp. 504–15.

F. McDonald and G. Zis, 'The European Monetary System: Towards 1992 and Beyond', *Journal of Common Market Studies*, 27 (1989), pp. 183–202.

R. I. McKinnon, 'Floating exchange rates 1973–74: the emperor's new clothes', Carnegie-Rochester Supplement to the *Journal of Monetary Economics*, 3 (1976), pp. 79–114.

R. I. McKinnon, 'Monetary and Exchange Rate Policies for International Financial Stability: A Proposal', *Journal of Economic Perspectives*, 2 (1988), pp. 83–103.

Richard A. Meese, 'Empirical Assessment of Foreign Currency Premiums', in Courtenay C. Stone (ed.), *Financial Risk: Theory, Evidence and Implications* (Boston: Kluwer Academic Publishers, 1989), pp. 157–80.

R. A. Meese and K. Rogoff, 'Empirical Exchange Rate Models of the Seventies: Do they fit out of sample?', *Journal of International Economics*, 14 (1983), pp. 3–23.

R. A. Meese and K. Rogoff, 'Was It Real? The Exchange Rate Interest Rate Relation, 1973–84', *Journal of Finance*, 43 (1988), pp. 933–948.

J. Melitz, 'Monetary discipline and co-operation in the European Monetary system: a synthesis', in F. Giavazzi, S. Micossi and M. Miller, (eds), *The European Monetary System* (Cambridge: Cambridge University Press, 1988), pp. 51–79.

M. Miller, 'Discussion – Competitiveness, Realignment, and Speculation: The Role of Financial Markets', in F. Giavazzi, S. Micossi and M. Miller (eds),

The European Monetary System (Cambridge: Cambridge University Press, 1988), pp. 247–249.

Terence C. Mills and Geoffrey E. Woods, 'Does the Exchange Rate Regime Affect the Economy?', *Review of the Federal Reserve Bank of St Louis*, vol. 75, no. 4 (1993).

A. S. Milward, *The Reconstruction of Western Europe 1945–51* (London: Methuen, 1987)

A. Moravscik 'Negotiating the Single European Act: National Interests and Conventional Statecraft in the European Community', *International Organisation*, 45 (1991), pp. 651–688.

R. Morgan, *West European Politics since 1945: the shaping of the European Community* (London: Batsford, 1972).

R. A. Mundell, 'A Theory of Optimal Currency Areas', *American Economic Review*, 51 (1961).

R. A. Mundell, 'The appropriate use of monetary and fiscal policy under fixed exchange rates', *IMF Staff Papers*, 9 (1962), pp. 70–9.

R. A. Mundell, 'Capital Mobility and Stabilisation Policy Under Fixed and Flexible Exchange Rates', *Canadian Journal of Economics* (1963), pp. 475–485.

R. A. Mundell, *International Economics* (New York: Macmillan, 1968).

M. Mussa, 'The Exchange Rate, the Balance of Payments, and Monetary and Fiscal Policy under a Regime of Controlled Floating', *Scandinavian Journal of Economics*, 78 (1976), pp. 229–48.

S. Nelson (ed.), with David Pollard and Anna Wheeler, *The Convoluted Treaties, Volume II, Rome 1957, Treaty Establishing the European Economic Community* (London: Nelson and Pollard Publishing, 1993).

W. D. Nordhaus, 'The Political Business Cycle', *Review of Economic Studies*, 42 (1975).

N. Nugent, *The Government and Politics of European Union* (London: Macmillan, 1994).

M. Obstfeld, 'Rational and Self-fulfilling Balance of Payments Crises', *American Economic Review*, 76 (1986), pp. 72–81.

M. Obstfeld, 'Competitiveness, Realignment, and Speculation: The Role of Financial Markets', in F. Giavazzi, S. Micossi and M. Miller (eds), *The European Monetary System* (Cambridge: Cambridge University Press, 1988), pp. 232–247.

L. H. Officer, 'The purchasing power parity theory of exchange rates: a review article', *I. M. F. Staff Papers*, 23 (1976), pp. 1–60.

B. Ohlin, *Interregional and international trade* (Cambridge MA: Harvard University Press, 1967).

A. M. Okun, *The Political Economy of Prosperity* (Washington D. C.: Brookings, 1970).

R. Owen and M. Dynes, *The Times Guide to 1992: Britain in a Europe Without Frontiers* (Times Books Limited, 1989).

T. Padoa-Schioppa, 'Squaring the Circle, or the Conundrum of International Monetary Reform', *Catalyst, a Journal of Policy Debate*, 1, 1 (1985).

T. Padoa-Schioppa, 'The European Monetary System: A Long-Term View', in F. Giavazzi, S. Micossi and M. Miller (eds), *The European Monetary System* (Cambridge: Cambridge University Press, 1988), p. 376.

M. Panic, 'The Bretton Woods System: Concept and Practice', in J. Michie and J. Grieve Smith (eds), *Managing the Global Economy* (Oxford: Oxford University Press, 1995).

L. Papademos, 'Discussion – Monetary Policy Within the European Monetary System: Is There A Rule?', in F. Giavazzi, S. Micossi and M. Miller (eds), *The European Monetary System* (1988), pp. 356–366.

Mark D. Partridge and Dan S. Rickman, 'Differences in State Unemployment Rates: The Role of Labour and Product Markets in Structural Shifts', *Southern Economic Journal*, vol. 6, no. 1 (1995).

J. Patel, 'Purchasing Power Parity as a Long-Run Relation', *Journal of Applied Econometrics*, 5 (1990), pp. 367–379.

T. Peeters, 'EMU: Prospects and Retrospect', in M. T. Sumner and G. Zis (eds), *European Monetary Union* (London: Macmillan, 1982).

M. Perlman, 'Party Politics and Bureaucracy in Economic Policy', in G. Tullock, *The Vote Motive* (London: Institute for International Affairs, 1976).

M. Perlman 'In Search of Monetary Union', *London School of Economics Financial Markets Group* (Special Paper No. 39, 1991).

T. Persson and L. Svensson, 'Why should a stubborn conservative run a deficit?', *Quarterly Journal of Economics* 104, 2 (1989).

S. P. Peterson, 'Forecasting dynamics and convergence to market fundamentals', *Journal of Economic Behaviour and Organization*, vol. 22, no. 3 (1993).

A. W. Phillips, 'The Relation Between Unemployment and the Rate of Change of Money Wage Rates in the United Kingdom, 1861–1957', *Economica*, 22 (1958), pp. 283–99.

H. Polemarchakis, 'Discussion – Competitiveness, Realignment and Speculation: The Role of Financial Markets', in F. Giavazzi, S. Micossi and M. Miller (eds), *The European Monetary System* (Cambridge: Cambridge University Press, 1988), pp. 249–251.

S. Pollard, *European Economic Integration 1815–1970* (Thames and Hudson, 1974).

J. Rasulo and D. Wilford, 'Estimating monetary models of the balance of payments and exchange rates: a bias', *Southern Economic Journal*, 47 (1980), pp. 136–46.

J.-J. Rey, 'Discussion – Inflation and the European Monetary System', in F. Giavazzi, S. Micossi and M. Miller (eds), *The European Monetary System* (Cambridge: Cambridge University Press, 1988), pp. 136–139.

D. Richardson, 'Some empirical evidence on commodity arbitrage and the law of one price', *Journal of International Economics*, 8 (1978), pp. 341–351.

W. Rieke, 'Discussion – Interventions, sterilisation and Monetary Policy in European Monetary System countries, 1979–87', in F. Giavazzi *et. al.* (eds), *The European Monetary System* (Cambridge: Cambridge University Press, 1988), pp. 288–291.

W. Roberds, and C. H. Whiteman, 'Monetary Aggregates as Monetary Targets: A Statistical Investigation', *Journal of Money, Credit and Banking*, 24, pp. 141–161.

K. Rogoff, 'Can exchange rate predictability be achieved without monetary convergence?: evidence from the EMS', *European Economic Review*, 28 (1985), pp. 93–115.

N. Roubini and J. Sachs, 'Political and Economic Determinants of Budget

Deficits in the Industrial Democracies', *European Economic Review* 336 (1989) 903–38.

M. Russo, and G. Tullio, 'Monetary Policy Coordination Within the European Monetary System: Is there a rule?', in F. Giavazzi, S. Micossi and M. Miller (eds), *The European Monetary System* (Cambridge: Cambridge University Press, 1988), pp. 292–356.

J. Rueff, *Balance of Payments* (New York: Macmillan, 1967).

P. A. Samuelson, 'Theoretical Notes on Trade Problems', *Review of Economics and Statistics,* 46 (1964), pp. 145–54.

P. A. Samuelson, 'Analytical Notes on International Real-Income Measures', *Economic Journal,* 84 (1974), pp. 595–608.

W. Sandholtz, 'Choosing Union: Monetary Politics and Maastricht', in B. F. Nelson and A. C.-G. Stubb (eds), *The European Union* (Colorado: Lynne Rienner, 1994), pp. 257–290.

T. Sargent and N. Wallace, 'Rational Expectations, the Optimal Monetary Instrument and the Optimal Money Supply Rule', *Journal of Political Economy,* 83 (1975), pp. 241–54.

T. Sargent and N. Wallace, 'Some Unpleasant Monetarist Arithmetic', *Federal Reserve Bank of Minneapolis Quarterly Review,* 5 (1981), pp. 1–17.

A. M. Sbragia, (ed.), *Euro-politics: Institutions and Policymaking in the 'New' European Community* (Brookings, 1992).

Kenneth A. Schulz, 'The Politics of the Political Business Cycle', *British Journal of Political Science,* 25, 9 (1995), pp. 79–99.

R. Schuman, 'Europe–A Fresh Start: The Schuman Declaration, 1950–90', (Luxembourg: Office for the Official Publications of the European Communities, 1990), re-printed in B. F. Nelsen and A. C-G. Stubb (eds), *The European Union* (Colorado: Lynne Rienner, 1994).

L. J. Sharpe, 'Fragmentation and Territoriality in the European State System', *International Political Science Review,* vol. 10 (1989).

K. A. Shepsle, 'Institutional Arrangements and Equilibrium in Multidimensional Voting Models', *American Journal of Political Science,* 23, 19 (1979), pp. 27–59.

David J. Smyth and Susan Washburn Taylor, 'The Inflation-Unemployment Trade-Offs of Union Members', *Journal of Labor Research,* vol. 73, no. 2 (1992).

J. E. Spero, *The Politics of International Economic Relations,* 4th ed. (London: Routledge, 1992).

G. Stigler, 'General Economic Conditions and National Elections', *American Economic Review,* 63 (1973).

J. Stiglitz and A. Weiss, 'Credit Rationing in Markets with Imperfect Information', American Economic Review, 71 (1981), pp. 393–410.

Alexander C.-G. Stubb, 'A Categorisation of Differentiated Integration', *Journal of Common Market Studies,* 34 (1996).

R. Stubbs and G. R. D. Underhill, 'Global Issues in Historical Perspective', in Richard Stubbs and Geoffrey R. D. Underhill, (eds), *Political Economy and the Changing Global Order* (London:Macmillan, 1994).

M. Sumner, 'European Monetary Integration' in *The European Economy,* in D. Dyker (ed.) (1992), pp. 137–153.

G. Tabellini, 'Comment on Hughes and Smith', *Economic Policy,* no. 13 (1991), pp. 454–457.

G. Tabellini and A. Alesina, 'Voting on the budget deficit', *American Economic Review* (1990), pp. 17–32.

F. W. Taussig, *International Trade* (New York, 1927).

M. P. Taylor, 'An Empirical Examination of Long-Run Purchasing Power Parity using Cointegration Techniques', *Bank of England Discussion Paper* (1987).

M. P. Taylor and P. C. McMahon, 'Long-run purchasing power parity in the 1920's', *European Economic Review*, 32 (1988), pp. 179–197.

P. Taylor, 'The new dynamics of EC integration in the 1980s', in J. Lodge (ed.), *The European Community and the Challenge of the Future* (London: Pinter, 1989).

M. Thatcher, 'A Family of Nations', in B. F. Nelsen and A. C.-G. Stubb (eds), *The European Union* (Colorado: Lynne Rienner, 1995), pp. 45–50.

Alun H. Thomas, 'Expected Devaluation and Economic Fundamentals', *IMF Staff Papers*, vol. 41, no. 2 (1994).

N. Thygesen, 'Inflation and Exchange Rates – Evidence and Policy Guidelines for the European Community', *Journal of International Economics*, 8 (1978), pp. 301–317.

N. Thygesen, 'Introduction', in F. Giavazzi, S. Micossi and M. Miller (eds), *The European Monetary System* (Cambridge: Cambridge University Press, 1988), pp. 1–20.

Treaty on European Union (1992), Office for Official Publications of the European Communities.

Niels Thygesen, 'International Co-ordination of Monetary Policies with Special Reference to the European Community, in John E. Wadsworth and Francois Leonard de Juvigny (eds), *New Approaches to Monetary Policy* (Alpen aan der Rijn: Sijthoff and Noordhoff, 1979), pp. 205–24.

R. H. Tilly, *Financial Institutions and Industrialization in the Rhineland, 1815–1870* (Madison, Wisconsin: University of Wisconsin Press, 1966).

The Times, 11 July (1978).

J. A. Trevithik, *Inflation, A Guide to the Crisis in Economics*, 2nd ed. (London: Penguin Books, 1980).

R. Triffin, 'Discussion – The European Monetary System, the dollar and the yen', in F. Giavazzi, S. Micossi and M. Miller (eds), *The European Monetary System* (Cambridge: Cambridge University Press, 1988), pp. 41–43.

L. T. Tsoukalis, *The New European Economy*, 2nd ed. (Oxford: Oxford University Press, 1993).

E. R. Tufte, *Political Control of the Economy* (Princeton, New Jersey: Princeton University Press, 1978).

Dave Turner, The Role of Real and Nominal Rigidities in Macroeconomic Adjustment: A Comparative Study of the G3 Economies, *OECD Economic Studies*, no. 21, Winter 1993.

Philip Turner, *Capital flows in the 1980s: A Survey of the Major Trends* (Basle: Bank for International Settlements, 1991).

Lars Udehn, *The Limits of Public Choice* (London: Routledge, 1996).

H. Ungerer, 'The European Monetary System and the International Monetary System', *Journal of Common Market Studies*, 27 (1989), pp. 231–248.

H. O. Ungerer, O. Evans, T. Mayer and P. Young, 'The European Monetary System: Recent Developments', *IMF Occasional Papers* (No. 48, 1986).

G. D. R. Underhill, 'Introduction: Conceptualising the Changing Global Order', in R. Stubbs and G. D. R. Underhill (eds), *Political Economy and the*

Changing Global Order (London: Macmillan, 1994), pp. 17–44.

H. Ungerer, O. Evans, T. Mayer and P. Young, 'The European Monetary System: Recent Developments', *IMF Occasional Papers*, No. 48 (1986).

D. Urwin, *The Community of Europe: a history of European integration since 1945* (Harlow: Longman, 1991).

H. Van der Wee, *Prosperity and Upheaval: The World Economy 1945–1980* (Pelican, 1986).

R. Vaubel, 'Real Exchange Rate Changes in the European Community – a new approach to the determination of optimum currency areas', *Journal of International Economics*, 8 (1978), pp. 319–339.

R. Vaubel, 'The return to the new EMS: objectives, incentives, perspectives', in K. Brunner and A. H. Meltzer (eds), *Monetary Institutions and the Policy Process*, Carnegie Rochester Conference Series on Public Policy (Amsterdam: North Holland, 1980).

R. Vaubel, 'Image and Reality of the EMS; a review', *Weltwirtschaftliches Archiv*, 125 (1989), pp. 397–405.

R. Vaubel, 'Currency competition and European monetary integration', *Economic Journal*, 100 (1990), pp. 936–946.

A. Velasco and A. Tornell, 'Fiscal discipline and the choice of exchange rate regime', *European Economic Review*, vol. 39, no. 3 (1995).

J. von Hagen, 'A Note on the Empirical Effectiveness of Formal Fiscal Restraints', *Journal of Public Economics*, 44 (1991), pp. 199–210.

J. von Hagen and Ian J. Harden, 'Budgeting procedures and fiscal performance in the EC', *Economic Papers*, 96 (Brussels: European Commission).

S. Vona and L. Bini Smaghi, 'Economic Growth and Exchange Rates in the European Monetary System: Their Trade Effects in a Changing External Environment', in F. Giavazzi, S. Micossi and M. Miller (eds), *The European Monetary System* (Cambridge: Cambridge University Press, 1988), pp. 140–178.

J. M. Wagner, C. K. Rowley and R. D. Tollison, *Deficits* (Oxford: Basil Blackwell, 1986).

H. Wallace with A. Ridley, *Europe: The Challenge of Diversity*, Chatham House Paper, No. 29 (1985).

B. R. Weingast, K. A. Shepsle and C. Johnsen, 'The Political Economy of Benefits and Costs: A Neoclassical Approach to Distributive Politics', *Journal of Political Economy*, 89 (1981), pp. 624–64.

Werner P. et al. (Werner Report), 'Report of the Council and the Commission on the realisation by stages of Economic and Monetary Union in the Community', *Supplement to the Bulletin of the EC* (3, 1970).

K. D. West, 'A Standard Monetary Model and the Variability of the Deutschmark–Dollar Exchange Rate', *Journal of International Economics*, 23 (1987), pp. 57–76.

J. Wheatley, *Essay on the theory of money* (England, 1807).

J. A. Whitt Jr, 'The Long-Run Behaviour of the Real Exchange Rate: A Reconsideration', *Journal of Money, Credit and Banking*, 24 (1992), 72–82.

D. Wiegal and P. Stirk (eds), *The Origins and Development of the European Community* (London: Leicester University Press, 1992).

T. D. Willett, 'Some Aspects of the Public Choice Approach to International Economic Relations', in R. Lombra and W. Witte (eds), *The Political Economy of International and Domestic Monetary Relations* (Ames: Iowa State University Press, 1982).

T. D. Willet, 'Exchange Rate Volatility, International Trade, and Resource Allocation: A Perspective on Recent Research', *Journal of International Money and Finance*, 5 (Supplement) (1986), pp. 101–112.

T. D. Willett and J. Mullen, 'The Effects of Alternative Monetary Systems on Macroeconomic Discipline and Inflationary Biases', in R. Lombra and W. Witte (eds), *The Political Economy of International and Domestic Monetary Relations* (Ames: Iowa State University Press, 1982).

John T. Woolley, 'Policy Credibility and European Monetary Institutions', in Alberta M. Sbragia, *Europolitics*, (ed.) (Washington D.C.: The Brookings Institution, 1992), pp. 157–90.

G. Wright, 'The Political Economy of New Deal Spending: An Econometric Analysis, *Review of Economics and Statistics*, 56, (1974).

C. Wyplosz, 'Discussion – The European Monetary System, the dollar and the yen', in Francesco Giavazzi, S. Micossi and M. Miller (eds), *The European Monetary System* (Cambridge: Cambridge University Press, 1988), pp. 43–47.

Index

219

ΑΘΛΕΣΗ 11.